Forest Rambles

Nottingham Forest
1959 – 1999

40 Years with the original Reds

Richard Pulk

The reminiscences and opinions of a middle aged supporter who can't believe that 40 years have passed since his first Forest match.

Touchline '99

First published in 1999 by Touchline '99

6, Brechin Close, Arnold, Nottingham, NG5 8GN

ISBN 0 9536646 0 0

Typeset by Richard Pulk at
Touchline '99

Printed by Anthony Rowe Ltd, Bumper's Farm,
Chippenham, SN14 6LH

Contents

~

Introduction :-

My first Forest match was our famous 1959 Cup Final win.

We didn't have a television in those days, so the family was transported courtesy of Nottingham City Transport from Carlton to the Bestwood Estate where I was plonked by my father in front of my cousin's black and white TV and instructed to watch.

I was a reluctant spectator – 7 years old and sporting a huge red and white rosette, but more interested in their train set. Forest won 2-1, but I wasn't particularly impressed.

The amazing reception in Slab Square, where I was hoisted shoulder high to witness Jack Burkitt and his team display the cup from an open top bus, was my first experience of what Nottingham Forest Football Club meant to so many people, and made a lasting impression. I've followed them ever since.

A few years ago I decided to write a book about the Reds and started jotting down notes. I thought it would be easy – but then again I used to think we were too good to be relegated.

The chapters that follow are personal reminiscences, reflections and opinions.

I've re-visited memory lane, aided and abetted by selective statistical input (essentially, and with thanks, Ken Smales "Nottingham Forest, the first 125 years") and driven myself mad trying to condense 40 years into a few pages of scribble. I hope that Forest fans of all ages can identify with the highs and lows which I've tried to capture, but if your particular recollection or favourite player is missing I'm sorry, but the Editor's decision has to be final.

Apart from checking statistics I've kept my nose completely out of any other Forest publication and any similarities are entirely coincidental.

All opinions expressed are my own and I would emphasise the old cliché, particularly for those who may disagree with some of my comments, (especially Notts fans!) that "Football is a game of opinions"

Richard Pulk

Beginnings

I recall Alan Bleasdale stating during a television interview that his teenage support of Liverpool kept him going during a difficult period and without wishing to go into specific detail it is true to say that my own support for Forest in the late 60s became an all consuming beacon that lit up an otherwise pathetically featureless existence.

As the decades have rolled relentlessly and terrifyingly on and middle age has maliciously sneaked up, the intensity and passion has diminished, but the fortunes of Nottingham Forest F.C. will always remain close to my heart.

Individual results, even defeats in Cup semi finals, will never again carry the "life or death" drama of the tearful devastation of our 1967 FA Cup exit against Spurs at Hillsborough, but it's still annoying when they lose (which has been far too often in recent seasons).

The chapters that follow are not intended to be a documented history or reference volume but a selection of experiences and opinions from a lifetime's interest in Football in general and my hometown club in particular.

I've missed or only skirmished with whole chunks of the Reds, but that's inevitable.

Jim Baxter's alleged dressing room comment to Matt Gillies, after an especially dire team performance - "don't worry boss, we can play a lot worse than that" – has belatedly surfaced from the deep recesses of my memory, not to mention a pig suddenly racing across the City Ground pitch, John Barnwell spontaneously sitting on the ball, or Robbo conducting the Trent End in song.

If your favourite match, player, or incident doesn't appear, remember that 40 years is a long time and my excursion is nothing if not subjective.

In case anyone doesn't know, Nottingham Forest Football Club are the Football League's 3rd oldest, behind another local team, whose name I forget, and Stoke City. My introduction came in 1959 with a family excursion, courtesy of Nottingham City Transport, to the Bestwood Estate where my cousin basked in the luxury of having a television set.

The purpose of the visit, as evidenced by the red and white regalia which decorated the house, both inside and out, was Forest's appearance in the 1959 Cup Final against Luton Town. My father, a dedicated supporter who scarcely missed a match, was predictably one of thousands of genuine Reds fans who were unable to obtain a Wembley ticket, even though the capacity at the time was 100,000 and corporate hospitality "tickets for the boys" yet to feature significantly.

Season Tickets were almost non existent and other "priority" methods such as programme or match ticket vouchers a scarcely viable alternative for a club that hadn't won a thing in the 20th Century and scarcely expected, despite Billy Walker's excellent stewardship, that this would be the year. (If we hadn't scraped a jammy late equaliser against non League Tooting and Mitcham in the 3rd round it would merely have been an early chapter in the long running saga of embarrassing cup exits – such is the almost surreal knife edge of fortune that can change the future in a split second).

Wembley ticket allocations were, for most, quite literally a lottery, with my father failing to secure the necessary good fortune in a postal ballot. Hence it was that the family was uprooted to the nearest available television set and "disinterested of Carlton" saw his first "live" Forest match, although he was more excited by the prospect of a journey involving a change of buses in town and the novelty of the Trinity Square Bus Terminal, departure point for the other side of the World.

For the record, Tommy Wilson and Roy Dwight (cousin of Elton John) gave Forest an early 2 goal lead and it appeared that Luton were about to be overwhelmed until that knife edge of fortune took a cruel twist and Dwight was stretchered off after 32 minutes with a broken leg after a seemingly innocuous tackle.

The Reds hung on for a dramatic 2-1 win in those days prior to the use of substitutes and at a time when fitness levels, particularly on the emotionally and physically draining Wembley turf, were at a far lower level than in today's game. It turned the 1959 Final into a memorable battle of drama and tension as Forest, now the underdogs, battled valiantly to protect their lead and become the first team to win an FA Cup final with only ten men.

Nottingham rejoiced and thousands packed Slab Square to welcome the returning heroes. The scenes of jubilation, unlike the televised match itself, had a magical and awe inspiring affect, and I can still see Jack Burkitt, Forest's captain, holding the Cup aloft, the open-topped bus surrounded by a seemingly endless sea of cheering masses. Roy Dwight, the wounded hero, sat with his outstretched leg in plaster, and was sadly never to recover fully from the injury, which finished his career.

Forest took the acclaim of the jubilant City of Nottingham from the Council House balcony. It was a celebration of civic pride, as well as a victory for the Reds and in a way it was a watershed between the post War years of austerity and drabness and the optimism and vibrancy of the 60s, reflected locally in massive slum clearance programmes.

Every Forest supporter should be compelled to learn, Michael Palin style, per his excellent "Ripping Yarns" series, the famous 1959 Forest cup winning team, so repeat after me :-

"Thomson, Whare, McDonald, Whitefoot, McKinlay, Burkitt, Dwight, Gray, Wilson, Quigley, Imlach".

My Forest Supporters Apprenticeship started the following season at the age of eight when my father insisted on taking me to a number of Home matches as a "treat", although in the early days at least the football was of less interest than the promise of a half time soft drink and a bar of chocolate.

I can't claim to recall my first ever game, but have distinct memories of the balding Jeff Whitefoot, another Geoff (Vowden), Johnny Quigley, ever present Bobby McKinlay and, at the tail end of his Reds career, Stuart Imlach.

For some reason Birmingham City spring to mind and I recollect that we were involved in some dour struggles against the Blues. They were not only difficult to beat at the City Ground at that time but also had an appreciation of the less subtle aspects of the game, an area that was to be honed to "perfection" (a misnomer if ever there was one) by Don Revie and his Leeds team of the 70s.

Memories of the early 60s are of an average to poor Forest side, happy to retain First Division status, with any end of season position above half way being considered a measure of some success.

I spent those days on the uncovered Bridgford End, a shallow expanse of terracing which legitimately acquired a reputation for being like a morgue, unlike the Trent End which was to develop during the 60s into a swaying, singing, chanting mass, the sound reverberating from under the low roof. Whilst Liverpool's Kop and Manchester United's Stretford End were numbers one and two respectively, by season 1966/67 the noise and atmosphere generated by Forest's compact Trent End arguably matched that of any other English club.

Well before that historic season I'd developed a passion for Nottingham Forest Football Club that intensified with every disappointment, always expectant that the next match, or maybe the next season, or rumoured transfer target, would change everything.

My father had quite rightly taught me to ignore the Notts County propagandists still living the legend of Tommy Lawton (but never getting off their backsides to make the trip to Meadow Lane) and to honour Wally Ardron who was Forest's goalscoring hero of the 50s, but always in the shadow of the black and white striped one.

My red and white bias was such that I began to nurture the beginnings of a dislike for County and their ever whingeing "supporters" who talked a good match without ever going to see one. Mind you, they knew that every Notts defeat was down to the referee.

The annual County Cup competition, run for charitable causes by the Notts F.A., and compulsorily involving Nottinghamshire's powerhouse trio of the Reds, Stags and Magpies was a focal point for my burgeoning antipathy towards Notts and I recollect Forest giving them a good thumping at the end of the 63/64 season, with Frank Wignall scoring a hat trick.

That season also encompassed my first away matches, Leicester (which more or less became an annual event) and, right at the death, Manchester United. Forest lost 3-1, my abiding recollection being of the vast expanses of covered terracing and a raucous home crowd. The modern Old Trafford is barely recognisable from that 1964 relic but at the time it was so imposing and intimidatory that it belonged to another world.

So, for that matter, did the Spurs double winning "push and run" side, a team that is a memorable contrast to Revie's cynical 70s outfit. I have vivid recollections of a sunny Saturday afternoon in 1962 (the records show it as September 29th) when a group of us were playing football on the local "Rec." off Valley Road, Carlton. A late arrival came with the sensational news that we were winning 1-0 at White Hart Lane.

I could scarcely wait to get home for twenty to five for the final score on the radio. (Nowadays most teams are still playing at five, or Sunday, or Monday, or whenever Murdoch dictates).

Had we managed to hang on? Even a draw would be superb. The familiar, nerve jangling, Sports Report music was quickly followed by the calm, measured, alphabetical announcement of the results, starting with "English League, Division One" (not a sponsor's name in sight!).

I could barely stand the tension as the list inexorably moved on, until "Tottenham Hotspur 9, Nottingham Forest 2" left me in a state of semi shock. It was my biggest disappointment so far as a Reds supporter and I wasn't exactly consoled by the fact that we'd scored first and last (Colin Hockey and Geoff Vowden). Jimmy Greaves, who scored more League goals against Forest than any other club, settled for a modest four.

Further dismay came my way on December 1st when I missed our home game against Burnley due to a viral infection. It laid me low and caused me, unusually, to take a couple of days off school (I hate people who skive with the merest hint of a sniffle and say they've had the 'Flu). Unfortunately, my mother argued, logically, that I wasn't fit for the match on Saturday.

As a result I missed one of the City Ground wonder goals, scored by "Flip" Le Flem, who played on the left wing. His effort would have been exceptional even by fellow Channel Islander Matt Le Tissier's standards, as he beat 5 defenders in a mazy dribble before steering the ball into the net. The newspapers went into raptures and my mate Phil couldn't wait to tell me all about it at school on Monday.

Le Flem's presence also inspired the appalling schoolboy joke :- "Look, Le Flem". "Where?" Revolting noise of throat clearing and other exaggerated bronchial sounds followed by the depositing of large globule of spit onto the pavement. "There".

Bobby McKinlay

Any so called Forest supporter who doesn't know that Robert ("Bobby") McKinlay holds the all time appearance for the Reds should be forced to watch Notts County.

He made his League debut on 27th October 1951 (I was just over 3 months old at the time) in a 3-3 draw at Coventry City and went on to make 685 appearances, just about all of them at what used to be called Centre Half. Ian Bowyer comes a distant second, 121 games behind, or approximately 3 full seasons, with 564.

McKinlay established himself during the 1950s, an era which also featured Nottingham's star forwards Tommy Capell and Wally Ardron, but only came into my consciousness during the 1960s when I came to understand that the first name on every teamsheet was R. McKinlay at number 5.

His record is phenomenal, with a staggering run of 9 consecutive seasons from 1959/60 to 1967/68 when he missed just one League match, a 2-1 Home defeat to Aston Villa. Our previous game, away at Sunderland, was his 265th consecutive appearance, a breathtaking achievement in any standard of football, let alone at the top Professional level. I've known players who could scarcely manage 265 consecutive minutes without breaking down.

He also missed one other match during that 1965/66 season, our FA Cup 4th round tie on February 12th against Hull City at Boothferry Park. We'd been beaten 5-3 at The Hawthorns in our previous game (a typical Reds v. Baggies special) so our defence wasn't exactly on top form, but it was a shock when Danny Wilson, who played only 2 matches all season, came out of the tunnel wearing McKinlay's number 5.

I remember the dismay of the Reds fans around us. We needed all the experience we could get against the lowly but ferocious Tigers and their deafening support in a full house of 38,055. We went out tamely, 2-0, and post match rumours surfaced that there had been "domestic bother" within the Forest camp en route to Hull. Whether that's all a load of cobblers I don't know, but it remains a mystery that could explain Forest's dispirited capitulation.

Anyway, it would be nearly 3 seasons before anyone else got their hands on that shirt, and who better than Terry Hennessey, who donated his customary number 4 to John Barnwell for the day on December 21st 1968. It was the first tangible sign that not even R. McKinlay could go on for ever and the end of an era was in sight.

McKinlay played his last game on November 15th 1969, a 3-1 defeat at Newcastle (Dave Hilley got our goal) watched by 24,307. His unbeatable appearance record, which featured a goal every 68.5 games (9 in the League and 1 in the FA Cup) ultimately owed everything to exceptional fitness and the good fortune to escape that one career threatening moment that can arrive out of the blue in any match.

McKinlay's upright, no nonsense, style and persona was strictly military. His tall, lean, Guardsman's frame patrolled a narrow furrow up and down the centre of the pitch, but rarely inside opposition territory – the archetypal traditional Centre Half. Strong in the tackle and in the air, his role was essentially as a stopper, creative ambitions usually satisfied by a simple lay off to a colleague or a thump downfield or into touch.

He retired from Football, appropriately, into the Prison Service, a reflection both on his character and the era in which he played. I can't imagine Des Walker, or even Steve Chettle, needing the security of a job in the Public Service Sector to eke out their meagre earnings from Football, but one thing that no amount of money can buy is Bobby McKinlay's permanent place of honour in the Nottingham Forest record books.

Bobby McKinlay was synonymous with an era that saw youngsters, including myself, arriving for big games with home made wooden boxes where we'd be precariously perched by our fathers. The state of the art construction was honed to perfection so as to fit snugly on the narrow Bridgford terracing, and the funereal atmosphere was irreverently enlivened by the machine gun clattering of whirling rattles.

It was also punctuated by cries of "Oy, watch it!!" as the occasional burst of juvenile over enthusiasm resulted in a near miss (or worse) and I seldom returned from a match without a couple of self inflicted bruises where I'd clouted myself on the head. For my pains I'd receive the sympathetic response that "where there's no sense there's no feeling". Nowadays there's a likelihood that "compensation" would be claimed from the manufacturer.

The earliest arrivals would claim a position hard against the low concrete wall surrounding the pitch, where they could clatter away with impunity, but even in those early days I appreciated the far better view from higher up, and would remain with my father some 20 steps back, just to the right of the goal.

The vast majority of the spectators arrived from the Trent Bridge end, on foot or by Public Transport (the Lady Bay Bridge was still in commission by the Midland Railway as one of its 2 Southbound routes). Most of them couldn't be bothered to walk round to the Pavilion Road turnstiles or try to push through the crowd to the gate – which might in any case be locked - in the fence that partitioned the Bridgford Terrace and so I learned the valuable lesson that even for popular games a decent view could usually be had by using a bit of common sense.

It was exactly the same at the Trent End, where all access funneled supporters to its Main Stand end. By walking to the furthest (i.e. East/Exec Stand end) of the 3 sets of entrance steps and emerging to the left of the goal it was usually possible to find ample room.

In later years I would despair at the mentality of the Police when TV highlights proved my comment at the game that there was loads of space left of goal, where I was standing, yet the Main Stand end was allowed to become a solid, surging, mass of fans desperately – perhaps dangerously-craning to get a half decent view. Late comers were accommodated in this already crowded corner when two thirds of the Trent End was scarcely half full by comparison.

Once the permitted quota was in, "Trent End full" would be announced, albeit that its overall capacity was substantially reduced from those atmospheric days of the 60s and 70s and regardless of sensible crowd apportionment across its 3 fenced sections – echoes perhaps of the infamous Leppings Lane.

All that was in the future. May 10th 1963 saw the debut of Ian Storey-Moore (or just Ian Moore as he preferred to be known) in our 2-1 home victory over Ipswich Town. I'm proud that I was one of the modest 13,055 in attendance, although I can't claim to remember much about his contribution other than him being a skinny lad wearing no. 11 and that we'd plucked him from non League Boston Utd. He didn't score, the honour going to Len Julians – our regular, (and often barracked), no. 9 before Frank Wignall's arrival in 1963/64 – and an own goal.

My earliest Forest hero was our no. 1, a goalkeeper who rates as one of the Reds greatest ever players, perhaps 2nd only to Ian Moore in our hall of fame. It might be true that early impressions and memories are often the most influential and enduring but the records dispel any suggestion that my recollections are clouded by rosy tinted nostalgia.

Peter Grummitt

There was never a doubt that a goalkeeper would feature in any choice of special Reds, but which one? There have been perhaps 3 exceptional Forest custodians during my time.

Hans van Breukelen fails to qualify as number one no. 1 due to lack of time served, but the big Dutchman otherwise displayed in his couple of seasons a massive presence. He was an excellent shot stopper, but his intelligent quickfire distribution, unsurpassed by any Reds keeper, was a special feature, as was his commanding personality – shades of Peter Schmeichel as he kept his defence organised in a quiet, unassuming, way.

Peter Shilton would be the majority choice, near enough 100% for anyone under 40, and his achievements can't be overstated. However, his weakness on crosses was only compensated for by the efforts of others. Messrs. Lloyd, Burns, Needham, etc., had aerial control in most situations, whilst the new unwritten refereeing directive spared his blushes on others. It was deemed (and still is) that any goalkeeper failing to cleanly catch a cross above head height, with an opposing player within 10yards, would be automatically awarded a free kick.

Thus it was one City Ground Saturday when Shilts charged off his line in a hopeless cause in an attempt to intercept a centre, leaping studs first into an innocent forward and pole-axing him. The ball ricocheted off Shilton's flailing arms, onto the back of his leg, and into the Bridgford net. Own goal or, at least - if the ref cocked up the Advantage rule - Penalty. No other possibility. The ref gave Forest a free kick for, presumably, "Keeper failing to catch the ball".

Such absurdities didn't feature in Peter Grummitt's day and that, amongst other reasons, is why the slightly built, unprotected, Grummitt gets my vote.

He arrived from lowly neighbours Chesterfield and replaced Chick Thomson, our veteran 1959 Cup Winners medallist, making his debut at the City Ground in Division One on 12th November 1960 against Bolton Wanderers. I was there with my father, perched on my wooden box at the Bridgford End.

18,812 are officially recorded as having turned up, but a good few hundred were still meandering into the ground, or queuing for programmes, or Bovril (arguably the vilest concoction known to Man), when Grummitt conceded his first top class goal, in what are surely unique circumstances. With barely a minute gone he was picking the ball out of the net, courtesy of an own goal by Forest's long serving midfield stalwart Jim Iley. Scarcely a confidence booster for the nervous debutant, but we recovered to record a 2-2 draw.

In truth I can't remember anything of the match, but my formative Forest years were dominated, goalkeeper-wise, by our new signing, who was to become **the** all time number one for the Reds.

Our new keeper, unassuming in demeanour and build, nervous and short on confidence, (Jim Iley's first minute contribution didn't help) displayed the equivalent of a goalkeeper's stammer, with a namby pamby girlie way of taking goal kicks that was wide open to ridicule, especially at away games. As he started his run up he'd hesitate, execute a mincing double footed shuffle, up on his toes like the Sugar Plum Fairy, before regaining his stride and belting the ball upfield. Like a golfer with an attack of the "Yips", but in Grummitt's case it was permanent.

Appearances were never more deceptive. Goal kicking eccentricities aside, Grummitt proved himself more than worthy of his place and immediately became a fixture, first choice no less than 26 times between his November debut and the end of the season.

He made 26 appearances again in season 1960/61, but over the next 6 seasons he missed just 11 League games, 8 in 1962/63 alone and just one in each of consecutive seasons 63/64, 64/65 and 65/66. He played every game in 1961/62 (the Winter of the Big Freeze and rock hard, rutted, surfaces) and also in our epic 66/67 Season, including 10 in the Cup for good measure.

Grummitt became a hero to every true Forest fan and I was a privileged follower from behind the goal. His slim build, youthful appearance and nervous disposition belied a steely disposition and strength of character that, allied to his unsurpassed brilliance as a shot stopper, could practically reduce the opposition to tears. I think it did once, at Leeds on 26th September 1964 when he gave the greatest display of goalkeeping that I have ever seen.

My father treated me to a visit to fortress Elland Road, where Leeds were undefeated in 33 games. Forest undid them 2-1, with goals by Wignall and Hinton, before a crowd of 32,778. So much for the bare statistics.

From our spot halfway up the open bank of terracing at the Kop end we saw Leeds overwhelm Forest with waves of attacks, yet finish on the wrong end of the scoreline as Grummitt kept them at bay with a string of sensational saves. The 2nd half was one way traffic as the Yorkshiremen (and Leeds probably had a few in their side in those days) poured forwards in a desperate attempt to preserve their unbeaten run.

Every time Leeds thought they'd equalised Grummitt produced another miracle – blocking the ball with his body, claiming it amidst a ruck of players, athletically flicking a header over the bar, hurling himself full length to push a piledriver round the post, or somehow deflecting a point blank "cert" to safety.

Leeds were roared on by their passionate support, staccato chants of "Leeds", "Leeds", "Leeds" ringing around Elland

Road, but their exhortations were in vain and were turned, on the final whistle, into acclamation for our Keeper. "Grummitt saves Forest" was a regular headline throughout his illustrious career, but it was never more appropriate than at Elland Road on 26th September 1964.

By the end of our glorious 1966/67 adventure he had played in 165 of our previous 168 League games, taking hefty batterings along the way from many an opposition hitman, aeons before the imbalance was over corrected and the current and ludicrous "free kick for goalkeeper not catching the ball" rule was introduced.

Injury inevitably caught up with him and in 1967/68 he was limited to 27 League appearances, dwindling to 17 in 68/69 and just 2 in his final season as he struggled and failed to recapture his previous level of fitness and athletic consistency.

On 27th September 1969, almost 9 years since watching his Forest debut, I witnessed his last match for the Reds, at the City Ground, in a crowd of 23,394. The opponents were Crystal Palace and fittingly Peter Grummitt kept a clean sheet, in an otherwise forgettable 0-0 draw.

Special memory – that performance at Elland Road.

~

The early 60s saw a sprinkling of excursions to away matches and one of my earliest memories is of a trip with my father to Villa Park. We went by Football Special from Victoria Station, at a time when Nottingham had a railway infrastructure, slap bang into the City centre, that was probably unparalleled. Strange to think that there are people serving jail sentences who are, morally at least, less culpable than those decision makers who walked away from their legalised destruction with nothing but big egos and fat wallets. Unfortunately, I see little prospect of future enlightenment.

At the time I was only concerned with the type of locomotive (steam, of course) that would be hauling us and was disappointed, but not surprised, to find that it was one of the ubiquitous "workhorse" Black 5s. We were also to find that the driver was barely capable of operating the thing and one reason that the trip stands out so vividly (if not the result of the game) is the constant juddering and ferocious stop-start braking that threatened to throw us from our seats. Only after a change at the controls for the return journey could it be argued that steam power could give new fangled Diesel a run for its money.

Villa Park, as with Old Trafford, had vast expanses of terracing that would look dated today but at the time were impressive compared with the City Ground. Even more so was our view from the Main stand where I enjoyed the unprecedented luxury of a seat. My first ever such indulgence seemed like the ultimate in decadence and the lofty panorama over the pitch had me awestruck throughout the match. Our exposed Bridgford End spot seemed prehistoric in comparison.

My first visit to Leicester City conveyed a similar impression, although I felt a little queasy as we gazed down from the front row of the upper tier behind the goal. City's veteran double decker is still there – until they move.

Visiting Leicester, as with our other East Midlands rivals Derby, was like entering a giant shoe box. Their cramped pitches were hemmed in claustrophobically by the terraces and stands, separated only by the narrowest of running tracks. The linesmen ("referee's assistants" in today's politically correct parlance) looked as though they were actually picking their way through the crowd, conspicuous only by their semaphore flags.

It was something of a culture shock to me, used to the open spaces of the City Ground with its huge playing surface and acres of running track. It was even more of a shock to find that their supporters were prepared to back their teams with a passion that was almost absent (until that famous 1966/67 season) at the City Ground.

Filbert Street buzzed with anticipation and excitement as Leicester sprayed the ball about with characteristic zip and precision, and Derby, in later years, (under you know who) were to perfect a similar style. Ironic that both clubs were to suffer the disadvantage of their compact, intimidating, stadiums as pitches became Winter quagmircs and Spring deserts.

For me, those early away trips, with their added adventure, whetted my appetite enormously and I found myself increasingly demonstrative in support of the Reds on foreign territory, prior to the proliferation and scourge of mob violence. Considerations of personal safety were scarcely an issue. In any case I was always looking for an excuse to travel somewhere further afield, whether it be trainspotting trips with mates to Grantham for the East Coast Main Line, bike rides to Lincolnshire or Derbyshire, or in support of the Reds.

Thus it was that on February 20th 1965 at the tender age of 13 I travelled alone to South London to follow Forest at Selhurst Park in round 5 of the FA Cup.

We'd beaten Norwich City 1-0 (scorer, Colin Addison, one of my favourite players at the time) at the City Ground in the 3rd round on a miserable rainswept day that was dramatically illuminated for me by a huge and colourful (hard to be anything else in yellow and green!) Norwich contingent.

There was no formal crowd segregation, but the bulk of their supporters were on the terraces in front of the old East Stand, absolutely soaked, but magnificent in their backing, punctuated at regular intervals by boisterous renditions of their unique and eccentric "On the ball, City", the like of which I'd never heard before. The gate of 28,574, in miserable conditions, included some 8,000 from Norfolk, temporarily leaving East Anglia with a severe tractor shortage.

If I remember correctly, Addison aquaplaned in and slid home the ball at the Trent End, where I was sheltering from the elements at the Main Stand corner – one of only a couple of occasions when I opted for what was one of the worst views in the ground. I can still recapture the excitement of the pre-match build up, the thrill of the atmosphere generated by the Canaries fans and the euphoria at our unexpected and undeserved winner.

The FA Cup held real magic in those pre television days. The rain turned my hand knitted - by my mother, not me, I hasten to add - woolen scarf into a soggy mess as I retraced familiar steps back up Arkwright Street towards the City Centre, but my mind was set only on Monday's 4th round draw.

Sunderland at fanatical Roker Park hardly inspired confidence, but we were going well in the League (with an excellent finish in 5th place) and the Mackems were brushed aside 3-1, Addison and Wignall adding to Charlie Hurley's own goal. The second that I heard the result I knew it was Forest's year and that I'd be there for the 5th round.

My friends were either not interested or not allowed to travel to deepest suburban South Norwood where in any case a Reds victory against such lowly opposition as Crystal Palace was a foregone conclusion. I also had the benefit of cheap Rail travel, the only perk of my father's employment.

The Eagles were one division below us, having risen from the old third, although ominously they were on something of a roll and had pretensions on achieving greater things. They were a Southern equivalent of Coventry City.

My only concern was the British weather, late February doing its best to put the mockers on everything with overnight snow. As far as I could tell in those pre – Teletext – pre almost anything – days the match was still on and as there were no discouraging blackboard notices at Midland station I boarded the almost empty train to St Pancras in lighter spirits.

By the time it arrived in London I was absolutely frozen, and still alone in my compartment, the heating having failed to respond to any number of permutations and beltings. There was also a cheerily whistling icy draft that couldn't be stifled by any means known to man. I wondered if I was perhaps suffering from the first stages of exposure and welcomed the crowded warmth of the Underground as Scott would have received an AA Recovery team.

I emerged back into Winter – albeit a diluted, Southern Softie, version – and onto another proper train, and another miserable effort, this time of shabby Southern Region suburban commuter stock. I arrived outside Selhurst Park some 2 hours before kick off, and was reassured to spot a few other desolate Reds fans amongst the gathering programme sellers, police and sundry match officials. The area was otherwise practically deserted – not a Palace fan in sight.

Anyone familiar with the area will appreciate that there's little to do for a couple of minutes, let alone 2 hours, so as soon as the gates were open I decided I'd rather shiver inside the ground than outside. I claimed a discreet spot on the terrace at the main stand side a few yards in from the corner flag, with the huge open expanse of terracing banked up behind the goal just to my left. I demolished the remains of my rations, alone apart from a sprinkling of Reds and a few stewards, and waited for the crowd to arrive.

By kick off 41,167 were wedged inside and my eardrums were ringing with the deafening chants of "Eagles, Eagles". I'd never remotely anticipated such fanatical home support, especially for a Southern team of such lowly standing, and it began to permeate my brain that it might not be such a stroll after all.

The gluepot pitch didn't stop Palace tearing into Forest with passion, pace and skill and it was the Reds who were outclassed. We went down 3-1, but I knew from early on, when Alan Hinton went down in the cold treacly morass just in front of me, that we didn't fancy it. Forest's answer to the creature from the black lagoon rose slowly to his feet, to a cacophony of derision, looking as though he'd rather be anywhere but Selhurst Park. I knew the feeling.

We were never in it and I learnt the painful lesson, to be repeated again next season, (and in many others) that being a Forest supporter means never being able to underestimate the opposition, no matter how inferior they may appear.

It's worth noting the Reds line up, which on paper was pretty convincing :-
Grummitt, Hindley, Mochan, Newton, McKinlay, Whitefoot, Addison, Moore, Wignall, Barnwell, Hinton.

I left on the instant of the final whistle, glad to put distance between me and the euphoric Palace supporters, and even gladder to be out of St Pancras on the Nottingham train. Pockets of lying snow flashed white through the window as we made thankful ground northwards and I shivered, but couldn't care less, in another unheated carriage.

It was déjà vu a year later, when on February 12th 1966 my father accompanied me on another away day special, this time to 3rd Division Hull City. (Interesting fact – Hull is the largest English city never to have hosted a top division football club, and anyone who thinks that it's because it's a Rugby League stronghold should have been there in 1966).

We'd beaten fellow 1st Division club Northampton Town 2-1 away in the 3rd round and I knew that we weren't going to suffer the indignity of a second consecutive FA Cup disaster against a bunch of also rans. It was purely coincidence that the weather conditions were very similar.

We travelled North by Football Special, a despised (by me) Diesel Multiple Unit. It did at least have the benefit of a working heating system, fierce blasts of tropical air surging through the shin level vents. I spent the journey with my legs contorted hideously so as to avoid the certainty of 1st degree burns. As we approached Hull the balmy influence of the North Sea put paid to any lingering patches of snow and I couldn't wait to exorcise the ghost of Selhurst Park.

We had time to wander around Hull first and marvel at their yellow telephone boxes, before travelling back by the local rail connection to the station at Boothferry Park, directly behind the ground itself. The stadium was years ahead of the City Ground, and we had a great view from the seats behind one of the goals.

The pitch was heavy, but otherwise in excellent condition, but the home support, in a full house of 38,000, was even more intimidating than at Palace. It was an unrelenting barrage of sound, and the Tigers responded, ripping Forest apart in a 2-0 win that flattered the Reds.

We were a pale imitation, and subsequent gossip was that there'd been something of a "domestic" in the Forest camp, with a somewhat strained atmosphere, euphemistically speaking, on the team bus (see earlier Bobby McKinlay feature).

I'd already suffered a few dire performances in my 5 years or so with the Reds but a precedent was set on that day by our taking the unspoken decision to leave some 5 minutes before full time and with the roars of the crowd still in our ears we boarded the train back into Hull.

It was packed with the happy smiling faces of the returning Forest faithful. The reflective silence was broken only occasionally by the wit and repartee of a throwaway jest of the kind we Reds fans are renowned :-

"What a bunch of effing spineless wankers"

The Hull City debacle effectively ended our season, and we slid to a worrying final League position of 18th, barely safe from relegation. There was however a glorious ray of sunshine on the horizon, and it was to illuminate the City Ground and inspire us to the most dramatic and thrilling season the club had ever had.

Joe Baker arrived some 3 weeks after our Cup exit and made his debut on March 8th in our 1-0 home victory over Burnley. The crowd of 28,246 was 7,000 up on our previous (and pre-Hull) home game, against Newcastle, and the legendary striker had already captured imaginations and repaid the first instalment of his fee. He was to capture the hearts of Reds fans in a whirlwind love affair that took our breath away.

The legendary striker hit it off with Ian Moore and with big Frank Wignall taking the knocks and Barry Lyons firing in crosses from the right as a replacement for Chris Crowe we had a forward line that was capable of frightening any opposition. Throw in Grummitt, Hindley, Winfield, Newton, McKinlay, Hennessey and Barnwell and that was essentially the 11 that was to turn the following season into a memorable epic and trigger a passion and atmosphere on Trentside that could previously be experienced only on opposition territory.

Joe Baker

My first recollection of Joe Baker is one of acute disappointment.

Back in those Golden days before saturation television stole the magic and extinguished imagination the only way to see a star in action was at the match itself, apart from the infant "Match of the Day" – some 30 minutes of grainy black and white highlights of one selected match (usually, Liverpool or Manchester United). I missed Baker's appearance in the very first one, playing for Arsenal against Liverpool.

Thus it was that my first live sighting of one of the game's legends was down at the City Ground. I expected a sculptured "Roy of the Rovers" Adonis. I got a midget, whose one memorable contribution nearly brought the house down, or at least the Trent End. I was only a few yards away, just left of the goal, as Baker, glamour centre forward of glamour North London giants Arsenal, turned quickly on the ball in front of goal, took an almighty swipe, executed a schoolboy air shot and fell onto his backside, the ball trickling feebly to the surprised and grateful Peter Grummitt. It was an open goal miss to match some of my best Parks Football howlers.

So that was the mighty Joe Baker, and after we'd all stopped laughing I scarcely gave him another thought until, out of the blue, Forest announced his capture in the early Spring of 1966.

He made a quiet debut on March 8th against Burnley (who were to feature significantly in the Baker folklore of the following season) at the City Ground, Ian Moore scoring the only goal of the game and thereby delivering instalment number one in what was to become a legendary Forest goalscoring partnership.

Like Moore, he was sensational in that never to be forgotten 1966/67 season. With Wignall and Lyons also hitting top form our attacking balance, once we'd got into our stride, was as close to perfect as it's ever been.

I'm not sure why Arsenal agreed to release him. Presumably, they thought they'd seen his best days, but he was re-born at Forest and crowned King of the Trent End. Never before or since (with the possible exception of "Psycho") has a Reds player been idolised to such an extent and although his Forest career was relatively short its legacy is a rich seam of memories.

Baker, and Forest, found their feet after a humiliating 4-0 drubbing at Anfield on November 5th prompted a soul searching dressing room inquest. It was the catalyst for a new team spirit and commitment and for Joe Baker to set the terraces alight.

The diminutive Scot showed us why he'd been a star, in Arsenal's galaxy of stars, and why Turin had flown him to Italy in days when the nearest that most players got to a foreign transfer was a tattoo of Sophia Loren. Baker could turn a defender in an instant, killing the ball with his marker tight on his back and in the same movement spinning through 180 degrees, pushing the ball past his flat footed opponent and catapulting away in a scintillating burst of pace.

As an alternative to fancy footwork he might greet a bouncing ball – often following a high punt downfield by Grummitt – with a flicked back header over his surprised minder, execute his familiar spin, and sprint away on goal. All the more impressive when comparing his 5ft 6in frame with his opponent's usual 6ft plus.

He'd finish with a variety of options – confidently tucking the ball away past the helpless keeper, crashing a shot against his body, hitting a thunderbolt into the roof of the net, or into the Trent, slicing it out for a throw-in, or nonchalantly rounding the keeper and popping it into an empty net. Or he might simply fall over the ball.

Anything could happen, and usually did. Baker did most things in a hurry, with an instinctive striker's flair for creating chances out of nothing. When he was on the ball there was a buzz of expectancy, his quick feet, slippery turn and blistering pace an irresistible combination. He wasn't averse to a slice of "bread and butter" close range poaching, Jimmy Greaves style, service usually courtesy of Messrs. Lyons and Moore, and of course **that** goal against Burnley.

We played them home and away in our Easter programme, following up our 4-1 City Ground romp on March 27th 1967 with a 2-0 win at Turf Moor the next day. Baker scored twice in each game. Our League and Cup charge drew home gates above 40,000 on 9 occasions and 41,586 flocked to Trentside for the first leg of the Burnley double. Under the City Ground floodlights he lit up a fabulous night's entertainment with a stupendous goal.

A right wing cross came in from the Main Stand side. Firmly hit, head high, it was destined to fizz harmlessly across the edge of the Penalty area. It had already beaten the incoming Baker, into No-Man's land behind and above him, or at least that was the unwritten script.

Baker hadn't read the plot. He never did, preferring to write his own story. As the ball flew behind him he simultaneously twisted and launched himself, like a spring heeled acrobat, into a spectacular overhead scissor kick. The odds on making contact with the ball were remote, at best, but with his back to goal he caught it superbly and volleyed an unstoppable shot into the roof of the Bridgford net.

Breathtaking. Outrageous. Unforgettable.

The ground erupted and Baker's goal was the talk of the town for the rest of the season.

He scored 16 in 34 League appearances in 1966/67, plus 3 in the Cup (before Brian Labone's tackle finished his season), to add to 5 in 14 in 1965/66. A return of 16 in 39 plus another 5 Cup gals in 19967/68 were testimony to Baker's continued significance, but as Forest's 1966/67 side disintegrated and adequate replacements were not forthcoming season 1968/69, his final one in a Reds shirt, witnessed a sad decline.

With neither age nor fitness on his side Baker was a pale imitation of his former self – just 4 goals in 30 injury hit appearances, littered with substitutions, before Sunderland signed him. His last game for us was the final one of the season, a 1-0 defeat at Elland Road on 30th April 1969.

He might have overstayed his welcome by one disappointing season but the City Ground welcome on his return as a guest at our Premiership match against West Ham was overwhelming.

"King" Joe was home, and those of us who worshipped from the terraces in those glorious black and white days were proud to pay homage again.

"Zigger Zagger" was back in town!

Never to be forgotten – that goal against Burnley.

~

The 1966/67 Season

The fireworks began after our Bonfire Night roasting at Anfield when we went on to lose only once in our next 28 League and Cup games. We finished the season with absolutely nothing, but our glorious, exhilarating, campaign left memories which aren't even eclipsed by the Cloughie era.

From a personal perspective, unhappy teenage days at school plus my parents disintegrating marriage heightened my need for identity, and having already attached myself lock stock and barrel to Nottingham Forest Football Club their unprecedented flirtation with glory nearly blew my mind.

Even for the less committed it was an adventure that swept them along as Nottingham discovered its own niche in the Swinging 60s, an East Midlands answer to The Beatles, George Best and the Manchester disco scene. Forest became the most talked about team outside the North West, and Match of the Day, in the shape of our 6th round FA Cup tie at home to Everton, would have the highlights of one of the greatest matches ever played.

Our meteoric rise came on the back of an initially largely unnoticed set of good results, but successive 1-0 wins against mighty Everton on December 23rd and 26th respectively saw us climb to the dizzy heights of 3rd in the League. Local interest was well and truly stimulated, with 36,227 at the City Ground on Boxing Day a staggering contrast with the 22,540 at our previous home game, a local derby against Sheffield Wednesday.

When we beat Leeds at home on January 14th it was our 6th consecutive win. 43,849 saw Ian Moore score the game's only goal. They also saw the appalling Billy Bremner, legend at Elland Road but loathed at the City Ground, (to name but one venue) sent off for a nasty foul on Grummitt.

As if our challenge for the Championship wasn't enough to set pulses racing we embarked on an equally dramatic FA Cup run that contained enough twists, turns and drama to cover a lifetime. Remember, we'd just scraped enough points last season to avoid relegation, for the 2nd year running we'd been humiliated in the Cup, and as recently as November we were heading rapidly nowhere again. To say it was unexpected was the understatement of the Century.

It began quietly enough, as it had in the League, with a low key and unconvincing 2-1 City Ground win in the 3rd round against Plymouth. Wignall and Baker were the scorers.

Mind you, the gate of 34,005 was evidence that the City was ready for something to match our League success, and 45,962 saw us demolish Newcastle, 3-0, thanks to Wignall, Barnwell and Baker. (There were 47,188 packed inside the City Ground a week later for our 1-0 League win against Leicester).

The crowds kept flocking in and our 5th round home draw against 3rd Division yokels Swindon Town saw another huge gate, 45,878, including a massive contingent of wurzel eaters. I couldn't remotely contemplate that, in the 3rd consecutive year of trying, and with home advantage, resurgent Forest could possibly fail to comfortably sweep aside these minnows. At the final whistle I trudged home despondent at the prospect of a replay at the cramped and hostile County Ground (even the name had unpleasant connotations) whilst the Railwaymen celebrated their 0-0 draw.

28,008 were packed in on the following Tuesday where Forest's new found resolve saw us hang on against fanatical West Country support to fight another day after a 1-1 draw. Peter Hindley was the unlikely scorer and whilst I didn't go there was no way that I was going to miss the next one.

It was arranged for the following Monday at Villa Park and my mate Phil and I both skived off school early with "dental" appointments. I can still hear the secretary's cheery "Enjoy the match" echoing after me down the corridor. There was no time for the game to be made all ticket, nor was it for some reason even considered necessary, but the whole of Nottingham was going and so, presumably, was Swindon, judging by their following in the City Ground game.

We went on one of the earliest departing supporters coaches – as far as I remember, it's the only time I've ever travelled away by bus – my prediction that it might be chaos proving correct. The Birmingham traffic snaked at snail's pace through Ashby and the numerous villages that punctuated a route that was notoriously slow and difficult even on a "good" day. The A/M42 wasn't even a twinkle in the planners eye at the time and the early Nottingham exodus was enough to bring traffic to a standstill.

Thanks to our foresight (for once!) we arrived in plenty of time for the scheduled kick off, unlike many of our schoolfriends who had not asked or been given permission to leave early. Swindon supporters, having further to travel, had generally made a day of it, but Forest's massive support had generally set off towards tea time. Huge numbers of our fans were turned back 10 or 20 miles short of the ground as the congestion became one huge shambles.

It wasn't much better at the ground, with less than half the turnstiles open, the officials surprisingly surprised and overwhelmed by the massive volume of support which had poured in from both Nottingham and Swindon.

We queued for ages to gain admission to the massive covered bank of terracing that was the Holte End, from where to gaze awestruck at the solid mass of Swindon fans already packing the open Kop at the other end. There was no formal segregation, but Swindon's early arrivals had quickly populated their adopted end and were all around the rest of the ground, including a substantial percentage around us. Thankfully, late arriving Reds gave the Forest support a much needed boost, but we were well outnumbered in an official attendance of 52,596 that excluded perhaps 10,000 from Nottingham.

Forest redressed the imbalance on the field in a surprisingly one sided game that had me wondering if Swindon were really a 3rd Division team. We'd forgotten how to capitulate to inferior opposition and ran out comfortable 3-0 winners with one apiece from Lyons, Baker and Barnwell. It was only the next day at school that I learnt what had happened to our missing support.

"Bastards!" was the cordial greeting to Phil and myself from Ken, who'd conscientiously worked a full afternoon before crawling by coach to some 10 miles short of Villa Park, there to be turned back, along with thousands of others, with the match already underway.

Ken, as usual, had been somewhat slow off the mark in contemplating a late afternoon visit to the dentist (he was to display similar qualities whilst playing up front in our Parks team) and the school had by then rumbled the "coincidence" of so many pupils requiring an early finish due to various sudden medical conditions. Still, we all had the 6th round draw to look forward to.

For the 4th time running, Forest's name came out of the hat first and we drew the tie of the round, against Everton, who would be desperate for revenge after our League double. Even I doubted that we could achieve the impossible by beating them 3 times in just over 3 months.

I got tickets for the Trent End, including one for my brother and one for our next door neighbour Richard, and counted the days down. The game, on April 8th, came on the back of 6 straight wins, including the fabulous Easter double over Burnley, and as the big day arrived it all seemed too good to be true – surely we were due a defeat.

The whole City was buzzing in expectation and on a grey drizzly day we were amongst the first in the Trent End, superbly positioned against a crash barrier halfway back and right behind the goal. We needn't have bothered.

By 2pm it was obvious that we might as well have turned up at five to three as the goal had all but disappeared behind a sea of people and it was almost impossible to move in any direction. If Crystal Palace and Hull City had been an education in terms of crowd passion then Reds fans were learning quickly and by 3pm it was obvious that this could be the game.

Everton's large following was liberally spread, in a sellout 47,510, along the East Stand terracing and interspersed with the Bridgford End supporters. 5 or 6 Scousers had somehow acquired tickets for the Trent End and were shouting themselves hoarse in a vain attempt to compete.

By kick off we had already endured over an hour of "sardines". At one minute past three, the first time that the ball was at our end of the pitch, a huge crowd surge sent my brother spilling off the end of our crash barrier and careering down the terracing, and we never saw him again until the final whistle.

By two minutes past three, Joe Baker, our predicted matchwinner, had been heavily clattered by Brian Labone (was it purely a mistimed challenge?) and was clearly struggling before eventually limping off. Soon afterwards Everton went 1-0 up, the Forest support had gone deathly quiet, the Scousers to my left were giving it full volume and my ribs were beginning to hurt.

Half time arrived with the score unchanged, the past 3 weeks bubble of anticipation well and truly burst. The Trent End gently swayed in stunned silence and the prospects of recovery for Baker-less Forest looked bleak.

Everton must have wished that half time had never arrived. Forest took them, and us, by surprise as they lifted their game, and the crowd, storming the Trent End. Ian Moore was about to write himself into our hall of fame with a virtuoso goalscoring performance and equalised early on with a close range tap in following a half stop by the keeper. The ground absolutely exploded in celebration and relief, the roof came off the Trent End, and my ribs stopped aching. Game on.

The game ebbed and flowed to a pulsating atmosphere, and I was vaguely aware that the whole of the City Ground, including the undemonstrative Bridgford End, was roaring us on, with the Toffees fans letting it rip in return. Vaguely, because the cacophony of sound from our end drowned out the rest of the crowd.

Ian Moore did it again midway through the half, hitting home a fierce drive. I know because I saw the highlights on TV, but at the time my last view of each goal was of him connecting with the ball followed by a simultaneous explosion of sound and waves of jubilant bodies surging down the steps.

The Trent End – in fact the whole ground – went absolutely mental and it was the turn of the Everton fans to stand in silent dismay and shock. At least it was until one of their own spirited counter attacks brought a late equaliser that sent their hordes into raptures and practically launched the half dozen Trent End Scousers into orbit.

I felt that we were as good as out of the Cup, the celebrating Evertonians clearly sharing my assumption that a Goodison Park replay would see us off. The desperate last few minutes ticked agonisingly by, for both sets of fans, until Ian Moore, with scarcely a minute to go, played his trump card.

The TV that night showed him surging through, only to have his shot blocked by a defender. He latched onto the rebound and crashed in a second effort, which spun into the air off the keeper. Still coming forwards, he headed the ball towards the empty net, only to see it rebound off the crossbar. Moore was first to react as everything seemed to go into slow motion. He threw himself forwards again and headed it into the back of the net.

From my position behind the goal the action consisted of an oncoming Ian Moore about to shoot, followed by a series of crowd surges, a sequence of agonisingly stifled celebrations, and then a huge and unremitting explosion allied with me being carried some twenty feet down the terracing in spectacular confirmation that we'd scored the winning goal of this drama packed epic.

Every Reds fan went up in a delirious, emotional, singing, chanting, clapping, backslapping riot of celebration. We'd ridden an unimaginable, unforgettable, roller coaster of a football match and hat trick hero Ian Moore had somehow contrived to save an almost unbelievable fairy tale ending until the very last act.

Don't let anyone say that Football's "only a game".

Re-united again after the final whistle we left the Trent End as we'd found it, transformed in a few short minutes back into a deserted bank of draughty concrete steps overhung by a low and basic roof structure.

Any sympathy we might have had for Everton (with the emphasis on "might") evaporated as we walked back towards Trent Bridge. We'd just crossed the road near County Hall when without the slightest hint of a warning Richard was suddenly knocked down by a punch in the face. A Scouse voice called out "Come along, William" (I remember how incongruous it seemed, even at the time. "Bill", or "Billy", would have sounded more in keeping).

Thankfully, Richard got to his feet with nothing worse than injured pride and "William", who was clearly not a good loser and was on the lookout for anyone in a Red scarf, obediently trotted off to rejoin his companion. I occasionally wonder, when re-visiting this match, what became of William and whether he ever grew up to accept Life's disappointments in more philosophical fashion.

It was only my second experience of violence at Football, following an incident on Boxing Day - appropriately - 1963 when Forest threw away a 3-0 lead to a late fightback by Sheffield United. Blades fans around us at the Bridgford End were somewhat over enthusiastic in their celebrations, punches were thrown and we escaped from the ensuing melee by scrambling over the wall onto the running track.

The Everton Quarter Final involved over four hours in a swaying mass of tightly packed humanity, going through just about every possible emotion, without a view of any of Forest's goals, all followed by my friend sustaining an unprovoked attack in the street by some looney.

It remains to this day as the one game I would choose to re-live.

The Semi-Final draw pitted us against Spurs at an ideal venue, just up the road at Hillsborough. All of Nottingham wanted to be there so there was no way I could take any chances on not getting a ticket. Apart from a minority of priority applications it was basically "first come, first served" and so as to be absolutely certain my brother and I queued all night, ironically taking our position directly behind the Trent End goal, with maybe a couple of thousand or so ahead of us. By first light there were thousands more behind us and our overnight vigil had clearly paid off.

Well into the morning, two hours or more after the scheduled time for sales to commence, it was obvious that something was wrong, as the queue wasn't moving, yet scores of people could be seen walking back over Trent Bridge towards Town, presumably with their tickets safely tucked away. After an eternity of panicky shuffling and shoving we finally reached a ticket window only to be told that the last of the terrace tickets had just been sold and only seat tickets were available. Between the two of us we scarcely had enough money to cover the cost of one seat and, like many around us, stormed off in furious disbelief.

Phil, who had declined our offer to join us the previous evening, had, we discovered, set his alarm for 5am and cycled down to the ground, picking up a terrace ticket after a modest couple of hours queuing. A secondary queue of latecomers had fed into the head of the original one and whilst those at the front had been able to do something about it the poor bastards like ourselves who were hidden around the corner from the mayhem had no idea what was going on. Nor, predictably, did the Police (or more likely they didn't give a toss) or stewards, if there were any.

Hot on the heels of my all time greatest Forest match came one of my bleakest Football moments. I can still taste the bitter injustice of it all and I'm getting wound up again just typing these lines.

55,000 saw Forest go out of the Cup 2-1, despite a late goal by Terry Hennessey, and I was reduced to following Forest's biggest match in eight seasons on the radio. Defeat by radio was harder to take than the real thing, where emotions can be released from the terraces, and I shed a few tears of frustration and disappointment before disappearing onto the Rec and walloping hell out of a football for the next couple of hours.

Our Championship challenge also faltered, but we had the consolation of finishing second in the League, behind Manchester United, a superb achievement in its own right, let alone coupled with our dramatic FA Cup adventure.

We rounded things off with a 3-2 win at Fulham on May 13th and I travelled down in a tribute to the Reds great season and as a perverse, and inadequate, substitution for my stolen Cup dream. Sammy Chapman, playing up front in those early days, got 2, and John Barnwell the other, and I proudly applauded at the final whistle until every last player had disappeared into the tunnel.

Sounds of the 60s

Our thrilling, unprecedented, flirtation with success in 1966/67 was the catalyst for the Trent End's mutation from a derisory handful of would be cheerleaders ("would be", because no-one else ever joined in) to one swaying, singing, chanting mass as Nottingham joined in with the naïve enthusiasm and self consciousness of the "Swinging 60s".

Imaginations previously had run little further than US College style chanting :-

"2,4,6,8, who do we appreciate?
F,O,R,E,S,T - FOREST!!"

Even worse :-

"We yell, we yell, we yell,
We yell, we yell, we yell,
And when we yell we yell like hell
And this is what we yell :-
1,2,3,4, who the `ell are we for?
F,O,R,E,S,T, - FOREST!!"
Stirring stuff, echoing feebly from 50 gallant souls.

By March 1967, a tightly packed sea of partygoers were lifting the roof and belting out their choruses – old, new, borrowed or, predictably, blue :-

"Whenever you're sad, whenever you're blue,
Whenever the Forest are playing,
You're out of luck, you'll fight like fuck,
To keep the Trent End swaying"
(Sung to the tune of "Just like Eddy")

Liverpool had the Kop, The Beatles and the Cavern. Manchester had the Stretford End, George Best and a vibrant nightclub scene. None of which mattered :-

"Oh, we're better than United & we're louder than the Kop
We're second in the League & we should be at the top"
(Cribbed from Man U to the tune of "McNamara's Band")

Opposition teams were subject to a Trent End serenading of a famous Mexican (I think) tune, thanks to the conveniently named Russian goalkeeping legend and man in black, Lev Yashin :-

"We all agree, Grummitt is better than Yashin,
Joe Baker is better than Eusebio,
And Leicester are in for a thrashing"

Well, 1-0, actually, but an incredible 47,188 of us were there to witness all time Forest great Ian Storey-Moore grab the goal :-

"Give it to Moore, give it to Moore,
He will score, he will score"

Highly sophisticated and imaginative though it may have sounded at the time, this simple Trent End spun homily has perhaps lost a little over the years, but even today's generation will recognise the Troggs in Trentside's two word tribute to our pacy number 7 :-

"Ba-ba-ba-ba-ba-Barry Lyons"

The diminutive, electric, electrifying, Joe Baker was the Trent End King, proudly proclaimed to the tune of "Excerpt from a Teenage Opera" :-

"Joe Baker, Joe Baker,
Is it true what Trent End say,
You are our King?
Oh, yeah, yeah"

The Irish got a look in as Molly Malone was hijacked in homage to the mighty atom :-

"In Dublin's fair city, where the girls are so pretty,
I first set my eyes on sweet Molly Malone,
As she wheeled her wheelbarrow*
Through streets broad and narrow,
crying :-
Joe, Joe, Joe Baker, Joe, Joe, Joe Baker!!"

(* It was subsequently purchased, in rather poor condition, by a team of songwriters from Meadow Lane)

Our tribute was sung slowly, deliberately and atmospherically, unlike the manic, immature, breathlessness of today's express paced songsters, where even Newcastle's traditional "Blaydon Races is stampeded to about 10 seconds flat.

A sea of hands is raised aloft as the punch line approaches. "Joe, Joe, Joe Baker!!" reverberates from 8,000 throats and captivates and lifts the entire City Ground in a phenomenon, as yet fresh and untarnished, that captures the mood of the times and changes forever the way we support our team.

Baker practically cornered the market in Trent End adulation during the second half of season 1966/67, partly due to the simplicity of his name. "Zigger zagger, zigger zagger, Joe Baker" had a nice phonetic ring that couldn't be applied with conviction to other players. Ian Moore had the embarrassment of one feeble dirge and a mention in the following :-

"Come on and cheer again, come on and cheer again,
`Cos we are here again to see the Forest play
Come on and score again, it's Ian Moore again,
And we are sure again, we're gonna win today"

This Trent End version of an original French song, "M`Lord", was as far as I'm aware unique to Forest and begs the question as to who spotted the potential of this catchy but relatively obscure tune, thought up the words and presumably got a few mates to sing along until the rest of the Trent End cottoned on.

All answers gratefully received.

There were plenty of other songs and chants springing up all over the country. Liverpool's "You'll never walk alone" was, and is, the definitive anthem. Now synonymous Worldwide with Liverpool, Gerry Marsden's UK hit was taken from the American Musical "Carousel" and is arguably the most unlikely song ever adopted.

Spurs "Glory, glory, hallelujah", another US import, was my earliest identification with one particular club, but I've no idea how it originally came to be associated with them. In part, I suppose it's down to names again – the chorus would scarcely fit around Hamilton Academicals.

Unfortunately, as in "Who the fuck are Man United", it's been stolen and contaminated and the signs were there in the 60s. Jim Reeves ballad "Distant Drums" was corrupted into a particularly distasteful jibe at opposition fans, but none of this can diminish the memories of those special Trent End days.

~

Out with a whimper

The following season saw normal service resumed and our expectations that Forest would build on their achievements were dashed. A decline set in as the squad fragmented, or players lost form, and consecutive League finishes, from 1967/68 onwards, of 11th, 18th, 15th & 16th were to be followed by an inevitable relegation, which duly arrived at the end of 1970/71.

There was no early strengthening of the squad, and with John Barnwell's appearances hit by injury Sammy Chapman was his struggling deputy until the arrival of the legendary Scottish hero Jim Baxter in early December.

The unfortunate Chapman became a favourite victim of the boo boys early in his Forest career, during which time he was dropped back from the forward line to midfield. I didn't rate him particularly, but had no time for the morons who made his playing life a misery.

Ironically, it was probably those same people who applauded his every foul when he moved yet further back, in later seasons, to his best position, at the heart of the defence. Disappointingly, he developed an all too frequent liking for the use of strong arm tactics, which endeared him to many but which in my opinion brought the club into disrepute. Even though Chapman was on our side I often wished he wasn't, and was pleased when Cloughie unloaded him.

As for "Gentleman Jim" Baxter, if Forest thought they'd made another inspirational signing to follow Joe Baker they were sadly mistaken. We saw flashes of his genius, most memorably a swivel and instant volley dispatched ferociously into the Trent End net, but he was otherwise a disappointment. Drink problems and lack of fitness had overtaken him and unlike Baker he wasn't about to hit an inspired purple patch late in his career.

Baxter did however give us another Trent End adaptation, written by Bob Dylan, sung by Manfred Mann :-

"Come on without, come on within,
You'll not see nothing like the mighty Jim"

At Elland Road on February 17th 1968 he proved us right, sealing our FA Cup 4th round exit with a silly foul that cost us the match. I was in almost the same spot as my previous visit to Leeds when Grummitt was the hero.

This time we were wedged into a capacity 51,739 crowd as Leeds fans were beginning to taste the fruits of the Don Revie era. Grummitt was hoofing a long punt safely downfield when Baxter for some reason pushed over a Leeds player in the Forest box, well off the ball and entirely unconnected with play. It was directly below our position on the Kop.

We couldn't miss it, but hopefully the ref would. No chance. Penalty, and out we went, 2-1. Baxter's motives were a mystery, and he was full of remorse afterwards, but knowing the way that Leeds often conducted themselves I suspect that "provocation" might have been involved.

Still, as a senior and International Pro he should have known better – perhaps taking a leaf out of a certain Leeds players book and slyly kicking his opponent on the back of the ankle when ref, linesmen and the crowd were otherwise distracted.

That was about it for the season, although on the theme of capacity attendances the City Ground had its highest ever gate, for the visit of Manchester United, back on October 28th. 49,946 are officially recorded, but it's known that some climbed in over the fences, making it the only home game in the history of the club with over 50,000 in the ground.

I couldn't get in the Trent End, and reverted to the guarantee of a spot on the Bridgford terrace half way back and just to the right of the goal. By kick off I was down near the corner flag, totally unable to move, other than as part of one compressed, swaying, mass. I remember being seriously worried for a time, and looking back I've no doubt that the ground was dangerously overcrowded. I dread to think what might have happened if additional fences had prevented the Bridgford End from surging outwards into the corners.

For the record, the Reds won 3-1, two from Baker and one from Wignall undoing United.

Jim Baxter stayed for another season, one which saw another relative minnow, this time once proud Preston, dump us out of the FA Cup, 3-0 in the 3rd round. He didn't make that game, and the team that played showed only one change (Chapman for Wignall) from our 1966/67 quarter final line up against Everton.

All was clearly not well in the Forest camp, and the Preston result, following an earlier run of 13 games without a win, precipitated the arrival of Matt Gillies in place of Johnny Carey.

The disastrous fire in the Main stand on 24th August against Leeds didn't help. I missed it, returning home from holiday that Saturday, but otherwise turning up at every possible home game and a good cross section of away ones, including our fixtures at Meadow Lane, which Notts kindly donated until the City Ground was back in commission on November 16th (minus still closed Main stand), where we lost 2-0 to Arsenal.

We played 6 matches at Notts ground and couldn't manage to win any of them. It started with a 3-2 defeat by West Brom in the League Cup before 23,970, which was to be our highest Meadow Lane gate. (We won 5-2 at the Hawthorns 4 days later in the League, just to continue the tradition of silly results against the Baggies). The best we could manage from the next 5 was 3 draws and only 17,651 saw our 4-2 defeat on October 6th at the hands of the northern Magpies, Newcastle United.

I stood on all 4 sides at Meadow Lane in a futile attempt to change our fortunes. It was ironic that Forest's newest stand had gone up in flames when Notts ramshackle, substantially wooden, constructions had lasted since the Vikings first sailed up the Trent. Neither ground of course had perimeter fencing and for the second year running, although no-one fully appreciated it at the time, Forest could be thankful.

The re-opening of the City Ground was welcomed with a collective sigh of relief, but we still managed to lose, and by the end of 1968/69 we'd scraped a dismal 18th place.

Grummitt had broken his thumb back on August 14th at Chelsea and our goalkeeping crisis saw Williamson, Grummitt, Sherratt and Marshall used in successive games.

There was a bright spot with the debut on 22nd March of yet another goalkeeper, Alan Hill from Rotherham United, who kept a clean sheet, 3-0 at home to the Baggies. The agile and brave Hill quickly endeared himself to the fans, but an arm injury at home to Everton the following February finished his career. He played in just 41 League games, but is still fondly remembered.

In 1969/70 we said farewell to Grummitt, Hennessey and Barnwell, with debuts by Collier, McKenzie, Ingram, McCaffrey and Cormack. Dave Hollins came on goalkeeping loan from Mansfield, Liam O'Kane became established, and Chapman dropped back into defence.

The season's highlight was the 2-0 away stuffing of Cloughie's Derby, but I had to give up my ticket due to an attack of Mumps, which I'd managed to avoid as a child and save for a really inconvenient time. 38,225 packed into the Baseball Ground, with the records showing a seated allocation for Reds fans of a derisory 20 tickets – that's less than sit on most Premiership benches these days.

We finished the decade in 15th, which wasn't bad all things considered, and there are no prizes for guessing the name of our top scorer.

Ian Storey-Moore

Ian Storey-Moore, or plain Ian Moore as he preferred to be called, was plucked from the non-League wilds of Boston in Lincolnshire but was to be adopted as a famous son of Nottingham.

As far as I can recall, his arrival prompted little more than the usual passing interest, as another skinny youngster with "promise" joined the club. His progress in the "A" team and Reserves was unspectacular and I'd scarcely heard of him when I saw him make a low key debut, aged 18, on 10th May 1963 in a Division One fixture against Ipswich Town before a meagre City Ground attendance of 13,055. (We won, 2-1, thanks to Len Julians plus an own goal).

Moore's League debut was his only appearance until Boxing Day 1963 when he also scored his first senior goal, against Sheffield United. Frank Wignall and Geoff Vowden got the others to put us 3-0 up, before Blades late revival to 3-3 saw an uncharacteristic explosion of Bridgford End fisticuffs and yours truly, aged 12, over the concrete wall onto the safety of the running track.

He made a modest 12 League appearances that season, but scored a far from modest 6 goals, noteworthy for a centre forward and eyebrow raising given his role at that time as an out and out winger. Nevertheless his progress was slow, problems of fitness and physique limiting him to 13 League games in 1964/65, but a still respectable goals tally of 4.

Another quiet season followed, with a modest 5 League goals, but a confidence building 23 games signalled that the Forest management saw him as a potential first team regular. He had grown up physically and was about to explode into Season 1966/67, co-starring in attack with the mighty atom, Joe Baker.

In from day one in that famous season, he scored 21

League goals in 39 games, but hit the target in only one of 8 Cup ties, the Toffees coming unstuck in a legendary encounter. He'd come of age, and thrilled Reds fans with his powerful, weaving, runs, swerving inside or outside his man before unleashing a ferocious shot, distance no object. I've never seen a player hit the ball better, and with such accuracy that scarcely an effort was wasted – at worst whistling past the woodwork, but usually threatening to burst the back of the net.

On 8th April 1967, before 47,510, he completed his sensational hat trick in the last minute of our pulsating 6th round FA Cup tie at home to Everton and Forest were through to the Semi-Final after the greatest match ever seen on Trentside (see "The 1966/67 Season").

Moore achieved hero status in that unprecedented, exhilerating, season, but our flirtation with glory was just that and we entered a decline that saw the team fragment, but which paradoxically illustrated what a great player Moore was, as he performed heroics in what was ultimately a losing battle.

We came 11th, 18th, 15th and 16th in consecutive seasons before relegation at the end of 1971/72, and Moore's departure, first with Brian Clough for a walk around the perimeter of the Baseball Ground ("Welcome to our new signing". "Oh no, he isn't". "Oh yes, he is". Oh no, he wasn't) and then, officially, to Manchester United, where injury problems quickly caught up with him.

Seasons of clatterings, at a time when you couldn't be sent off for anything less than attempted murder, ended his career. (Mind you, it might have helped if he'd persevered with the idea - first introduced donkeys back at Nottingham Forest by Samuel Weller Widdowson, or someone very similar - of wearing his shinpads, instead of rolling his socks down to his ankles).

It was a painful irony that Forest's brightest, and by that

time only, star was denied the opportunity to shine with a galaxy of stars at Old Trafford, and earn the regular England caps to which he was entitled. He'd remained loyal to Forest's sinking ship, an isolated target man, for Forest and opposition alike. ("Stop Moore and you stop Forest.") He kept us afloat with 17 League goals from 26 games in 1968/69, 11 in 30 in 69/70, 18 in 33 in 70/71 and 13 in 30 in our relegation season 71/72. A one man show in an increasingly disjointed and dispirited Forest side.

Those deprived, through accident of birth date, of seeing Forest's greatest player in the flesh might imagine a far classier and more effective version of Andrei Kanchelskis, perhaps the nearest modern equivalent of Moore's build and direct attacking style. They should also picture a player with an exemplary temperament and, even by the yardstick of the times in which he played, endearing loyalty to the Reds.

His Christmas Holiday goal at the Bridgford End in 1971/72 against Arsenal, nonchalantly tucked under the advancing keeper after a thrilling solo run from deep inside Forest's half, was far and away the highlight of that dismal season, but 3 failed attempts equally characterise his phenomenal abilities to conjure something from nothing.

The inauspicious occasion of a County Cup Final against the Pies is an unlikely recollection. We were awarded a free kick, almost on the touchline, in front of the old East stand and level with the Bridgford Penalty area. County's defence retreated naively, anticipating the floated centre, as Moore placed the ball, one eye on the inviting channel that had opened up.

He took a couple of paces back before stepping up and hitting a venomous drive from some 35 yards that ricocheted off the chest of the startled Notts keeper before he could blink, let alone try to save it. One foot either side, it was a goal. The astonished Notts defenders watched in relief as the ball cannoned miles to safety.

It was a similar story when Cloughie's upstart Derby County gave us a City Ground footballing lesson, Moore providing our only credible repost. Picking up the ball on halfway, on the Main stand side, he made ground before cutting inside and unleashing a ferocious long range effort that crashed back off the Trent End crossbar. Typically, it came from nothing, and no doubt helped persuade Mr. Clough that Moore was the man for Derby, which of course he wasn't – even Forest's management couldn't allow such sacrilege, although it resulted in the Baseball Ground walkabout debacle.

Bramall Lane was treated to Moore missing the ball altogether, but in spectacular and fearless fashion. Forest attacked down the right and a half clearance was smashed back, as an attempted shot, across the face of the Kop goal. Moore, at the near post, instinctively threw himself into a head first dive in a vain attempt to deflect the ball into the net. The ball rocketed across the area and out for a throw in and Moore thus avoided decapitation. Blades fans around me were unanimous in their admiration of his kamikaze effort, which was entirely in keeping with his 100% commitment to the cause of Nottingham Forest F.C.

He's currently back with the club in a Development capacity after a temporary exile with turf of a different kind, in the shape of Ian Storey-Moore, Bookmaker, and if his efforts produce a fraction of his success as a player then Forest will be well rewarded.

Special memory – that winning goal against Everton, the most dramatic moment in my 40years with the Reds.

~

The 1970s (The Wilderness Years)

The early to mid 70s were to encompass Forest's lowest fortunes for many years, with relegation to Division 2 (as it then was), plummeting gates, unrest amongst supporters and staff alike and a playing squad which, with a few notable exceptions, was not up to the job.

Paradoxically, our Second Division status was not to diminish my own support. The novelty of new opposition and the ease of gaining admission to most grounds led to a string of away trips, the purpose of which was generally a lads day out, with Forest as the excuse.

The 70/71season saw the Reds consolidate in Division 1, finishing a semi-comfortable 16th, with Ian Moore, as usual, top scoring, backed up by Peter Cormack. It also featured the debut of a certain John Robertson, coinciding with the final appearance of our fierce tackling stalwart midfielder Henry Newton.

Forest fans, apart from the 1959 Cup win and the tantalising promise of 1966/67, didn't harbour aspirations above their station, but neither did we expect, despite it becoming a regular feature, yet another "Reds Cup shock". Millwall were the lucky no-hopers to draw us out of the 71/72 3rd Round hat, but at least we had the consolation that Cold Blow Lane was every bit as inhospitable as it sounds.

Worse was to follow, with relegation from the 1st Division, and to add insult to injury a 3-0 drubbing at the hands of the Pies in the County Cup Final. Only Moore's goal against Arsenal, and a typical high scoring Baggies encounter (4-1 at home, with Martin O'Neill scoring on his debut) lifted the gloom.

Once the reality of relegation had hit home it was almost unthinkable that we wouldn't bounce back within one or two seasons, but in fact it took five long years before we re-entered the Big League.

There was much to be endured - and occasionally enjoyed - in the meantime. 1972/73 opened with the visit of Portsmouth, and a naively expected easy win, which turned into a dour 0-0 draw. As the season progressed, so reality filtered through the rose tinted mists of optimism and a clear picture emerged – it was going to be bloody hard getting promoted from this division.

Relegated teams tend to fall into one of two camps – either they're immediately up there challenging for re-entry to the higher flight, with sustained, or even increased, support, retention of key players and strengthening of the squad, or they fall away, spectator interest dwindles, good players are replaced by mediocre ones and a dangerous vicious circle sets in and becomes almost impossible to break.

Forest fell into the latter category.

Ian Moore had gone the previous February, Man U bound as our relegation loomed ever larger, and Matt Gillies resigned in October 1972 following a run of pitiful Division 2 results that were already ringing relegation alarm bells again.

Dave McKay took over in November and steered us to relative success, in that we didn't get relegated to Division 3. That dismal first season found us in a final position of 14th. The attendance for our last home game (against Sunderland) was 10,306, a world away from those almost surreal 35/45,000 plus gates which were commonplace in the late 60s.

Strangely enough, our own motley group stayed largely loyal and some half a dozen or so would meet up at one minute to three, where unfortunately we were guaranteed an excellent view from the thinly populated East Stand terrace. Like all long suffering supporters, we found comfort and humour in adversity. A slow handclap (which seems to have disappeared from the modern supporters repertoire) broke out during one particularly dire interlude and Phil spontaneously broke into a rhythmic chant, a la Negro Spiritual, of "A-Men, A-Men……". Within seconds there were a few hundred fellow gospel singers in the choir.

When times are really bad, expectations are low, and the team performance even lower, there's a kind of perverse masochistic delight in taking the proverbial out of the misfortunes of the team and fellow spectators alike, and the early 70s gave endless opportunities. They also brought us to despair.

Phil's usual stoicism snapped once as we were walking across Trent Bridge following a particularly awful display. He had been unusually sullen during an increasingly desperate and rain soaked second half and hardly spoke a word as we left the ground. Midway across the bridge he dramatically tore off his scarf and hurled it petulantly into the murky depths of the Trent.

"That's it, finished. I'm not wasting any more of my time and money watching that crap".

"See you on Wednesday then?" I ventured as we returned home.

"Suppose so" was his reply.

By the end of the season he'd bought a new scarf.

1973/74 showed more promise in the League, with a final placing of 7th, but is memorable for an inspired FA Cup run that came to an end in disgraceful and dramatic fashion.

It was déjà vu in the managerial stakes. Dave McKay departed to fry bigger fish in October and Allan Brown took over in November. He inherited a mixed squad which at last had some team spirit and was capable of causing the odd upset, and we'd surely have clinched our 3rd Wembley Cup Final but for outrageous events both on and off the field.

The 1966/67 Cup run belongs to Ian Moore. 1973/74 belongs to Duncan McKenzie.

Duncan McKenzie

Car jumping, chain smoking Duncan McKenzie lit up the City Ground in season 1973/74 with a brand of eccentric, electric, football that owed its origins to the circus rather than the training ground.

He'd been semi dormant since his debut, aged 19, in our 2-1 defeat at Roker Park on 20th September 1969, which was also his only game of that season. 5 League appearances and 2 goals were clustered at the tail end of 1970/71. We were relegated next season, McKenzie picking up 7 League goals in 31 appearances, and also the departed Ian Moore's shirt for our last 12 games, commencing with a 1-0 defeat at West Brom.

I was there, frozen to death, pissed off and soaked by heavy sleet as early March lived up to its usual promise of Spring and the Arctic Hawthorns to its role as England's highest League ground. To complete a perfect day, we were attacked by Blues fans (of the Birmingham City variety) in the Bull Ring subway, barely diving to safety over the barriers into New Street station.

After relegation, McKenzie played 27 League games in 1972/73, scoring 6 times. The pressure of wearing Moore's famous number 11 was shared by no less than Martin O'Neill, Barry Lyons, George Lyall, Alan Buckley and Miah Dennehy. John Robertson played 28 times and never got a sniff.

Like Moore, McKenzie suddenly burst out of the shadows to illuminate a depressing period of mediocrity, and launch us dramatically towards the Twin Towers. Moore came of age in 1966/67. McKenzie blossomed in 1973/74. He stole the show, scoring 26 in 41 in the League, but, like Moore, saving his best for the Cup – a modest goals tally of 2 in 9 games, but a breathtaking contribution in one very special match. Moore demolished Everton, McKenzie took Manchester City apart.

As in 66/67 it all started quietly, with not a hint of the magic yet to unfold. Our usual cluster of diehards gathered above the tunnel on the East Stand terrace in a meagre gate of 10,792 for our opening League fixture, a deceptively easy 4-0 win against Luton. McKenzie got one, Tommy "flat on his backside" Jackson got 2 and Neil Martin the other. No-one gave much thought to McKenzie's newly acquired talisman – Lucky 7.

He lay claim and wore it all season bar, curiously, Millwall at home on 6th October when Steve Peplow had the privilege and McKenzie wore number 10. Forest won 3-0, McKenzie got 2, and Frank Saul, scourge of our 2-1 Semi Final defeat against Spurs in 1967, got himself sent off. McKenzie reverted to number 7, and failed to score, when they dumped us out of the League Cup 10 days later, after a 0-0 at the Den.

We flattered to deceive in the League, secure but disappointed in 7th place. George Lyall's 11 goals from midfield was the only other contribution in double figures.

We lost the plot in the FA Cup too, not only forgetting to lose in the 3rd Round against "inferior" opposition (Bristol Rovers) but also, for the first time at the City Ground, playing on a Sunday, 6th January. It was an unqualified success. We shaded a thriller 4-3, before a cracking attendance (easily remembered, too) of 23,456. I can't claim to remember much of McKenzie's contribution - Neil Martin with 2, Sammy Chapman and George Lyall were the scorers - but no-one would forget his performance in the 4th Round.

The Bristol Rovers victory triggered a palpable sense of expectancy amongst Reds fans and the visit of 1st Division giants Manchester City on Sunday January 27th drew 41,472. 41,472 of them left the City Ground incredulous at a performance by one individual which ranks alongside Moore's as the greatest ever by a Forest outfield player (Peter Grummitt's performance at Leeds is the goalkeeping equivalent).

Duncan McKenzie simply tore Man City's star studded team to shreds in a one man show that had the match finished by half time and the packed, swaying, terraces delirious with adulation.

Leo Sayer's "One Man Band", popular in late 1974, was made for McKenzie. Individual, unpredictable, he'd take on entire defences single handed in a compelling, often frustrating, mix of master juggler and red faced clown, first bamboozling by sleight of foot, then getting a face full of custard as he fell over the ball.

Against Manchester City his act was flawless, a once in a lifetime virtuoso display of every trick in the Football book. He could do no wrong, shredding their shell shocked defence with an array of impudent flicks, feints, dummies, twists and turns, leaving opponents spinning like tops in his wake. His set up for Ian Bowyer's first, especially sweet against Bowyer's former club, was sensational.

On the halfway line, tight against the Main Stand touchline, he drew gasps as he contrived to kill an impossible, overhit ball, simultaneously swivel through 180 degrees and set off down the line, all in an instant, leaving a baffled marker flat footed.

He danced a tightrope along the line, shimmied past another defender, and wound up in typical McKenzie fashion with nowhere to go, and defenders snapping at his heels, in the Bridgford corner. He cut inside, performed an exquisite nutmeg, and suddenly his wiry frame was bearing down on the near post.

As the keeper closed down the angles McKenzie made the most difficult part look absurdly easy. He glanced up, before nonchalantly rolling the ball back across the box for the incoming Bowyer to joyously sidefoot home. The City Ground exploded and Forest went on to wallop one of the country's top teams 4-1, McKenzie adding his name to the scoresheet for good measure.

38,589 turned up for the next City Ground celebratory Sunday where McKenzie's penalty, the only goal of our hard fought 5th Round tie against Portsmouth, was proof that he could deliver in less spontaneous circumstances.

Dramatic, eccentric, times and the elastic, slightly built, McKenzie would have taken us, on the crest of a tide of passion and emotion, like Sunderland in 1973, to Wembley, but for outrageous bureaucratic injustice in the face of mob rule, and that shocking travesty at St James Park.

Duncan McKenzie left the Reds after the season, for the deserved pastures of the 1st Division, but left us the rich legacy of his halcyon season and that special, undefeated (including our 3-1 win at Newcastle) FA Cup run.

~

The infamous 6th round tie at Newcastle was our first quarter final since Everton, and every bit as dramatic. Forest were written off as no-hopers by the neutrals, but there was a growing sense of expectation amongst Reds fans and some 12,000 travelled to Why-aye Land to mix with 40,000 fanatical Geordies in a sellout crowd.

Our interested group had swollen to about a dozen, so yours truly suggested hiring a minibus, and naturally ended up driving the thing. It seemed like a good idea at the time.

Nottingham on the Friday night was alive with Forest fans, fuelled on booze and confident of giving the Geordies a bloody nose, but it was as nothing compared with the near hysteria of the Newcastle fans, already swarming into the local pubs several hours ahead of kick off. As far as they were concerned they'd as good as already won the Cup and Forest were a minor 2nd Division irritation to be contemptuously swatted aside.

The City centre was in absolute turmoil, with thousands of Magpies followers drunk on the scent of victory and Newcastle Brown. The window of the Strawberry pub erupted outwards into the street in an explosion of shattering glass, and a policeman was seen to carry the offending missile, a chair, back inside, before quietly retreating as the mayhem continued.

Foolishly, naively, and with misguided bravado, our little party wandered the city decked proudly in red and white. We came to no harm, Newcastle fans content at worst to shout ridicule at these idiots from Nottingham who were about to see their team wiped off the face of the planet.

A lady assistant in Woolworth's, where we escaped for food and sanctuary, sought us out and earnestly warned us to be careful as the atmosphere had been building to fever pitch for days. There was not even a 1% possibility in the minds of these, at the most low key of times "volatile", supporters that Newcastle weren't already through to the

Semi Final. The city had gone mad and it was a frightening case of mass delusion.

Our misguided route to the open Gallowgate terrace where the Reds support was mainly housed (along with a substantial Newcastle contingent) took us round the back of the notorious Leazes End where we had first hand experience of the fervour into which the Geordies had worked themselves. It was still largely good natured, but the current of absurdly over confident ridicule and contempt for Nottingham's 2nd Division also rans made it clear that if things didn't go Newcastle's way - and we honestly thought we'd got a great chance – they just wouldn't be able to cope with it.

The atmosphere on the packed terraces was incredible, Reds fans shouting themselves hoarse as Newcastle struggled – just as we'd done so many times – to assert themselves against fiercely committed underdogs on top of their game.

Our star of the moment, Duncan McKenzie, failed to shine, but Newcastle daren't take their eyes of him, perhaps unaware that the likes of Liam O'Kane, Georgie Lyall, Neil Martin, Ian Bowyer, Martin O'Neill and John Robertson could also play a bit.

We were the better side, and sensationally held a 3-1 lead well into the 2nd half, thanks to Bowyer, O'Kane and Lyall, with Newcastle's centre half (whose name stubbornly refuses to trip off the end of my tongue) sent off. All over bar the shouting, and that was all coming from 12,000 demented Reds.

Suddenly, with Forest as good as through and Newcastle ragged and dispirited, there was a crescendo of commotion at the opposite, Leazes, end, and all hell broke out. Hundreds of mardy yobs, unable to live with their broken delusions, and accept defeat to a better side, poured across the pitch towards us. A Forest player was punched and most of the others were jostled or verbally abused.

The situation was potentially horrific and inevitably the game was stopped (but not abandoned) and by the time the pitch had been cleared and a very shaky Forest team re-emerged Newcastle were scenting victory – by fair means or foul, it didn't matter.

They ran the shell shocked Reds ragged in the remaining quarter, urged on by their fanatical and disgracefully shameless support, who had apparently forgotten already that rioting is not a legitimate weapon in changing the result of a football match (or so I foolishly thought – it was, of course and the end was to justify the means).

Even then, after they'd levelled at 3-3, and with only a few minutes remaining, we were awarded a free kick on the edge of the box just in front of us. George Lyall hit it quickly and precisely, and it was fizzing into the bottom corner before their keeper made the save of the match and miraculously turned it round the post. Still time for the thieving Magpies to re-group, mount another attack and score a hollow and late "winner".

We just stood totally stunned and speechless. We'd overcome all the odds - the rest of the country had written us off without even a shout – and beaten them fair and square on their own patch, and now we were expected to play the crowd as well.

We trooped back, scarves prudently hidden from the baying, unashamedly triumphant, Geordies, who could not rationalise that use of mob violence (including directly or by intimidation at the players themselves – pity poor Jim Barron having to stand in front of the Leazes after that lot, Geordie or no Geordie) was somehow against the rules.

No blame on the ref – if he'd abandoned the match there and then, there would likely have been bloodshed. For the same reason Allen Brown was right in agreeing to let his shocked players return to the St James Park madhouse.

As the inevitable post match inquiry was announced Reds fans knew that justice could take one of two forms, either Newcastle be thrown out and Forest through to the Semi or, perhaps, the last 20 minutes be re-played behind closed doors, from 3-1.

There was no other possibility, so we were devastated when we heard of the craven capitulation to mob law and the ruling that a full replay would be held and, to add insult to injury, at Goodison Park, a pig of a venue to get to from Nottingham. Even more shocking, if that were possible, was that most Newcastle fans seemed to think that they'd been robbed by the verdict which, if I remember correctly, included a role by Newcastle's own Lord Westwood.

All that was to come. In the meantime, as we endeavoured to pick our way home through the Newcastle traffic, I was forced to evacuate our happy tribe at speed up a side street to avoid brick hurling morons. We drifted cross country until we came to the industrial village of Stanley, where a local hostelry was clearly in full swing, despite licensing laws to the contrary.

We tentatively approached, and were given a real old fashioned welcome, even to the extent of a rousing chorus of "Blaydon Races" when we told them the "result". Warmed by this traditional North Eastern hospitality we left in better spirits, seeking out Durham and its many pubs as the evening's next - and final – stop.

It was approaching midnight when we left, the idiot driver finding himself for some reason heading back north up the A1 towards Newcastle. Sod the Highway Code, there was only one quick fix – wait for a gap in the traffic and execute a U-turn across the central reservation, almost grounding the vehicle in the process.

Trevor Woodford, a friend of my brother, had been harping on about doing some of the driving back, although I wasn't convinced that he was insured under the hire agreement (in fact I was bloody sure he wasn't), but as my eyes began to glaze over I finally gave in and pulled into a lay by, where we swapped seats. Hardly anyone noticed, either asleep or semi-comatose.

So, it seemed, was Woodford. He'd failed to appreciate that the A1 didn't have a hard shoulder, and that I'd pulled into a short parking lay by. Mr. Nonchalant confidently accelerated away, head turned back 90 degrees checking for non existent traffic, and drove straight off the pull-in and onto a steep and rutted embankment.

It was only the weight of 12 bodies that kept us barely upright as we pitched and bounced like some kind of demented bronco, before he somehow wrestled the vehicle back onto the carriageway, executed a series of screeching slaloms, and managed to point us back in a straight line.

Miraculously, and no doubt due to their relaxed alcoholic states, no one behind us suffered worse than bruising, although to say they were shaken was an understatement.

"I'll be alright, now", said Woodford in mock cheeriness, chastened but insistent on staying in the driver's seat. As for my intended couple of hours kip, I spent the rest of the journey wide awake, watching eagle eyed and nervously checking every few minutes that my seat belt was fastened.

His excursion into the countryside had induced a certain amount of heaving and throwing up amongst the passengers, the results of which I had to attend to at 8am on Sunday morning (frozen sick is particularly difficult to remove from paintwork) before returning the vehicle, walking 2 miles back home and awaiting my lift for a 10am Sunday League kick off.

Needless to say, all this was forgotten by the time of the Goodison Park replay and whilst then, as now, I knew that we'd already won the tie I had to stick with the Reds and see if we could win it again.

Our party had diminished only slightly, to a creditable 2 car loads, with Woodford taking the wheel of his own pride and joy, a bottle green Austin 3 Litre Automatic. Having driven it, I could vouch for its power, once its huge mass was up and rolling, but the merest touch on its primitive super light power steering would practically spin it round. After Woodford's antics in the minibus I could only marvel that he kept it on the road.

Not to be outdone, I hired a 2.5 Granada and we rolled into Liverpool, scarves defiantly flailing from the windows, miles ahead of kick off. Most of Newcastle was already there. A large mob of Geordies saw us approaching and charged out into the road ahead. This time, Woodford got it right.

He flicked on his main beam stalk and held it firmly in place, thumped his other hand against the horn, and jammed his right foot down onto the accelerator pedal. He reckoned his "Straight 6" consumed half a pint of petrol with each prod of his right foot, but I reckon a full pint disappeared in those vital, tyre burning yards.

Close on his tail, I saw the gap between us dramatically increase as the Woodford-mobile surged away. I dropped a gear, floored the throttle, and charged after him, Ford chasing Austin in a duet of blaring horns.

Newcastle fans loved to announce their collective presence to the chant of "Geordies here, Geordies there, Geordies every fucking where", and so there were, scattering like ninepins in the path of over a ton of fast accelerating machinery. Any keeper worth his salt would have been proud of their acrobatics, and it's a miracle no-one was hit.

We blasted on, to find sanctuary in a distant residential street, where we parked, still shaken. Woodford however, glowed in the satisfaction of his Clint Eastwood style "make my day, Geordie" encounter. I daresay that if I'd been leading we'd still have the scars to prove it.

"What if they hadn't jumped out of the way?" I ventured.

"I'd have run the bastards over" he retorted. He would as well.

There weren't any official signs welcoming us to Liverpool, but we instantly recognised those words which bring a lump to the throat of any expatriate Scouser :-

"Mind yer car, mister?"

"Piss off you little sods" came the knee-jerk reply, which condemned us to another tour before we finally homed in on an "official" match day car park. Normally, we hated paying for the "privilege" of organised parking, where the queuing time for the exits could exceed the length of the match (albeit often better value for money), and would go to almost fanatical lengths to find free street parking, even if we had to walk 5 miles to the ground.

This time it seemed like a good idea, but our reward was a meeting with busloads of Geordies, a substantial number of whom could best be termed "hostile". We adopted a scarves hidden, ignore them and they might go away, strategy, but they could smell fear and some 20 or so followed us across the road, intent on giving us a good kicking.

The ringleader, a gangly, craggy youth of some 6 foot plus, bore a remarkable resemblance to Jimmy Nail and I've sometimes wondered if it was him, given that he was a prominent "bovver boy". Whoever he was, his colleagues joined in with his unanswered insults, quickly followed by a series of increasingly firm "ankle taps", as we walked on in frightened silence.

I could almost feel their breath on the back of our necks, and Andy received a nasty kick on the back of the calf as it began to get serious.

We knew that to panic and run would bring the mob down on us, to turn and face them would be suicide, and to do nothing was equally impossible. I've seldom been more frightened in my entire life.

Nor have I been so relieved to see a few dozen Forest fans, arriving on 2 asthmatic "cowboy" coaches and pouring out to the Beck-esque strains of "And it's hi ho, we hate Geordies, everywhere we go it's aggro".

The cavalry had arrived in the nick of time, tough lads from North Notts who wouldn't be running from anyone, and who were joined at the double by a small group of fellow Reds wearing brown trousers. "Jimmy Nail and Co" backed off and kept their surly distance.

I was usually quick to criticise Forest's yob element, but I was proud to hear the obscenities hurled out at the now sullen Magpies.

What came across strongly, and appalled us, was that most Newcastle fans seemed to think they'd been robbed, whereas the exact reverse was the truth, and were nursing bitter grudges and irrational feelings of injustice at having to play again.

The whole episode caused a Forest - Newcastle enmity that has taken years to subside, which is particularly sad given the large exiled Geordie community in our area, and the previous traditions of good natured rivalry. (Fortunately, the atmosphere at recent games has been generally excellent, helped by "Psycho's" transfer and testimonial).

Thanks to our involuntary escort we reached the ground without further trauma, and joined the few thousand fellow Reds on the Gwladys Street terrace, Everton's popular end. Most of the rest of the ground, in an attendance of 40,681, was thickly black and white, Forest fans predictably well outnumbered.

We did however have the lukewarm support of a number of locals, a good few of them sporting the red and white of Liverpool F.C., but their initial enthusiasm faded as the match developed into a dour attritional battle, Forest to their credit demonstrating that our victory at St James Park was no fluke.

We even had a goal disallowed, although I can't remember whether it was for offside or for allegedly taking a free kick too quickly. Whatever, it was becoming clear that Forest's name was not to be in that coveted semi-final line up.

As the match progressed, my naivety concerning our new found Scouse support disappeared. Their indifference to the match, and Forest's cause, was reflected in an inability to remain in one place for long. I kept my hands firmly over my pockets for most of the rest of the match.

Even as we wended our way back through dark streets liberally strewn with broken glass and debris we were put in fear by the local mafia. We asked directions of 2 angel faced youngsters. Scarcely 4 feet tall, God knows what they were doing out alone at that time of night.

"It's up there, mister" came the reflex response, deliberately pointing us completely the wrong way.

"Is it bollocks" we retorted wittily.

"Hey, they're Forest supporters they are, Forest supporters over there ". The infant Scousers screamed it out at all and sundry, and 8 fully grown adults made double quick time from 2 evil little shits of scarcely seven or eight years old.

We eventually arrived home in the small hours, exhausted but thankfully safe, and thrilled by the prospect of work in a few short hours time. Not surprisingly there was little enthusiasm, either within our own group or in general, for the second replay, particularly as the all knowing decision makers had decreed that it would again be at the easily accessible and welcoming surroundings of Goodison Park.

Only my brother and myself determined to see it through, in pursuit of a just outcome, although we were by then only going through the motions as there was a feeling that somehow Forest wouldn't be allowed to progress. We went by special football train and I remember being cheered by a large "Good luck, Forest" banner displayed from a trackside factory window just outside Midland station.

We were less cheered by the lines of empty Newcastle specials in the sidings approaching Lime Street. Newcastle Brown cans taunted us through the windows of every one of the dozens of carriages.

If we'd been outnumbered at the first replay, it was nothing compared with this one. No wonder the North East marathon is so popular – they don't know when to give up.

The gate was down by over 9,000, at 31,373, mainly missing Reds plus some locals. We "lost" 1-0, but at least no-one tried to kill us – two is in any case a far more anonymous number – and I could take some comfort from the fact that I didn't live in the vicinity of the "Scotty" Road.

To be truthful, we just wanted the whole thing over and done with, and players and fans alike were mentally exhausted.

At the final whistle the thousands of Geordies celebrated emotionally and at full volume. They thought they'd won. They hadn't. Forest hadn't either (or so the official statistics erroneously tell it).

The game had lost.

We walked back to Lime Street over a sea of broken glass. Empty bottles were everywhere and cheeky little Scouse rascals were flitting impishly in and out of the shadows, hurling missiles against the windows of passing coaches.

Despite our warm Liverpool welcome I was an honorary Scouser for the Wembley final, after Newcastle had predictably beaten Burnley in the "easy" Semi, just as Forest would have hoped to do.

Malcolm MacDonald and Co talked a cracking match before being annihilated 3-0 in one of the most one sided Finals ever (Newcastle were lucky to get the "Nil") as Liverpool proved what ordinary, 2nd Division, Forest had already shown – it was all hype and little substance.

If it appears that I'm still bitter and twisted about the whole affair, well I must say that time, and subsequent events, both on and off the field, have put this 6th round clash into perspective, but yes;

WE WERE ROBBED!!!!

Apart from the Newcastle epic the early to mid seventies were punctuated by any number of low key away trips at uninspiring venues with sparse crowds and little at stake beyond 2nd Division respectability.

My old school friend Phil had moved to South London where he had taken a "bijou" (as in, all he could afford) flat just off one of the grottiest parts of the Old Kent Road and within comfortable (if that's the right word) walking distance of Millwall's equally bijou Coldblow Lane establishment.

A colleague spotted a British Rail "Theatregoers Special" whereby a return to London could be had for one third of the normal price subject to the outward journey departing after 4pm. Three of us left work early, arrived in St. Pancras just after 6pm, taxied across London and arrived by suburban train in New Cross in time to meet Phil and, regrettably, make the kick off.

The Den's renowned, intimidating, atmosphere was totally absent for such an inauspicious occasion, Forest's total complement of supporters perhaps numbering an almost invisible 50, and the match being so irredeemably awful - it finished 0-0 – as to stifle any passion, hostile or otherwise. My major concern was to avoid falling forwards down the crumbling, almost vertical, weed infested terracing, and to wonder that the ground still had a licence.

Perversely, I made the trip 2 seasons running, and failed to see a Reds goal, which at least avoided the problem of trying to look like a pissed off local whilst wanting to leap 2 feet into the air with a huge cry of "Yeeeess!!".

Kenilworth Road was another "nice day out, shame about the match", my brother and friend completing a threesome by hired car. We allowed plenty of time to stop for a pub meal, and with me as always having an almost paranoid aversion to missing the kick off, left it until just short of Luton.

A 2pm departure would clearly see us inside the ground by 2.30, but by 3.00 we were still a mile away, due to horrendous roadworks. After abandoning the car in a side street we tore through a maze of narrow terraces and found ourselves, breathless, on the open Kop behind the goal, distinctly less than awestruck at Luton Town's own version of "bijou".

The first half was already over 20 minutes old, so it's possible that we might have missed something interesting. The remaining 70 wouldn't have recognised "interesting" if it had strolled up, tapped them on the shoulder, and introduced itself, and Forest went on to clinch "Nil", which was a shame as Luton had already scored.

Cardiff City was almost certainly the biggest shambles. 5 of us filled our temporary Austin Maxi (the car hire company at the bottom of Westdale Lane had a lot to answer for) and once I'd learnt the formula for selecting the required gear - somewhere south of Birmingham – it was clear that we'd be there hours ahead of schedule.

We'd left early enough to travel half way round Britain, only to realise, with increasing disbelief, that due to over indulgent refreshment stops and the misguidedly relaxed attitude of the driver we were still seventy miles short with only an hour to go.

We arrived outside a seemingly deserted Ninian Park well into the 2nd half, with just a few disinterested policemen patrolling. We explained our predicament in expectation of being granted leave to park, but the natives had little time for English visitors and we were less than politely told to seek alternative arrangements.

Ten minutes later we were back, having found a spot half a mile away and run back, only to become embroiled in a furious argument with a steward, who refused to let us in. He finally capitulated, after pressure from one of the Police, and opened the gate.

We saw the last twenty minutes of what, to judge from the crowd's reaction, had been a pretty dire affair and which according to one of the Cardiff supporters stood at 1-1. As neither team scored again (although Ian Bowyer put a header just wide) we assumed that that was indeed the result, but none of us was by that time really bothered, and I'm not even sure that we checked in the papers the next day.

At such times I don't consider it constructive to apportion blame, particularly where simplistic members of the party might question the driver's planning. One or two of them had taken literally my observation that by setting off at 7am we would be comfortably in Cardiff by lunchtime, giving us ample time to visit a cross section of the City Centre hostelries before taking in the match.

As always, we made the best of a bad job. After all, isn't that what being a Football supporter's usually about? Rather than waste a couple of hours "dead" time waiting for Cardiff to open up, we began the homeward trek, but this time via Abergavenny to Hereford, which seemed a likely place to stop for the evening.

A local yokel almost instantly attached himself to us in Hereford and wouldn't let go. He insisted on being our guide and protector around the pubs, allegedly to keep us out of the way of the local lunatic fringe who would love to have a go at an isolated group of Nottingham Forest supporters.

We simply couldn't get rid of him.

By the end of the night he had made the decision that he was travelling back to Nottingham with us and, furthermore, would be playing in our Sunday Morning League team. (The latter suggestion did have its attractions – like most Parks teams we were frequently short, and given that we wouldn't be back until gone 3am, with one or two somewhat the worse for drink, there wouldn't be a shortage of volunteers willing to sacrifice the honour of playing for an extra 3 hours in bed).

He climbed into the back of the car and declined any attempts to coax him out, but an unspoken committee decision was unanimously taken that he'd have to go, proposed by the faces of the other three back seat passengers.

We stopped, some time around midnight, a few miles north of Hereford at a Service Station for a "toilet break", but the second he disappeared into the gents we scarpered back to the car and drove off. Callous, but sometimes, as the saying has it, you have to be cruel to be kind. I feel guilty again writing these notes, but hopefully he made it back home safely.

We played an away match at one of the bigger Bulwell Hall pitches on the Sunday morning and with at least 5 of our team either knackered or knackered and hung over we were losing 5-0 at half time. We went on to fight back to 5-5 by the final whistle. What it proves, I don't know, but it's "strange, but true".

Another expedition in which Forest played only an incidental role was one of my several visits to Craven Cottage, which was totally unplanned and came about purely because of my beliefs.

At that time, and with some justification, I was of the firm conviction that the Catholic Club on Carlton Hill sold the cheapest beer. I was practicing my faith one Friday evening when, during a chance conversation, a casual acquaintance, fellow Red and leader member of CAMRA advised me that I was in line for a free trip to Fulham the following day.

All I had to do was take the place of their mini bus driver who'd broken his arm earlier that day (and had the plaster to prove it) and convey their party of Forest/CAMRA supporters - not necessarily in that order - to the ground, all expenses paid (i.e. admission). Such an offer, on the back of several pints, was too good to refuse and the following morning off we went

The whole experience was somewhat surreal, although the trip down and the match itself passed without event. If I remember correctly, we lost 2-0. It was just one of a whole catalogue of away trips where the football was utterly forgettable, unlike Craven Cottage, which is the closest rival to the City Ground, with its superb riverside setting.

If the football scarcely sparked lively discussion, the choice of a post match "real ale" pub was the subject of an intense and heated debate. My skirmishes with CAMRA had drawn the conclusion that frivolous luxuries such as carpets, upholstered seating, wallpaper and inside toilets were for namby pamby Lager drinkers (i.e. such as myself), who wouldn't know a pint of "Old Disgusting" from a bowl of dishwater (is there a difference?).

Someone knew of a suitable dive somewhere in North London - it might have been Tottenham way – but not before one of our party suddenly leapt out of the back with the cry "gone for a football paper", and off he vanished.

I was presumably expected to halt a 15 seater minibus on the North Circular whilst 3 lanes of traffic politely manoeuvred their way around us. No chance. Caught up in the tide of vehicles, desperately checking my mirrors for signs of our erstwhile passenger, I lumbered along as slowly as possible until, some two or three junctions ahead, he suddenly appeared, like a triumphant homing pigeon, Sports Extra tucked under his arm.

Results digested, and Forest a little further down the table, we eventually stumbled across a North London pub which seemed to fit the aforementioned CAMRA criteria, i.e. it and the beer were both revolting. Duly topped up (driver excepted) with sufficient quantities of "Vile and Murky" the party were ready to press on to the next one.

Unfortunately, the brew was already having an effect, and a temporary London Transport bus stop, complete with concrete base, was uprooted from its position ahead of some roadworks and manhandled into our vehicle. Whilst I didn't personally consider it the best of ideas, "democracy", and the beer, prevailed, and it was to remain with us, playing a more active role later in the journey.

Next stop was an olde worlde country inn just off the M1 which, despite having deep carpets, comfortable seats, running hot and cold water, etc, was deemed suitable as it also sold "Bullocks Truly Awful".

We stayed the rest of the night, mixing amicably with a group of Spurs fans and deafening the locals with a raucous closing time rendition of "Jerusalem", for which we surprisingly received generous applause.

Halfway back up the motorway the engine developed a misfire which developed into a sickly cough before, spluttering and kangarooing, it packed up altogether and I was forced to pull in to the hard shoulder which, naturally enough, served as an impromptu toilet.

Someone professed to know about engines, muttering about "blocked jets" or something, and I let him get on with it, turning the ignition key and flooring the gas pedal when instructed. After a few minutes tinkering he told me to try again and it roared into life and continued to rev freely. All set again, and not a second too soon. Motorway hard shoulders vie with free fall para gliding as my idea of fun.

We looked to round up the others and were greeted with a tragi-comic scene. Whilst we'd been trying to get the engine started they'd plonked the bus stop alongside the inside lane and were standing in a queue, arms outstretched, as conveys of blazing headlights sped past within feet. Would be kamikaze members plus bus stop were back in the vehicle in double quick time and I spent the next few minutes anticipating the appearance in my mirrors of a flashing blue light.

Thankfully the journey was completed without further incident, and this account may shed some light on the mysterious appearance of a London Transport bus stop in the garden one Sunday morning of a house on Standhill Road, Carlton.

That Fulham trip was a microcosm, albeit an eccentric one, of our seventies awaydays, and in many ways they were the best Forest times. When the football is of a mediocre standard, in a mediocre division, and expectations are minimal, supporting takes on a different dimension. It's more of a laugh following a club with little at stake, but when the rewards are suddenly greater, as with the Newcastle episode, the intensity of the result overwhelms everything else.

That's not to say that I'd relinquish one second of the Clough glory years but mediocrity does have its compensations and I'd always support my local club, through thick and thin. Rather follow, say, Plymouth around the country than join the West Country "instant glory" (and entirely superficial and meaningless) Man United brigade.

At the time we were mainly unmarried, without commitments, and admission at away games could easily be obtained on the gate, so trips were often last minute ideas, sometimes even on the Saturday morning.

One trip to Bolton, with my brother, was a double whammy, taking in a Moody Blues concert at the Gaumont in Hanley, Stoke on Trent, on the way back. I can still remember the concert (it was one of keyboard player Mike

Pinder's last tours before he left, to be replaced by Patrick Moraz). I can also vividly recall a fierce thunderstorm as we drove down from Bolton, but the Forest game typically lived up to forgettable expectations. It didn't diminish our enthusiasm though.

2 consecutive away trips in 1973/74 were dominated by ferocious gales, Blackpool and Sunderland respectively illustrating that West coast or East coast, it makes no difference in a British Autumn.

Four of us travelled to Bloomfield Road intending to pull in the match and then spend an evening along the seafront, but the weather was atrocious, with leaden skies and torrential rain putting the match in doubt. It cleared from the west in time for kick off, but the pitch was a mudbath and we were wet through and frozen on the exposed terracing behind the goal.

For once, Forest cheered us, with a fighting 2-2 draw after big John Galley had gone in goal following an injury midway through the first half to Jim Barron. By the end of 90 minutes we also had the luxury of being dry, thanks to a gale that had been picking up throughout the game.

Our plans to see the "sights" of Blackpool, if there were any, (I've never been back to check) were thwarted as the October gale assumed near hurricane proportions. It was literally almost impossible to stand up, not to mention dangerous, as miscellaneous flying objects crashed about our ears.

The promenade was closed for safety, with high seas and sand swirling horizontally over the front. Seeking sanctuary in a parallel side street we still had to run the gauntlet, at every exposed crossroads, of the veritable sandstorm that was roaring in. Bodies stooped, heads down, eyes tightly closed, we battled like lost souls from a Bedouin tribe, searching for the one pub that might have some people in it. There weren't any.

With most of Blackpool now resembling the beach we struggled back through the elements to our car for the dark and windswept journey home. Thus ended a day in the life of a travelling Forest supporter.

It was only the tremendous enjoyment and value for money that kept us going.

I travelled alone, and by train, to Sunderland a few weeks later and Blackpool gale's identical twin was there to greet me. In fact, it was raging from early morning onwards, buffeting the 3 car Diesel Multiple Unit as it entered Grantham station where I was to change for the Newcastle train, followed by a short local hop to Wearside.

With the forecast for severe weather in the north, causing structural damage, only an idiot would have travelled. I contemplated that fact as our Deltic hauled express struggled to make headway, rocking from the blasts of pressure and arriving some 30 minutes late into the shelter of Newcastle station's huge canopy.

I battled through to Roker Park (my first and only visit, hence my determination to go) where the conditions were the most difficult, blizzards possibly excepted, in which I have seen football played. The entire local league programme was abandoned and it was a mystery as to why this game was uniquely played.

Just one example sums up the absurdity of it, not to mention the danger if part of a stand roof blew off, as looked quite possible. Jim Barron used every inch of the Area before belting the ball flatly into the teeth of the gale. It simply came to a complete stop, mid flight, before being lifted as if by a giant hand and hurled back over the Forest crossbar for a Sunderland corner.

The game finished 0-0, which seemed entirely fair to me as the whole thing was a travesty, but apart from the weather it was memorable for an explosion of hostility and rage from the Sunderland fans when an innocuous throw in decision went against them. It's known in the North East as "passion", and I was glad not to be in the linesman's shoes, as he went through hell for the rest of the game. I shudder to think what would have happened if it had been a penalty decision.

Thus it was with the "wilderness years" of the early to mid 70s when Forest's falling from grace and the indifferent standard of football generated an inevitable change of emphasis as far as the remaining supporters, myself included, were concerned.

I remained loyal, as did many of my friends and acquaintances, but in order to adapt to the sometimes rock bottom performances on the pitch the football itself was increasingly incidental, particularly where away trips were concerned.

Duncan McKenzie left us at the end of 1973/74, the season when Allan Brown had a possible Wembley Cup Final stolen, and just over a year later, with the Reds fortunes seemingly in free fall, Brown followed.

A certain Tony Woodcock had made his debut towards the end of 73/74, and another local youngster, Viv Anderson, was to emulate him early in 74/75. John Robertson, Martin O'Neill and Ian Bowyer were already becoming established, but seemingly going nowhere.

What we couldn't possibly appreciate was the massive potential from these five unpolished gems, soon to be realised under the brilliantly eccentric management of an opinionated (now there's a novelty) Yorkshireman.

Robertson, O'Neill and Bowyer are my personal identification with the mind blowing transformation that was to take place.They also experienced the desolate days of the early 70s, and all 3 played in that bitterest blow of the period, the St James Park robbery.

~

The 1970s (Glory, Glory)

It was business as usual during the 1974/75 season. Duncan McKenzie had gone and the squad lacked obvious quality and strength, unexploited potential notwithstanding.

We expected the Reds to build on the moderate achievements of 1973/74 but instead we had a frustrating run of poor results, with the "relegation" word again beginning to feature. The dour Allan Brown was unpopular with the fans and by the turn of the year, with home gates hovering around 10,000, things were as grim as I can remember.

On December 28th 1974 Notts County came to the City Ground and demonstrated what Reds fans had feared for some time – they were the better team. A Christmas holiday crowd of 25,013 witnessed the humiliation as an abject Forest capitulated 2-0 on a cold, drizzly day that ranks as one of my most miserable ever with the Reds.

Including that shambles, we'd played 27 League and League Cup games, winning 9, drawing 7 and losing 11, and had only managed 1 win in our last 6. Notts was the final straw, but it was also perhaps the best result in Forest's history as it was the catalyst for unimaginable change.

The impenetrable gloom, according to local soothsayers, was soon to be illuminated by a brightly burning star from the North. We rejoiced in the post match dismissal of the unfortunate Allan Brown, held our breath, hung onto every word thrown out by the gathering media circus, and joyously greeted the official news from the Forest Committee that our saviour had truly arrived. A little late for Christmas, but surely Heaven sent.

Brian Clough was the new manager of Nottingham Forest Football club.

We were suddenly famous, the focus of intense media attention as the man in the green tracksuit top set about the colossal task of re-building our crumbling club.

Cloughie's first match in charge was an against the odds victory, 1-0 at White Hart Lane in an FA Cup replay, thanks to a Neil Martin header. Local opinion in some quarters was that Forest could now go on to lift the Cup, gain promotion, and perhaps even arrange an end of season trip to the Moon, all courtesy of Brian's magic wand.

The realists amongst us, not least Clough himself, quickly dispensed stark reminders that Forest's squad was, euphemistically speaking, "poor".

Mighty Fulham soon proved the point, knocking us out of the Cup in the next round, 2-1 at the City Ground on February 10th in a third replay. (No such thing as Penalty shootouts – we'd have played until June if necessary). I went to 3 of the 4 Cup encounters, to add to my visit to Craven Cottage in the League on January 11th – Barry Butlin scored the game's only goal - and reckoned I'd seen enough of Fulham to last a lifetime.

By the end of the season we'd secured a relegation proof 16th in the table and Cloughie was fully appreciative, if he wasn't already when he first arrived, of the enormity of his task.

We also achieved the dizzy heights of a 2-2 draw at Meadow Lane in our return League fixture on March 25th, the attendance of 20,303 an indicator that Reds fans outnumbered the Pies by some four to one. I was disappointed that we didn't gain revenge for the City Ground debacle and from my view half way up the Kop I could confirm that Notts had as usual brought their own referee.

With both teams in the same division, and Notts temporarily in the ascendancy, there was an impassioned plea to the Football Post letters section from a County die-hard. He warned that Notts had better look lively as there was a whisper on the Red side of the Trent which would rise to a crescendo over the forthcoming seasons and swamp Notts. Prophetic words, which I did not afford myself the luxury of believing at the time.

Speaking of Newspaper letters brings to mind a couple of "unusual" exchanges of correspondence.

David Skinner, brother of one of my closest school friends, and a fanatical County supporter, emigrated to the East End of London – or what was left of it – and gloried in the fact that his Tower Block was officially designated the worst in Hackney, itself one of the most deprived boroughs in the entire country. I suppose he felt comfortable there, having spent so many afternoons in the surroundings of Meadow Lane.

As a form of escapism he took to supporting West Ham and sent thinly disguised correspondence, for my benefit, extolling the virtues and silky skills of the Irons, as against the crude efforts of the Reds. I duly rose to the bait and replied suitably, introducing an anti Notts theme into the argument. To his credit, he's still loyal to the Magpies, despite years of watching proper football at Upton Park, and visits the Lane whenever he can.

A particularly whimsical episode involved a heated debate between two parties of absurdly opposing views, which I happen to know were written under assumed names by one and the same person (and it wasn't me). Whether the Editor ever suspected, I don't know, but it generated a lively additional correspondence.

That was as nothing compared with the furore that was aroused by a fanatical Notts fan who, sick and tired of being an oppressed minority, set about rectifying matters in an exquisite demonstration of the pen being mightier than the sword.

Again under a false name, he purported to be a long standing Forest fan, persuaded reluctantly to accompany a friend to watch Notts at Meadow Lane, only to be overwhelmed by the friendly atmosphere, sporting fans and exciting play. It was a revelation, and he was immediately converted to the Magpies, discarding his Reds scarf for the Black and White of Notts. Yes, sir, it would be County all the way now for him.

The writer then sat back and had a good laugh at the tirades of "Judas" that followed from outraged Forest supporters. Their venom and invective brought him a sublime satisfaction that no pub argument could achieve and provides evidence, should anyone need it, that you can't believe everything that you read in the papers, even the Sports letters.

Brian would soon be wiping the smile off the faces of the Notts fans and, for that matter, Liverpool and Manchester United as well, but not before another season of consolidation.

1975/76 saw us a comfortable, but disappointing, 8th in Division 2 and our ritual FA Cup exit at the hands of minnows was this time carried out in a third round replay at London Road, Peterborough. I travelled by train with a work colleague, and we were convinced that Forest, backed by massive support, and the even more massive thighs of Bert Bowery, would overwhelm the Posh, but out we went, 1-0.

Despite the setbacks the squad was slowly gathering strength. The waif like John McGovern and the robust John O'Hare followed Cloughie to the City Ground in February 1975, shortly after his arrival, and 75/76 saw Frank Clark, the World's best ever free transfer acquisition, claim the number 3 spot. The temperamental (mardy arse, some might say) Terry Curran flattered to deceive, but for a while we thought he might be the next Ian Moore.

Colin Barrett came on board just before the end of the season, and with Peter Withe and Larry "where's yer blazer" Lloyd (initially, on loan) in the ranks by Autumn of

1976/77 surely we had to make it this time, if only for Brian's credibility.

We did, but by the very tightest of margins, and if our 1959 Cup win hinged on that dramatic 3rd round equaliser against Tooting and Mitcham, our promotion from Division 2 owed much to the riverside setting of the City Ground.

There was much water to pass under Trent Bridge in the meantime, and a milestone was achieved on December 15th when we picked up our first piece of Silverware under Brian, the prestigious Anglo Scottish Cup.

It was a 2 legged final against those intrepid Celtic warriors, Orient, (now thankfully Leyton Orient again) and we hammered them 4-0 at the City Ground after a 1-1 in the first leg. A modest 12,717 turned up, but it was a psychologically significant achievement and we celebrated enthusiastically.

Southampton knocked us out of the FA Cup, 2-1 in a replay at the Dell, after a staggering 38,284 had seen a thrilling 3-3 at the City Ground. That made for 5 games in the competition, given our 3rd Round clashes with Bristol Rovers, 1-1 home and away and 6-0 at Villa Park in the second replay before a derisory – and not including me – 5,736.

For once I didn't mind our usual early exit, Promotion being the only thing that mattered, but they were nail biting times as we shadowed that elusive third place (an automatic promotion spot in those pre play-off days), tantalisingly failing to break into the top 3.

2 games were particularly significant.

On February 16th Southampton went in at half time 1-0 ahead in one of those vital games which we just had to win, but which was turning into an anguished, frustrating, nightmare. Shortly after the re-start someone remarked "there's a fire somewhere". "That's not a fire, it's fog", remarked my brother, as the first grey swirls crept in from behind us, almost hesitantly, as if shyly stopping to take a prior look around either end of the East Stand.

Within seconds, having gathered its forces together, the eerie grey menace enveloped the City Ground and obliterated the proceedings. The match was abandoned and rearranged for March 22nd. We won, 2-1. Maybe the gods were now on our side.

The other turning point was April 6th. Four consecutive wins, commencing with the Southampton game, had catapulted us back into contention after it seemed that we'd missed the boat again. Bolton Wanderers were ahead of us in a promotion place and we simply had to beat them.

24,580 endured 80 minutes of negative, time wasting, spoiling tactics from Bolton, who were more than happy to settle for a draw, largely thanks to their "uncompromising" defence. They only needed Sammy Chapman to swap sides to have a full set.

For once, natural justice prevailed and Bolton's cynical, and unnecessary tactics – they were a good footballing side – backfired, as Forest ran out deserved 3-1 winners and we went home ecstatic. O'Neill, Bowyer and Withe were the heroes.

3 days later, in front of 32,518 at Meadow Lane, Notts were the villains, putting an almighty spoke in our resurgent promotion drive with a lucky 1-1 draw. It got worse, consecutive 2-1 and 1-0 defeats against Chelsea and Cardiff more or less putting the lid on it.

The pendulum had swung excruciatingly back and it looked like we'd blown it again. With just 4 to play we were out of the top 3, but 3 wins and a draw, including a scrappy 1-0 at home in our last game, against Millwall - and then only thanks to an own goal by Moore – saw us still in there. If I remember correctly, Bolton needed to win their last one, an evening game shoe-horned in after the others.

They didn't, and Nottingham went mad. Forest **were** back!

1977/78 – Champions!

I prepared for the 77/78 season by investing for the first time in a season ticket, specifically the East Stand terrace. Like many fans I was apprehensive concerning our prospects back with the big boys but Mr. Clough, now joined by Peter Taylor, reassured us that there was nothing to be worried about.

Kenny "stitch that" Burns added steel at the back, and was to play the best football of his career for the Reds. We made a sensational start, winning 3-1 at Goodison on the opening day and going on to lose only one of our first seventeen League and League Cup fixtures, 3-0 at Arsenal on September 3rd (our dog's birthday).

Not only that, but the Reds were playing uninhibited attacking football, the like of which hadn't been seen since 1966/67. A good maxim is to keep strengthening a successful side, but we were still surprised when a record fee was suddenly paid for a goalkeeper.

Peter Shilton scarcely had a shot to save on his debut, a comfortable 2-0 win at the City Ground on September 17th against Aston Villa, but it proved to be an inspirational signing, as was Archie Gemmill's a couple of weeks later.

The team almost picked itself, every one of them playing at the top of their form and with supreme confidence and team spirit. It's interesting to note the size of the squad, and the number of games played, compared with the top heavy and largely ineffectual numbers of a couple of years back, which played fewer games, at a lower level of competition.

The nucleus was :-

Shilton, Anderson, Clark/Barrett, McGovern, Lloyd, Burns, O'Neill, Bowyer, Gemmilll, Withe, Woodcock and Robertson, plus Needham and Woods helping out in the League Cup.

There's more than that on the Manchester United bench these days.

The bubble just refused to burst, Forest kept on winning, and a former Arsenal goalkeeper was forced to eat his words. Unfortunately, he was also punched in the face by a Forest "supporter" outside Wembley before our League Cup final against Liverpool.

It was Roy of the Rovers stuff as we stormed to the top of the League and stayed there. Incredibly, defeat by Leeds on November 19th was our only one in all competitions apart from our 6th Round FA Cup reverse against old friends West Brom.

The 4-0 victory at Old Trafford just before Christmas was the result that turned the fairy tale into reality and convinced us that our wildest Nottingham Forest fantasies were to be realised. If there was any (unspoken) doubt in the Reds camp then it was surely dispelled by that performance, in front of over 54,000 on England's biggest League stage.

Just to add to the interest, we were doing quite nicely in the League Cup as well, a competition that hitherto had completely bypassed Forest. We beat West Ham (5-0), Notts (4-0) and Villa (4-2) in successive home ties, before disposing of Bury, 3-0 at Gigg Lane.

Leeds barred our path to Wembley in the Semi, but Forest, backed by tremendous support, overwhelmed them in the first leg at Elland Road, 3-1, thanks to a couple from Withe and one from O'Hare. O'Hare's effort, a fierce - and untypical - volley at the opposite, Kop, end sent the Reds fans into raptures.

We expected the return leg to be a formality, which is how it looks, judging from the 4-2 scoreline, but Leeds scored first and caused more than a few flutters before Forest got their act together. Withe, Bowyer, O'Neill and Woodcock were the scorers and I left the ground in a dream. Forest were going to Wembley and I'd be there.

We stormed on in the League, but our League Cup Final, against Liverpool, was the only match on my mind.

Unfortunately, things didn't go as planned, and my first ever Wembley trip was soured by a couple of cock-ups.

First, my advice that we should leave an hour or so earlier than planned was ridiculed by a work colleague, to the extent that we stuck with the original timings. (I discovered subsequently that his party had actually set off earlier, and avoided most of the traffic problems that we encountered).

We then made the wrong decision when the Motorway ground to a standstill.

All this was compounded by the fact that I'd acquired 2 additional tickets for "exiled" Reds, old schoolfriends Ken and Phil, who were scheduled to meet us – and their tickets – outside our gate at Wembley from 1.30 onwards.

It all started superbly, scarves flapping from the windows as our party headed for the M1 in a gathering convoy of red and white. The motorway was a thickening stream of Reds fans – cars, vans, mini- buses and coaches, many plastered top to bottom in flags and banners.

The M6 was also a stream of red and white (although less ostentatiously – Liverpool had "been there, bought the tee shirt" often enough to become somewhat blasé. Besides, it was only a Mickey Mouse competition – at least that was their subsequent excuse) and the point where the 2 motorways converged became one solid jam.

Traffic ground to a complete stop, occasionally crawling agonisingly forwards again for a few yards before grinding to a halt. Hundreds of supporters, many exhibiting various stages of drink related behaviour, were wandering up and down the carriageways, playing impromptu games of football or simply relieving themselves on the hard shoulder.

It took something like 2 hours to cover 3 or 4 miles, and panic was beginning to set in, particularly thinking of our appointment with Ken and Phil. We decided to take the next exit - if we ever got there - and found ourselves heading for Wembley by the double-barrelled route – Milton Keynes, Leighton Buzzard and Hemel Hempstead.

Like many of my suggestions, it seemed like a good idea at the time. Admittedly, we weren't to know that the M1 ahead was about to start freeing up, or that our suburban route was a Saturday morning bottleneck at the best of times, and was currently riddled with roadworks.

My stomach knotted in frustration and disbelief. My Wembley dream had become a nightmare. We didn't even have the company of any other football traffic, just one isolated car with Red and White scarves drooping forlornly – we never went fast enough for them to flap – from the windows.

We arrived in Wembley, complete wrecks, just before kick off, and parked surprisingly easily in a side street. It was eerily quiet, apart from a couple of dozen fellow Reds, equally frantic and desperate for instructions to the ground.

We ran the mile or so through the empty semi detached Wembley suburbia that I was to come to know quiet well over the seasons, and suddenly, over the brow of a hill, there it was, my first ever sight of the World's most famous football stadium.

No time to savour the occasion, but despite all the panic I was surprised to notice that the noise of 100,000 people was a muted whisper, almost entirely contained within the huge concrete bowl. Ken and Phil were still waiting, literally on the verge of buying tickets from a tout, as the post kick off prices began to tumble. They'd gone through agonies watching the fans arrive, and like me they'd waited 20 years to see the Reds at Wembley.

The nightmare still wasn't over. There then followed a furious row with the stewards who wouldn't let us into our allocated upper terracing section behind the goal. "Sorry, full". We couldn't believe what was happening. This was, surely, our National Stadium, and we had legitimate tickets.

The mood turned ugly, and a vehement row broke out, some 20 or so Reds fans by now prepared to inflict serious damage on a couple of bloody minded "jobsworths". They grudgingly backed down, but we were led into a different section, the bottom front of the lower tier, actually emerging into daylight from the players tunnel itself.

I was immediately struck by the waves of noise ebbing and flowing under the canopy, and around the huge Wembley bowl. Chants, songs and oohs and aahs from the Liverpool end were answered at full volume from behind, above and around us by Reds fans and the pre-match atmosphere must have been something to behold.

We were like gate crashers to a party – no-one had noticed us arrive, things were already in full swing, and we were left on the side-lines, not really part of the proceedings. Sweating profusely, it took me until half time to settle down, by which time the pattern of the match was evident – Liverpool attacking consistently and Forest fighting a stubborn rearguard action, with young Chris Woods, deputising for the cup-tied Peter Shilton, playing a blinder.

Forest hung on to 0-0 through extra time and, drained and exhausted, I nevertheless began to plan my trip to Old Trafford for the replay.

It was held on the following Wednesday night and this time there was no mistake, arriving with a work colleague and friend well ahead of kick off. The organisation, at least compared with Wembley, was excellent, and we were shepherded efficiently into our spot directly behind the goal at the Scoreboard End.

Liverpool had the Stretford End, and the sides were allocated approximately 50/50, so there was no shortage of atmosphere, or support for the Reds, in a crowd of 54,375.

It was another dour, hard fought encounter, but Forest were at least holding their own, although a breakthrough seemed unlikely.

Midway through the 2nd half the pacey John O'Hare, deputising for the injured McGovern, suddenly burst clear on goal, only to be deliberately upended - as he admitted afterwards - by Phil Thomson.

I felt my stomach tighten in the split second before the referee pointed to the spot, although subsequent television evidence showed that Thomson's cynical foul had been well timed, just outside the box. (Mind you, Robbo would have scored anyway from the free kick, so I'm not sure what all the fuss was about).

Five minutes later, after Liverpool's uncharacteristic(!) protests had died down my stomach was tied in knots again as Robbo stepped up to take the kick. "Don't miss, don't miss, don't miss" was playing round and round in my head as he commenced his short run up.

He dispatched a typically firm and precise shot inches inside the keeper's right hand post, slap bang in front of us, and Forest's support exploded.

Liverpool threw everything into a last ditch effort to salvage something, but the Reds defence was superb, particularly Lloyd and Burns, who got their heads to everything as Liverpool were reduced to knocking in hopeful high balls.

I counted down every last one of the remaining 15 minutes as time seemed to stand still, and when the final whistle came we practically blew the roof off. Reds fans let rip with an unrestrained outpouring of relief and joy and at last I knew what it felt like to follow a winning team.

The only sour note was a mob of Liverpool fans who were running wild as we returned to our car. As Forest fans turned and ran, we actually made the right decision. We continued to walk on, and they charged straight through us, presumably, and as intended, mistaking us for fellow Scousers.

I was walking on air for days afterwards – now to wrap up the League.

Barring an absolute calamity we were certainties to clinch our first ever (and probably last) English League title and the great day duly arrived on April 22nd 1978.

We needed just one point from Coventry City at Highfield Road, but a jaded Forest were granted no favours by the determined Sky Blues, who were perhaps unlucky not to claim both points (as it then was).

Peter Shilton, by now recognised as one of the best signings ever made by Nottingham Forest Football Club, proved it yet again with a stunning point blank save to tip Mick Ferguson's header over the bar. Coventry could scarcely believe it, and nor could I – we were League Champions!

I didn't travel to Coventry, content to follow the anticipated celebrations by radio, but once it was clinched I let off steam by decking the dog in red and white and jogging around the streets of Carlton in a triumphant lap of honour.

Kenny Burns, a reformed but occasionally still miscreant character, was rightly honoured as player of the year, and Forest supporters spent the close season in something akin to a religiously euphoric trance, black and blue from self inflicted pinch marks.

Thus ended season 1977/78, one in which just about all my footballing dreams (shame we couldn't win the FA Cup as well!) came true.

I never remotely contemplated that we might claim an even bigger prize next season.

~

John Robertson

It's time for a word or two about JR.

Football has Peter Taylor to thank for spotting the potential of a lazy, overweight, under performing, could-be genius, and along with Cloughie shaping him into the most skilful player that I have ever had the pleasure to watch.

I was in the meagre crowd of 16,618 when he made his debut at the City Ground in a 3-1 First Division victory over Blackpool on 10th October 1970, with goals by 3 Reds favourites, Peter Cormack, Barry Lyons and Ronnie Rees, and a farewell appearance from fiercely competitive midfielder Henry Newton.

Despite the result, Forest, and Robbo, were on a slide, and we were relegated next season. If anyone had suggested that Robertson would set up Forest's winner in a future European Champions Final (and it was Champions in those days) and score the only goal in the following year's, the men in white coats would have been summoned.

Robertson liked a fag and a drink, didn't care much for training, and epitomised the lack of pride and professionalism that blighted Forest immediately pre Cloughie. He might have remained in the wilderness, a supreme talent unfulfilled, had his potential not been spotted and correctly harnessed.

The portly midfielder was moved wide to the left, effectively as a swap for Ian Bowyer, who was to excel in a left sided midfield role which gave full rein to his natural battling qualities.

Robbo hugged the touchline like a long lost friend, and the historic haunt of Stuart Imlach, "Flip" Le Flem, Ian Moore and Alan Hinton was now home to a stooped, jinking, magician whose sleight of foot left mesmerised defenders for dead and whose ability to put the ball on a chosen spot remains unsurpassed by any player in World football.

Robbo was the archetypal Scot, embracing the myth by refusing to give possession to the opposition. I generally deplore the Americans pointless obsession with statistics, but if a World table could illustrate percentage retention and accurate distribution Robertson would come top by a country mile.

He could dribble too, and one example typifies his art. Shilton rolled it short to the edge of the box and Robertson set off almost nonchalantly upfield in his familiar half walk, half run - jockeying for position, checking, looking up, shimmying, shuffling, first left, then right, but always within spitting distance (which admittedly can be quite some distance for the more accomplished exponents of this revolting practice) of the touchline, and always with defenders backing off, fearful of making the tackle that would see them on their backsides whilst the little fat man sped off into the distance.

Over halfway and Robbo was still playing on his own, tempting the tackle that never came, and weighing up his next move. It came as the defence compressed ahead of him, tightly guarding the penalty area. A feint to the right, a drop of the shoulder, then a sudden explosive, but perfectly balanced, surge to the left round the outside of his markers, and a whipped in left foot cross on the run that caused mayhem in the box.

Almost 100 yards from Trent End to Bridgford End in a seemingly half paced shuffle that was the unique style of the genius who is equalled only by Ian Storey-Moore in a Reds number 11 shirt.

Of all his attributes – perfect balance, fierce acceleration over the vital first few yards, two footed, a razor sharp appraisal of any situation, and extraordinary stamina, his temperament was perhaps his greatest, and least praised, strength.

Week in, week out, he was Forest's main outlet, and as the post-Europe side declined often the **only** outlet, the easy option for anyone in trouble. Knock it left to Robbo, ad nauseum, and even with 2 or 3 defenders snapping at him he'd control it, slow the play down, weigh up the options, take the pressure off the team and set us rolling again. He was Forest's safety valve.

His penalty against Liverpool at Old Trafford is special as it secured our first proper trophy since the 1959 FA Cup win.

I took penalties in our Parks team – 16 scored, one missed, the only plus in the career of a crap player virtually devoid of talent in every area of the game – but even at our level I knew the responsibility and gut wrenching pressure that can only be stood by the very strongest of us.

Well, perhaps not, but I was once threatened with GBH by several members of the nastiest team we ever played, and I'm ashamed to say that they were a Nottingham Forest Supporters side.

We endured 90 minutes of thuggery and verbal abuse, and the ball was kicked off the spot as I was commencing my run up. I was terrified, but only of missing, lest it be taken that I'd been intimidated by a bunch of scumbags. Fortunately, I scored, and justice was done, with a 2-1 win.

Robbo clearly received the odd word from one or two Liverpool players. I could even read Phil Thomson mouthing "good luck mate, you deserve it". Spurred by this encouragement, and rested by the few minutes break in play whilst Liverpool discussed the decision with the referee, he dispatched it precisely into the bottom corner, in front of 54,375 people.

Best moment – that penalty, to clinch our first trophy.

~

1978/79 – To Munich! (and Wembley again)

The season was pre-empted by the traditional Charity Shield curtain raiser at Wembley, against Ipswich Town. 64,438 were there, including my future wife, Lynn, whose definition of "treat" was not to concur with mine, as evidenced by her one match every ten years subsequently.

She also let the side down by typically girlie sympathy for "those poor men in the blue" as Ipswich got walloped 5-0. I was shouting for a 6th whilst Lynn was pleading for a consolation goal at the other end.

One thing I couldn't disagree with was her opinion of the hovel that passed as our National Stadium, not having had time to fully appreciate its squalor on my previous visit. I can't wait for it to be pulled down, and as for the Twin Towers, good riddance.

Wembley was a disgrace, and so was the ever rising tide of mob violence, which raised its vicious head from our very first League fixture.

If any game could be picked to follow that glorious 77/78 adventure it was surely our curtain raiser on Saturday August 19th at the City Ground against Tottenham. Spurs were back in the top flight after an unthinkable relegation and a season in the (then) 2nd division.

Drunk on promotion and the glamour signings of their Argentinian debutants, World Cup duo Oswaldo Ardiles and Ricardo Villa, half of North London was pouring towards the Bridgford terrace. It was hot and sunny and the stage couldn't have been more perfectly set.

Unfortunately, the Spurs fans hadn't read the script. By 2pm, as I stood outside the Outlaws Bar at the corner of Trent Bridge, waiting for Bob, I'd been spat at and verbally abused by any number from the columns swaggering arrogantly past. The Police did nothing to check them (now there's a surprise), content merely to contain this venomous snake.

In those few minutes before Bob arrived my usual first instinct of self preservation (cowardice would be a better description) was overwhelmed by a barely contained fury and outrage that these vile, gesturing, posturing, teenie yobs (most looked scarcely sixteen) had at a stroke ruined the opening day of a season that I'd anticipated since the last kick of the old one. Not just for me, but for thousands.

The match finished 1-1, but was overshadowed by possibly the most intimidating atmosphere ever generated by away fans on Trentside. Forest's yobs were all too happy to join in. There was trouble before, during and after the match and many Reds fans, in a bumper attendance of 41,223, vowed that this first match of the season would also be their last.

Like Northern Ireland's "Troubles", Football's version seemed to be an incurable malaise, and they surfaced with a vengeance on that sunny afternoon, destroying any memories of the game itself.

There wasn't much to remember in our next 4 matches as Forest couldn't stick it in the opposition net. Still, they couldn't stick it in ours either, and fans were treated to an exhilerating succession of nil – nils, broken by our elimination of Oldham in our first League Cup defence, and then a home victory against Arsenal in the League.

Next match, next (and new) competition, our first leg Champions Cup tie against Liverpool, our new "old enemy". Written off by most of the media, we were to be Liverpool's instant revenge for last season, but Garry Birtles put us ahead, and when Colin Barrett volleyed the ball into the Bridgford net for our second, with minutes remaining, I knew we'd dumped the Scousers again.

Bob was dumped by Scousers outside Anfield after Forest's battling 0-0 draw, and sustained a nasty eye injury after a vicious punch. Many years later he needed an operation on a detached retina, almost certainly a legacy of the incident.

I chose to stay in Nottingham, but couldn't cope with the nerve jangling ordeal of the radio commentary :-

"The cross comes over" (background crowd roar)

"Can Burns get his head to it?" (crowd noise intensifies)

"No, he can't! It spins loose" (noise rises to a crescendo)

"In comes the shot!!" screams the commentator, to a background explosion of sound

"Shilton punches it away" (agonising pause) "and McGovern hacks it clear".

We've only survived the first five minutes and already my nerves are shot. I spend the eternity that is the rest of the first half counting down the minutes, flicking the radio on and off, awaiting updates on the score :-

"And Liverpool are still surging forwards in search of that vital opening goal".

Thank God, still nil-nil. Radio off again for a few minutes. Half time finally arrives. Still nil-nil. Take the dog around the block to relieve the tension (mine, not the dog). Back to the radio. An hour gone, and back round the block, to the surprise and delight of one Golden Retriever.

Back to the radio for the last ten minutes and we're still holding the fort – reminiscent of last year's League Cup Final replay. I count down every last, excruciating, second until those magical words "we're into stoppage time" tell me that surely we've done it. Even Liverpool can't score twice now.

"There goes the final whistle………"

I don't hear the rest.

"YES,YES, YES!!!"

Walkies again, but this time in a state of euphoria for both of us (the dog always did go practically orgasmic at the sight of her lead) and a gallop across the open fields - until some bastard builds on them - of Carlton Forum.

Then it's the TV highlights, and I'm still terrified that Liverpool will score every time they attack.

Not until the following day, when I beg, steal or borrow every newspaper I can get my hands on, does the reality sink in and thoughts turn to the next round.

AEK Athens came out of the hat next and this time Forest were favourites to progress, which left me typically worried, especially as we'd won four in a row since Anfield, including a 5-0 thrashing of Oxford in round 2 of our defence of the League Cup.

Untypically, John McGovern got our first in Athens, and when Garry Birtles added another, in a 2-1 win, I thought we were home and dry – and so we were, 5-1 at fortress City Ground, and another couple for our number 9.

"Are you watching, Liverpool?" sang the Trent End, an original Trentside piss-take quickly plagiarised Nationwide and which endures to this day.

We dumped the other Scousers, Everton, out of the League Cup, 3-2 at Goodison, and after all the European excitement I began to fancy another big occasion at Wembley, but this time with a view to arriving before kick off, and soaking up the atmosphere.

Back in the bread and butter world of the Football League, a win, draw and win against Spurs, QPR and Bolton saw us to an unprecedented 42 game unbeaten League run, equivalent to exactly one full season's fixtures at the time, and surely a record that can never be beaten. Ominously, Liverpool away beckoned next.

December 9th 1978 saw a tired and weakened Forest side inevitably succumb, 2-0, at a passionate Anfield, but in a way it was a relief. The Scousers had their revenge (of a sort) and released the claustrophobic pressure of avoiding defeat that was stifling our play in the latter stages of our magnificent run.

We were straight back on the League Cup Wembley trail next game, defeating Brighton 3-1, with McGovern repeating his Eoropean feat by getting the first. Robertson and Birtles got the others.

I was always pleased when the much maligned McGovern scored, never more so than once when we were at home to Coventry and he was receiving full throated abuse from the Neanderthal next to us.

Barely had the witty jibe "Get off the field, you're fucking crap McGovern" issued forth when he unleashed a fierce shot into the Trent End net. I couldn't contain myself, turning to address our comic genius :-

"Who was that who just scored?"

Silence.

"Sorry, didn't hear you".

"Fuck off".

Ah, McGovern. Nice one, John".

Fortunately, he was sufficiently embarrassed not to punch me in the mouth.

To bait players, week in, week out, with torrents of witless invective takes the mentality of the playground bully. McGovern, with his slight build, unassuming demeanour and style of play became such a victim and the more that Cloughie defended him the more it fuelled the morons.

Despite everything, he never shirked or buckled, and conducted himself impeccably throughout his Forest career.

Wembley was on the horizon again as the New Year kicked off and Villa were beaten 2-1 at the City Ground in the 3rd Round of the FA Cup, Clough's bogey competition.

In the League Cup only Watford barred our path to a 2nd consecutive final and we beat them 3-1 on aggregate. All the goals came in the City Ground first leg, accompanied for the benefit of their chairman by the Trent End's "Song for Elton", "The League Cup isn't everything".

York City in the FA Cup were sandwiched between the Watford ties and we duly polished them off, 3-1, earning a tasty 5th round draw at home to Arsenal. It was the end of yet another FA Cup dream, "One nil to the Arsenal".

That left us with just the League, League Cup and Europe.

Swiss champions Grasshoppers Zurich were squashed 4-1 at the City Ground and with the second leg looking a formality Wembley again dominated my thoughts. Southampton were our League Cup Final opponents.

Ex Red Terry Curran was apparently going to run rings around our veteran left back, Frank Clark, by exploiting Wembley's tediously cliched "vast open spaces", leaving poor Frank adrift on an ocean of turf.

Two factors never entered the heads of the exponents of this absurd argument :-

Firstly, Forest had one of the largest playing surfaces in the League (behind Doncaster Rovers) and The Dell had one of the smallest, along with Arsenal and Derby. Forest's pitch may well have been bigger than Wembley's.

Secondly, and perhaps more important, Frank Clark had a footballing brain and Terry Curran hadn't, at least not on the day. Our free transfer acquisition from Newcastle was to give the temperamental winger a footballing lesson, with the hapless Curran sunk without trace well before the final whistle.

I set the alarm for 7am on Saturday, March 17th. No messing up this time. 8.30 lift on Carlton Hill then bomb down to Harrow for 12.00 rendezvous with Phil and Dennis, another old school friend, (except that Dennis never turned up due to his own local difficulties). A few drinks, then tube to Wembley. No problem.

7.01 and after I've finished strangling the alarm all's quiet. Too quiet. Out of bed. Open curtains.

"Shit, shit, shit, it's bloody snowing".

Like all kids, especially the male variety, that never grow up, I've always loved the magical transformation that Winter's white blanket brings, especially when it sneaks in unannounced, overnight. Except today. Surely not today. For a start, it shouldn't even be Winter any more.

"Look at it. Inches of the bloody stuff".

Unrelenting, and from leaden skies, heavy, thick flakes piled up on the ledges, perceptibly deepening and climbing up the windows. Into Corporal Jones mode – "Don't panic, don't panic!"

Radio on, flicking from Nottingham to Trent (despite its puerile adverts, any port in a storm) until a traffic report confirms that conditions are dreadful in Mapperley, Woodthorpe and Carlton – predictable, given our Himalayan terrain – but Carlton Hill is passable with care. The Sports report, live from Wembley, never even mentioned the weather, so despite the Arctic conditions in our garden it was presumably OK in the deep South.

I trudged, head down against the blizzard, and somehow made the summit of Ernest Road – "Big Ernest", as this steepest section of this roller coaster road is known locally – and onto the exposed Alpine plateau of Standhill Road. There I was cheered by the sight of a moving vehicle, soddened scarves hanging limply from its windows, slewing drunkenly through the white expanse towards the reputedly safe passage of Carlton Hill.

Deflated and discouraged by these surreal conditions, I felt the big match adrenalin begin to kick in as I awaited my lift – the sparse traffic sloshing by was 95% Wembley bound, as were the huddled pedestrians, albeit less red and white than white.

I could still just about feel the windward side of my face when Mick arrived, only a few minutes late, from low lying Bingham, cossetted by heavily gritted main roads and surprised at the chaos and conditions in hilly Carlton.

By the time we'd crossed the North-South divide that is Trent Bridge, barely a couple of miles away, road conditions had improved, although the heavy snow continued unabated and the countryside was blanketed. So it remained until just south of Charnwood Forest, when snow became sleet, then rain, then drizzle, and by the time we arrived in Harrow it was a dry and comparatively pleasant day.

Everywhere was a sea of red and white. Phil turned up as planned and we enjoyed a cracking atmosphere in the local pub, Phil and Saints fans alike surprised at our accounts of the weather conditions "up North". Southern softies, or what!

After the breathless shambles of last year the lingering walk up Wembley Way was sheer indulgence. A boisterous red and white street party slowly converged on the famous Twin Towers. "Oh when the Saints go marching in" rang out triumphantly, answered by a monotone, self mocking, chorus of "Robin `Udd, Robin `Udd, riding through the glen....".

We might have had the best team, but when it came to club signature tunes we had to get by with a 1950s Childrens TV adventure theme, sung only by Reds fans as a comic piss take.

We unofficially adopted, long before "You've lost that loving feeling" came into vogue, a Scousers song written about Scotland. "Mull of Kintyre" was imaginatively(!) corrupted to "City Ground, oh mists rolling in from the Trent" and whilst I thought it was exclusively cribbed by the Reds I subsequently noticed that Charlton Athletic have their own version.

Phil queued for a hot dog. I contented myself with the tantalising aroma of fried onions and memories – which in the interests of my starving mate I kept to myself – of my last experience of a hot dog, purchased outside the City Ground, where investigations of an unusually crunchy bit revealed a spent match.

Phil seemed well pleased with his cordon bleu offering, if not the matching price, and we parked ouselves on the concrete steps, to drink in the atmosphere and a few beers.

Klaxons blared. Someone, dressed as Nottingham Forest circa 1959, vigorously swung a traditional wooden rattle, threatening decapitation to anyone within six feet. Nobody minded. Both sets of fans seemed to be out to enjoy themselves and were high on pre match anticipation. At 2pm both teams were destined to lift the trophy.

At 2.30 we settled on the upper tier terracing directly behind the goal, where we should have been last year. We'd squeezed through the clanking, prison camp, turnstiles, climbed the squalid concrete stairways and paddled to the "Gents" through rivers of urine before reaching our allotted section where, it has to be said, the view was terrific.

We were herded to pitch level against Liverpool, and I'd taken seats, knees up around my chin, and with inevitable obstructing metal post, for the Charity Shield. Now we were in prime position, with a superb aerial view over the lush green turf. The steps were surprisingly high and I realised that the red and white wall of packed humanity behind the opposite goal was a mirror image of our end.

A low rumble of sound slowly intensified and poured towards us across the pitch and around the echoing canopies:-

"Oh when the Saints go marching in…….."

Our reply was immediate:-

"C'mon you Reds, C'mon you Reds……." reverberated deafeningly back, drowning the sound from the other end.

The terraces were packed shoulder to shoulder and when the teams came out Wembley exploded in a riot of sound and red and white. The League Cup had a lower status, but it was the "supporters cup final". Wembley's current 77,000 all seater capacity (with its demolition thankfully imminent) can't emulate the atmosphere of the sixties and seventies.

Then again, with a guaranteed seat a dozen blind drunk yobbos can't suddenly force their way abusively through the masses at one minute to three and decide that they're going to occupy your spot.

Like unwanted gatecrashers at a party their idea of a good time didn't match the occasion – "C'mon you bastards, sing up!" screamed one of them, oblivious that we had been, and that the match had kicked off, to a crescendo of sound. They scarcely knew which way to face, or which team was which. "Fucking wanker, referee!" greeted Southampton's first free kick, as we craned our necks for glimpses of the pitch.

Thus it was for the first 20minutes or so but as the match ebbed and flowed so did our friends, by now hoarse and subdued, until, by half time, they'd quietly dispersed, presumably to throw up and sleep it off.

Out on the pitch it was Forest who were feeling sick as Saints scored first and half of Wembley went mad, waves of noise attacking us from behind their goal. It's a strange, almost surreal, experience, like watching a mass celebration of your own funeral as you stand dejected and silent whilst another world, 100yards away, is in uproarous, joyful, tumult.

Then Forest find their feet, and their passes, and we chant defiantly back, knowing that we've got the better team.

When I 'phoned Phil to confirm our arrangements I promised him that Garry Birtles would be our hero, and when he equalised early in the second half, as Forest poured forwards towards our goal, we were ecstatic – for about 2 seconds. Offside - but the tide was turning and we could all sense it.

Stung by this setback Forest upped a gear and mounted waves of attacks, urged on by a barrage of sound. Southampton were being pummelled and when Birtles got the equaliser that counted, the ear splitting eruption nearly blew the roof off. We leapt into the air, arms aloft, in a thunderous release of emotion, and I could taste victory. Our end was going mad, and it was Southampton's turn to stand silently and watch.

Totally dominant, and with incessant vocal backing, Forest turned it on, Birtles, again, and Woodcock sending us delirious. A late Southampton consolation was irrelevant and for most Reds fans it was the first witnessing of our heroes lifting a major trophy at Wembley.

Sheer, undiluted, delight. Forget work, domestic problems, the gas bill, the Cold War, even the rise and rise of Margaret Thatcher – we've won the Cup!!

After the match we parted company with Phil, who I'd last seen at Wembley for the Liverpool final, and I arranged to meet him again next year – "same place, same time" – which I duly did.

The M1 north was a slow moving ribbon of red and white and although the sleet returned as we climbed over Charnwood it couldn't dampen our spirits.

It was snowing steadily when Mick dropped me off on Carlton Hill, but the major roads were clear and the lying snow was scarcely deeper than the 3 or 4 inches of the morning.

A solitary figure trudged, head bent against the driving, wet snow, and slithered, without crampons or ropes, down the face of a silent Ernest Road and home, where a single line of opposing footprints greeted him as he re-negotiated the tricky passage to the back door, snow still piled high against its ledge.

Like returning from holiday – "just think, 8 hours ago we were sweltering in Tenerife" – it all seemed like a dream. As dreams go, it was pretty damn good. As my Wembley visits go (seven, all with the Reds) it was the best of the lot.

I'd scarcely come down to earth when we were anticipating a European Cup semi final against IFC Cologne, courtesy of our expected 2nd leg formality in Zurich, where a low key 1-1 draw was good enough.

It set up a titanic battle against the Germans, as the great adventure just ran and ran.

We'd fallen adrift in the League, at least compared with last season's breathtaking gallop to the Championship, but a typically strong finish would see us achieve runners up spot. We faced the Germans in the City Ground 1st leg on April 11th undefeated in eleven matches since Arsenal's FA Cup win.

Our last 5 League games included thumping home wins against Coventry, 3-0; Chelsea, 6-0 and Aston Villa, 4-0. Only Bolton took anything from fortress City Ground, where a certain Trevor Francis scored his first goal, a last minute equaliser no less, since his £1m transfer – give or take a few quid, depending on whose story is believed – from Birmingham City. A 3-1 victory at Chelsea on the preceding Saturday set us up nicely and 40,804 expectantly packed the City Ground on Wednesday night.

John Robertson declared himself available for selection despite the death of his brother and played a vital, if uncharacteristic, role in salvaging something from what was becoming Nightmare on Trentside.

Despite goals from Birtles and Bowyer Forest's normally solid defence, founded on the rock that was Peter Shilton, foundered on that same rock as the Germans scored an unthinkable 3 away goals.

Their last was scored by their substitute, a Japanese striker, inspiring the media headline "Jap sub sinks Forest". His feebly hit long range effort somehow squirmed under Shilton's body and into the Trent End net.

All this after Robertson had put us ahead 3-2, tripping over his bootlace and scoring what to the uninformed looked remarkably like a perfectly executed diving header into the Bridgford net. After an initial moment of disbelief, and a few thousand "did Robbo actually head that?", a rapturous City Ground urged Forest forwards in a late charge for the 4th goal that would give us a healthy 2 goal cushion in Cologne.

If Robertson's header was a turn up, it was equalled by Shilton's clanger, and only a jubilant pocket of Germans in the old ramshackle, pre-Exec, East Stand were celebrating at the final whistle.

We trooped despondently homewards, the great European adventure as good as over, but in a moment of absurd delusion I predicted to a group of over confident Cologne fans that Forest would win the return leg 1-0.

After I'd said it, spontaneously and defiantly, I began to believe it. Tonight was an aberration. We'd won 1-0 often enough, and kept clean sheets against Liverpool twice in League Cup finals and twice in Europe. That was it then. Simple. We score, they don't. Clough and Taylor would have it sorted and the impossible dream could still be lived. I was almost cheerful.

I was ecstatic by quarter to five the following Saturday as our sparkling League run continued in the best possible way, with a successful raid into Sheep territory, 2-1. The matches continued thick and fast – home to Leeds on the Monday night (0-0) and Man Utd on Wednesday (1-1), then St Andrews on Saturday (2-0) as preparation for Wednesday night in Cologne.

Alex Ferguson would have apoplexy if his huge squad were subject to such an intensive programme. Forest just got uncomplainingly on with it, Cloughie accepting the price of success with the comment that playing would replace training.

By the morning of Forest's biggest ever match Nottingham expected, or at least believed that we were in with a fighting chance, and there was an air of anticipation as the day wore on and kick off time slowly approached. I was desperate for work to finish, and when I was finally released from my slow motion time warp pre match nerves kicked in and time accelerated.

I rushed into Slab Square for the bus, grabbing a "Yo-Po"

(Newsvendor-speak for "Evening Post) en route.

I'd become something of an expert on the calls of Nottingham's newspaper sellers cries whilst imprisoned in Market Square House one hot afternoon. I saved myself from Business Interruption Insurance Induction Course - Induced Insanity by listening to the unique calls emanating from the newstands dotted about the Square and drifting in through the open windows.

I wonder what became of the young lady – also an accomplished pavement artist – whose plummy, ringing, exhortation "Evening Post" contrasted so vividly with the rest, of which "Ge'dger Po, Mi'day Po", repeated over and over again in a gruff monotone, was a typical example?

The man near the Theatre Royal would wait until a passer by – preferably of nervous disposition, or old and infirm – was within a couple of feet before screaming, like some demented Town Crier, "POST!!!". I wonder how many people he killed.

My Yo-Po of Wednesday April 25th, as always, started on the back page, although I think that Forest were also promoted to the front, testimony to the most prestigious match in our 113 year history.

We were a headline story on Birmingham based "Midlands Today" (our "local" BBC TV News programme before the advent of dedicated broadcasting for the East Midlands) and allegedly carried the Nation's best wishes, except perhaps in Derby, Leicester and the Red half of Liverpool. Not to mention jealous Notts County fans, any number of Wolves fans, following a bust up at the City Ground a couple of seasons back, ditto Spurs, etc, and a Leeds acquaintance who hated Forest.

Yet local rivalries and yob culture aside most of the footballing nation did genuinely wish us well, unlike today when all non- Man U fans (i.e. the other half of the country) want them to fail at the first hurdle.

Trouble is, Europe is now rigged to a money crazed League basis for the benefit of the big clubs. In the eyes of many genuine fans the whole thing stinks, and is a massive turn off. My own views are unprintable.

By kick off I'd decided that I couldn't endure ordeal by radio – Liverpool was bad enough, and we'd started that one with a 2 goal lead. I took the dog for an excursion, returning early into the 2nd half. Switched telly on. Couldn't concentrate. Switched it off. On with the radio, heart pounding. As always, it was an eternity before the score was revealed, still 0-0 and on a knife edge.

When I switched on again, late in the 2nd half, the tone of the commentary had changed and I was swamped by a surge of adrenalin :-

"Lloyd brings it away. Finds Burns. He finds O'Neill, out wide on the right. O'Neill takes his time, then plays it long for Woodcock to chase. Woodcock can't get there, but it's another precious few seconds used up by Forest"

We're winning, and suddenly the tension ratchets up a stomach tightening notch. Bad enough at nil-nil, but almost unbearable when the prize is within grasp. Please, don't let it slip now, I couldn't stand it. Ten minutes left, and Cologne can't get on with it quickly enough, pouring forwards for the winning equaliser on the away goals rule.

Ten agonising minutes during which I learned that Ian Bowyer had scored, with a stooping close range header, the most important goal of his illustrious career.

Nerves shredded, I hung on to the commentary, twitching and agitating in a state of advanced torment, and yelling futile instructions into the radio as the ball bobbled around our area. "For Christ's sake clear the bloody thing!"

Forest duly did, time after time, in those last few desperate minutes, and when the final whistle went it triggered demented celebrations the like of which hadn't been seen in my house since the Scousers bit the dust at Anfield.

In the days that followed Reds fans basked in the glory of reaching the absolute pinnacle of European Club football, the European Cup final, whilst Forest prepared themselves for Saturday's League match, against Liverpool no less.

The attendance of 41,898 was the last occasion, barring future redevelopment on an unlikely scale, that over 40,000 were inside the City Ground. Our reward was a disappointing goal-less draw, although Trentside revelled in reminding Liverpool and their fans of what they were missing :-

"To Munich, to Munich" rang out in celebration of our showpiece finale, with victory surely a foregone conclusion against the unlikeliest opposition, English coached Swedish champions Malmo. I can't even remember who they beat in their semi as they quietly sneaked through to the final.

I do remember the bitter-sweet feelings as half of Nottingham made their preparations for the Olympic Stadium and that bloody song broke out every few minutes during each of our 3 remaining home fixtures, Liverpool, Southampton (1-0) and Manchester City (3-1).

I wasn't going.

Overdrawn, underpaid, and a complete idiot where money – amongst many other things – was concerned, I could never see the point in saving or planning ahead, for reasons that are nothing to do with this book. Suffice it to say that I'd got a mortgage and associated commitments that I could scarcely fund, averting Gas and Electricity disconnections only by a promise to pay when funds were available. The Public Utilities were to their credit sympathetic and practical, and at least I'd have the telly and a hot meal.

I'd always found money for Forest's domestic campaigns but as my financial circumstances plummetted to a new low, Forest's fortunes reached an unimaginable high. At the time it seemed an appalling injustice, as well-heeled (i.e. just about everyone compared with me) "supporters" popped out of the woodwork everywhere, excitedly planning their slice of Forest's great adventure.

"Mr. Radio Nottingham", Dennis McCarthy, described the colourful open air carnival that was Munich, as thousands of Forest followers, heavily outnumbering their Swedish counterparts, took over the Bavarian capital. My absence was solely down to me, although I could plead mitigating circumstances, and I resigned myself to sulking, and watching the match on TV.

No-one doubted that we would win against the Swedish part-timers, but a jaded and unimaginative performance was lifted only by a typical piece of John Robertson magic down the left touchline and a perfectly judged Trevor Francis header, and both sides seemed to accept that 1-0 to Forest was honourable.

As a spectacle for Europe's vast television audience it was dismal stuff, and particularly disappointing, in the light of so many exhilerating performances, that we couldn't save one for this unique occasion. Still, we were Champions of Europe.

Not bad for a provincial, small time, club that had been plunging into oblivion "B C" (Before Clough) and counted seasons 1958/59 (FA Cup winners) and 1966/67 (FA Cup semi finalists and Football League runners up) as its greatest achievements in over 100 years of trying, not counting our first FA Cup win back in the Victorian era.

In the 2 seasons 77/78 and 78/79 Forest were Champions and runners up in the League, had established that incredible 42 match unbeaten League run, won the Charity Shield, won the League Cup twice and now, at the first attempt, the European Cup. Even a "Roy of the Rovers" storyline based on our achievements would have been ridiculed.

I should have been "Over the Moon, Brian", but watching, via a 19inch TV screen, 30,000 ecstatic Reds fans celebrating as John McGovern lifted the European Champions Cup, and imagining the scenes in the streets and bars of Europe, left me feeling pathetically sorry for myself. The impossible dream had come true and I wasn't at the party.

Ten minutes after the final whistle they were setting Munich alight and I was watching some crap announcement about some crap American film that was about to follow the biggest match in my club's history. It was my own fault, but it didn't lesson my self righteous indignation at the distant hordes who were living my dream.

"Where were you at Roker Park?"

The feelings of resentment quickly subsided after the team, and triumphant followers, returned and we collectively bathed in the glorious afterglow of our season's climax. I even touched the Cup, which was left casually on display on a wall outside the Carlton Pub (it was, loosely speaking, in the custody of a well known Forest executive) and to all intents and purposes, unless specifically questioned, "I was there".

An interesting post-script to the Munich final was latched onto by the media when we were drawn against Bayern Munich in the EUFA Cup in the early 90s. A Reds fan had been arrested at the Malmo game for drunk and disorderly behaviour, or some similar offence.

He was given a choice of sentence, and rather than pay a fine he chose Community Service, utilising his trade skills to such good effect that he was offered permanent employment. He accepted – given no doubt the bleak prospects in Britain at the time – and was still there, living just south of Munich and eagerly anticipating Forest's visit to the Olympic Stadium.

There are stories galore, no doubt most of them apocryphal, of Scotsmen scattered to the farthest corners of the World following (failed) World Cup campaigns,

Rangers or Celtic tours, etc, but as far as I am aware this is the only example of a Forest fan securing a free transfer abroad.

I can visualise his post card home :-

"Dear all,

Got pissed. Got arrested. Got Community Service. Got a job.

Not coming home.

Auf wiedersehen.

P.S. Don't forget to feed the cat"

Having visited Southern Germany I'm sure he made the right decision – a life's course changed by a bizarre quirk of fate.

Back in Nottingham, the old City Ground was beginning to change, and about time too. Cologne and Munich threw into sharp focus the inadequacies of our outdated relic. We were deficient even by comparison with Hull City's Boothferry Park, or Turf Moor, Burnley, not to mention rising stars such as Coventry City's Highfield Road, itself now dated and scheduled for replacement as the next wave of redevelopments take place.

Cologne and Munich are also now outdated, with Ajax currently lauded as one of Europe's flagship stadiums, and the current City Ground awaits "only" a new state of the art Main stand, perhaps with an infill at the Trent End corners, to bring it into line with England's best.

Work started on our first new stand – and sadly we had to wait quite a while for the next one – after the Liverpool game on 28th April 1979. Demolition of the old East stand and closure of our largest and steepest expanse of terracing permitted desultory attendances of only 20,288 and 21,104 for Southampton and Manchester City respectively.

The passing of the East Stand was hardly lamented. It comprised a barn like structure perched at the back of the terrace and housing rows of wooden benches stylishly sub divided into individual seats by painted lines. The roof overhung a good portion of the terracing and when it rained we all scuttled upwards for protection, squashed and steaming, leaving scattered remnants, indifferent to the elements, dripping on the open expanse below.

As youngsters at Reserve matches we relished the opportunity to clamber over the dividing partition and lord it in the luxury of the seated area, fascinated by the disparity in width of the allocated portions. The man with the paint clearly didn't use a tape measure, and adjacent seats catered for visits by Laurel and Hardy.

From its ashes was to rise the pretentiously named "Executive Stand" (whoever lumbered us with that absurdity?). Thankfully, it's now been re-named, in 1999/2000, in honour of Brian Clough.

Its completion took an age, although I daresay there was more to it than I appreciate. Concrete pillars emerged slowly and starkly from the bare site and gradually the superstructure filled in. Fired by my Munich debacle I determined to scrape together the reddies for a Season Ticket in our new pride and joy, utilising a new (to me) concept known as "saving". I could "trade in" my Terrace ticket for my seat, once it was ready, and although the price was naturally higher it was relative peanuts compared with today's prices.

Unfortunately, I was at the "wrong" end, i.e. just opposite the Bridgford penalty area, and only a few rows from the back, and by the time it was declared ready for occupation, well into Autumn of 1979/80, the roof was still nowhere in sight, at least from my lofty and windswept perch.

Gulls circled lazily below, frightened to climb to the gale swept heights of row 26, Upper Tier. Still, the view was, and is, superb, although over the seasons I graduated below the snow line to row 11, almost on halfway, where the view is just about as good as it gets.

The part time, arthritic, one-legged vertigo sufferer responsible for the roof started at the Trent End and worked his way towards us, covering the ground at the speed of an elderly and severely asthmatic snail. At every home match we'd ponder glumly on his progress as the roofline crawled towards us, like the hour hand on a clock, invisible to the naked eye, but getting there, slowly.

The Executive Stand was officially opened by Brian Clough on August 20th 1980 (Forest 2, Birmingham City 1, attendance 26,561), although it had been as good as finished since the Spring, so perhaps it didn't take an eternity – I just happened to be sitting at the wrong end.

One question has always been uppermost in my mind, relating to safety. It takes forever to empty, and whilst it's of Fire Resisting Construction I wonder what the implications might be in terms of another emergency, e.g. genuine bomb threat, storm damage, etc.

Watching the 1998 World Cup on TV I was taken with the "V" shaped stairways at the brand new Stade de France in Paris, which conspicuously broadened towards the exits. A simple but no doubt effective feature for alleviating the familiar and potentially dangerous, and definitely time consuming, bottlenecks. Hopefully a new Main Stand will incorporate this design.

At the close of 1978/79 I couldn't wait for the start of the next season, for our new stand to be up and running, and for my shiny red plastic seat to be ready.

We'd be starting 1979/80 as Champions of Europe!

~

Martin O'Neill

I saw the 19 year old Law student from Northern Ireland make his debut at the City Ground on November 13th 1971 in our League match against West Brom. It was a typical Baggies encounter, Forest winning 4-1 and O'Neill scoring one of them.

I can't claim to remember anything about his goal, or his overall performance, but the records show that he went on to make 10 League appearances plus 7 as sub in that dire relegation season, and that he scored one other goal, in our 3-2 defeat at Old Trafford on December 4th.

What I can remember from his early Forest days is his strong running from midfield and fierce shot from distance, struck stylishly off the outside of his right foot – the exact opposite, for the same inswinging swerve, of Stuart Pearce's instep hit left footers. Unlike Pearce, it never became his trademark, a dead ball being harder to hit O'Neill style, but he scored his share of vital goals from open play.

He couldn't kick with his left, and refused to head it unless absolutely unavoidable, ducking into any contact as if the ball was made of concrete. Sometimes one of the loudest cheers of the game was for what passed as a Martin O'Neill header.

His heading prowess was a "quality", high on entertainment value, that he shared with his opposite number, John Robertson, but his real strengths were formidable. He tormented defences with his weaving, almost crablike, runs, the ball always under the close control of that right foot, before bursting through with an explosive injection of pace.

He could tackle a bit, too. Fiercely competitive, he more than punched his weight, taking it as a personal slight if he lost a challenge, and displaying endless reserves of stamina.

He struggled through those bleak days of the early and mid 70s before flourishing under Clough and Taylor. His preferred central midfield role was forbidden and he was pushed wide to the right where he became the perfect, if reluctant – the "O" stands for obstinate – foil for Robertson.

It was a particular feature of the Clough era that most of the players - of both teams – were usually compressed towards the benches (sometimes it looked almost ludicrous, from our high vantage point) and it made for contrasting performances from O'Neill and Robertson, who would almost invariably enjoy their best 45 minutes driving down the wide open spaces of the Exec.side.

At least, that's how I remember it, with O'Neill attacking the Trent End and Robbo the Bridgford.

I can't remember him ever giving less than 100% for the Reds, and his commitment and persistence, whether on a good or a bad day, earned him immense popularity with the fans, although not necessarily with Mr. Clough, who didn't appreciate his complaints that his natural game had been sacrificed in favour of the Team Plan.

My own view is that Clough and Taylor got it right, in the interests of team and, ultimately, player, and we saw the best of him in his disciplined role. O'Neill's love-hate relationship with the right touchline struck a necessary balance with Robertson, although O'Neill never hugged his touchline with quite the same conviction.

Cruelly robbed by injury and suspension of a European Cup Final appearance, having played in all 4 semi finals, he can still reflect proudly on a Forest career as a lynchpin in the most glorious run in the club's history.

He made his last appearance, in front of 25,357, at the City Ground on 21st February 1981 before his transfer to Norwich City, going out with a bang against the Gunners, with a double, in our 3-1 victory.

His subsequent move into Football Management, teaming up again at Leicester with his old mate JR, has been equally successful. Stubborn, animated, articulate, passionate, and like many top managers suffering from the very persecution complex that drives them to succeed, he's often quick to point an accusatory finger at the referee, and shameless when the TV replays prove him wrong.

We wanted him, and his tubby mate, back at the City Ground, and most Reds thought he was on his way, but it wasn't to be, Premiership Leicester – the team that O'Neill built - and their proposed new stadium proving the bigger attraction. Perhaps there was also the likelihood of a greater prize - he'll never be short of offers.

He also makes a decent Television pundit and I confess to watching in the hope that one day he'll exchange fisticuffs with Alan Hansen.

Strangely, my fondest recollection is of his return to the City Ground in Norwich City colours. He was only half fit, and couldn't play a full part, but the standing ovation from all around the ground was testimony, if any were needed, to his place in the Forest Supporters "Hall of Fame".

~

1979/80

We were back in Munich on August 1st 1979, where we lost a pre-season friendly 5-0 to Bayern Munich, a foretaste of their visit to the City Ground in the 90s when they walloped us out of the EUFA Cup.

Back in 1979 the disappointment was less acute, but the shock of a full strength Forest going down so heavily raised a few eyebrows, and no doubt a few voices in the post-match dressing room – or if Cloughie was there, perhaps one of his withering silences.

Either way, we stormed into the new season on the back of successive friendly wins against Botafogo, (whoever they might be) Dynamo Bucharest and Montpelier, with 4 straight wins – Ipswich away, Stoke and Coventry at home, and a 5-1 thrashing of West Brom at the Hawthorns, scene of an outrageous injustice several seasons previously.

I was behind the Forest goal when an Albion forward, unable to make legitimate contact with a speculative cross, blatantly and theatrically punched the ball into the Reds net, witnessed by 21 other players and everyone else in the ground – well, everyone bar two.

By an amazing statistical freak those two were the referee and linesman. As the guilty party retreated to face Forest's free kick it became apparent that a goal had been awarded. The ref was immediately surrounded by an outraged Forest defence and although he stuck by his decision, much to the amusement of the crowd, (most of them, anyway) he must have realised that he'd dropped an almighty clanger.

Never mind Maradonna's "Hand of God" incident, it was as nothing compared with "The Baggies hand at the Hawthorns". Forest were so traumatised by the affair – stress counselling wasn't commonly available in those days – that our expected challenge for the Championship never materialised.

Incident was never far away on trips to the Albion and the walk from and back to Smethwick Rolfe Street Station through the terraced streets of the largely Asian community was always "interesting", as gangs of mainly white Baggies infiltrated in search of a punch up.

Our threesome was ambushed one deceptively pleasant, sunny day by a gang of some 20 or so. Our standard ploy of looking confident and mingling incognito with the locals was completely shot when my idiot of a mate, Steve, removed his jacket in the warm sun, revealing his Forest scarf tied neatly in a belt around his waist.

We were spotted and surrounded, and sought help from a group of nearby Police, who basically told us to piss off - thanks, gentlemen, for trying so hard to protect innocent citizens. Rescue came courtesy of a couple of good Samaritan Albion fans who led us down a narrow alleyway across some private gardens where we laid low for a while, Steve's scarf now hidden firmly down the back of his throat.

Another season, familiar story. 2 of us this time were with some 50 Reds on the Rolfe Street platform when a similar number of Baggies came down the steps from the road. Someone threw a stone and before long missiles were being exchanged with increasing frequency and intent, and a serious confrontation looked inevitable.

They held the high ground and station exit and I was very aware of being trapped, particularly if local reinforcements arrived and we became seriously outnumbered. Our only option would be to run for it along the railway track.

Instead, we all ran for it, as a gathering thunderstorm suddenly broke with a ferocious downpour. Reds and Baggies dashed for the tiny shelter where we crammed in like sardines, mocking those outside, red and blue alike, who scuttled under whatever remaining shelter they could find, or gave up the futile attempt and stood dripping like the proverbial drowned rats.

By the time the train arrived any conflict had been reduced to sarcastic exchanges between wet and dry, and a bond of mutual dislike for Albion's local rivals, Wolves.

Enough of West Brom, and back to 1979, and our next League game, 0-0 at home to Leeds. Enough of Leeds.

Either side of West Brom our annual League Cup run to Wembley had started in confident manner, Blackburn Rovers being polished off 6-1 on our patch after a 1-1 at Ewood Park in the first leg. So far only Bayern had got the better of us, but Norwich City gave us the bird at Carrow Road, Tony Woodcock getting our consolation in a 3-1 defeat.

Our relative slide in the League was to continue, with a final position of "only" 5th, but 2 Cup Finals out of 3 competitions would be a tolerable effort.

Oesters Vaxjo bit the dust 2-0 at the City Ground in the first leg of the European Cup, but as defending holders our gate of less than 22,000, even allowing for modest opposition, was disappointing. The match was unexceptional, so those who stayed away doubtless felt vindicated. Bowyer scored both goals, and Woodcock got the away one in a 1-1 draw. Year 2 of our European adventure was up and rolling.

So was League Cup Wembley trail, year 3, a Woodcock hat trick demolishing Middlesbrough 3-1 at the City Ground.

Back to Europe, and another big name, Arges Pitesti, came out of the hat and duly fell as scripted, 2-0 at our place (Woodcock and Birtles) and 2-1 away (Bowyer and Birtles), before the Winter break put Europe on hold.

Sandwiched between the European games, in addition to a couple of League fixtures, was the next round of the League Cup. On Tuesday October 30th 1979 four of us left work mid afternoon for a first time visit to Ashton Gate, where

Forest salvaged a 1-1 draw, from an embarrassingly poor performance. John O'Hare's goal kept us alive.

The slog home into the early hours, with the prospect of the 6-30 alarm, did nothing to encourage a repeat excursion, but after we'd overcome City 3-0 in the replay (O'Neill, Anderson and Woodcock) the same foursome convened for a trip to Upton Park in the next round.

Unfortunately, things were turning gloomy in the League. First, our unbeaten home run of 57 games was ended. Our incredible run couldn't last for ever, but we went down with something of a whimper, against unlikely opponents – as is so often the way – who only saved themselves in the very last match of season 1996/97 from plunging out of the Football League altogether.

Yet the Seagulls crapped on us on 17th November 1979, hanging on for a record ending 1-0 win. It was also, sadly, Tony Woodcock's last appearance before his transfer to Cologne.

Things went from bad to worse.

After Brighton rocked us, the Rams stuffed us, 4-1 at the Baseball Ground. A 1-1 home draw against Arsenal slightly lifted the gloom and then another early finish at work saw us hitting the road again - specifically, the A1.

We parked somewhere near West Ham's ground, amidst a maze of terraced streets - remnants of the old, now fragmented, East End, but still with more than a hint of the traditional working class Cockney aura that wraps itself around the "homespun" Hammers.

It was to us outsiders an intimidating atmosphere, and four citizens of Nottingham in unfamiliar, dimly lit territory didn't waste words as they sought anonymity in a thickening tide of gor blimey expectancy converging on an invisible stadium.

Suddenly, we were directly behind one of the stands, trying not to look lost as we furtively checked our tickets to find our entrance. We pushed and shuffled through to our turnstile, a geriatric, clanking, piece of machinery that reluctantly clattered aside to swallow us up through its absurdly narrow passageway into the bowels of a dingy relic of a stand. (Still, at least some prat wasn't allowed, when it was still in its infancy, to name it the Executive Stand – that would be simply ridiculous).

For a second, I thought I was at the Baseball Ground.

We emerged, after a climb up drab, depressing stairways, onto our row of cramped wooden seats, and the reassurance of East Midlands accents. Our little pocket of fans were high above, and at the side, of the pitch, under the low overhang of the roof. It was nothing if not old fashioned.

For all that, Upton Park under floodlights was a dramatic sight. We gazed down on a postage stamp pitch hemmed in tightly by its compact surroundings. The sellout Boleyn Ground was heaving. 35,856 souls – less a couple of thousand Reds – were anticipating a right old knees up, with the Irons set to hammer the nails into Forest's League Cup coffin.

The terraces behind the goals were a solid, swaying, mass and such was the volume of noise from both ends that I couldn't tell which was the "popular" one. Forest's standing support, tucked away in one of the corners, was overwhelmed by an East End barrage of sound, exploding all around the ground as the teams came out.

West Ham fans were on a big night out and the intense, jellied eels flavour of it washed all around us, courtesy of the intimate "surround-sound" architecture of the pre-modern Upton Park.

If Forest looked complacent and jaded at Ashton Gate, Hammers fanatical support was double edged, shaking the Reds out of any such lethargy, and this was a real tooth and nail Cup tie. It was a backs to the wall defensive battle with never a second's relaxation, for team or supporters.

Bums were permanently on edges of seats. There were loads of oohs and aahs – those wooden seat edges could have done with a rubbing down – and the football supporters paradox, paying good money and valuable time for an away trip and then wishing away every minute of the second half, as Forest hung on for a fighting 0-0, subduing the crowd and surviving a late cavalry charge.

We stole quietly and quickly away after the match, and were soon belting back up the A1 towards our first drop off point in Bingham. Back home I reflected on our East End experience, if not the subtleties of the match itself, and its echoes of the 60s.

West Ham Utd on December 4th 1979 was traditional, passionate, working class football fare with no frills – light year's from today's sanitised, all seater, corporate diseased, over priced, over hyped, media circus. I wouldn't swap today's seat for yesterday's terrace, or yesterday's hooligan problems (although only a fool would suggest that it's fully under control), but I'd take much of the rest.

After West Ham, Forest were back in London, but with not a jellied eel in sight, the semi-detached suburbs of South Norwood this time proving inhospitable as the Eagles brought us down to earth in the League, 1-0. It might not have had the reputation of Upton Park or The Den, but Selhurst Park could be pretty hostile in those days, and 34,840 witnessed the Reds demise.

Our 4th successive encounter against London opposition was a flattering 3-0 win in the West Ham replay, Forest only breaking the deadlock in extra time, courtesy of O'Hare, Birtles and O'Neill. If I remember correctly, it poured, but I was warm and dry (at least, on the outside) at an inescapable Insurance Institute do, bemoaning the missed opportunity of a wet December night in the gods under the open skeleton of steelwork that mockingly awaited the arrival of the one-legged roofing contractor.

Indifferent form in the League – win a couple, lose a couple – was overshadowed by a plethora of Cup fixtures – FA Cup, League Cup semi final (2 legs), and European Super Cup (2 legs). The odd friendly was also thrown in for good measure.

Full strength teams were fielded in Cologne on December 18th as part of Tony Woodcock's transfer deal, and in Gravesend on 8th January to inaugurate their new floodlights. Our 6-1 win in Kent was sandwiched between an emphatic 4-1 victory at Elland Road in the FA Cup 3rd round and a 3-1 defeat of West Brom at home in the League. We completed a handy Cup and League double over Leeds by beating them again in Yorkshire, 2-1, before our 3rd consecutive League Cup semi final beckoned.

Yet again fate had pitched us into a mighty tussle with Liverpool, and as with Europe last year we were at home in the first leg. The Scousers were desperate for revenge, but Robbo repeated his 1978 Old Trafford feat, scoring the only goal of the game with a coolly struck penalty, in front of 32,220.

Like a bad penny, Liverpool just kept turning up. Four days later we "entertained" them (a strange expression that belongs to the "Executive Stand" category of misnomers) again on Trentside, this time as our 4th round FA Cup opponents.

The gate was up by 1,057, and it was the Scousers turn to steal the game, 2-0, and a fellow Red's car. Alright, there's no proof, but it didn't need Hercules Poirot to point a finger of suspicion in the direction of some anonymous "Scally" heading back to the North West – Forest's electronic scoreboard even used to post special Police warnings at Liverpool and Everton fixtures.

Boosted by their FA Cup success, confidence was high on Merseyside that Forest would be swept aside in the League Cup return, but we had another trophy to win first. It was a double header against Barcelona in the totally forgettable European Super Cup, a pointless exercise staged presumably for financial reasons between European and EUFA Cup (I think) winners. Whatever it was, Barcelona had presumably won it last.

23,807 saw on loan Charlie George score the only goal at the City Ground, and Kenny Burns netted at the Nou Camp before 90,000 to earn a 1-1 draw, and another piece of silverware. Just time to squeeze in a League match, 0-0 at home to Bristol City, before the second League Cup leg, where a packed Anfield expected.

I didn't fancy being "entertained" by Liverpool, despite their famous hospitality – "mind yer car, mister?" – particularly after Bob's experience last season, and couldn't face ordeal by radio with only a one goal advantage.

Instead, I stayed in the bar at Carlton Forum after a typically scintillating display at our Tuesday night 5 a side – saving a certain goal with a perfectly timed tackle one minute then drilling home a precision shot at the other end. At least, that's how it seemed after a few pints.

News came over the tannoy, to a rousing cheer, that Forest had scored, and I arrived home to find that we'd drawn 1-1 and were back at Wembley. Easy, and I'd hardly broken sweat, except in the 5 a side – and there may be witnesses who'd even dispute that.

Our goal was from yet another John Robertson penalty. He scored 14 penalties in "proper" matches that season, a testimony to some superb refereeing – the bloke at Anfield must have had a death wish – and Robbo's nerve.

Back to League action for a change and after a 2-2 home draw against Middlesbrough, guess what – another trip to Anfield, our 4th Liverpool clash in 8 games. We lost 2-0, but we'd claimed the big prize, Wembley, and taking into account our home win in the League back in September honours were even. Played 5, won 2, lost 2, drawn 1. One win each in the League, one knockout each in the Cup.

The matches just kept coming and I could hardly keep pace. I'd scarcely collected my League Cup Final ticket before Europe awoke from its Winter slumbers, in the shape of Dynamo Berlin. Hardly a mouthwatering prospect, and positively jaw dropping after a shock 1-0 City Ground first leg defeat sent me home despondent and, for the first time since our European adventure started, anticipating our exit.

Still, we walloped Spurs at home in the League 4-0 in our next match, which cheered me up, and Miller got himself sent off, which cheered me up even more, as I was never an admirer of his "unsophisticated" style of play.

Wolves next, in the League Cup Final, and having waited an eternity to see Forest at Wembley I was now set to make my 4th visit. Wolves would be a walkover and I took it for granted that the Reds would achieve the distinction of winning the League Cup three times in succession.

I agreed my annual rendezvous with Southern based Phil and after the scarf flying exodus down the M1 – undiluted Red and White to junction 19, then mingled with Old Gold and Black – we met again in Harrow, anecdotal home of a large Chinese community :-

Immigrant Chinaman arrives at Heathrow. "Harroh" he says, in cordial greeting to taxi driver. "OK, Guv", says our Cockney Sparrer, and proceeds to deposit him in Harrow, where he lives happily ever after.

Our trip down had gone like clockwork. No timing cock ups, and no blizzards. It was all too easy. We didn't even have a group of drunks park themselves on our toes right on kick off. Unfortunately, we had an uninterrupted view of a feeble Forest performance against an equally unimpressive Wolves outfit. We'd beaten them 3-1 in the League back in October and they were surely there for the taking.

Until Wolves scored what proved to be the game's only goal I thought we were destined to break the deadlock, click into top gear, and sweep them aside, but a moment of pure farce changed everything.

Another unimaginative punt upfield from Wolves drifted harmlessly towards the edge of the Forest box and Shilton left his line in anticipation of collecting it. Due to a "lack of communication" the unfortunate David Needham, playing his first match in eleven, as replacement for Larry Lloyd, simultaneously chested the ball back, to where Shilts no longer was. Both players were stranded on the edge of the Forest box as the ball ran gently towards the empty net.

I remember the agonised split second of realisation as the awful reality dawned.

"Shit, the bastard can't miss."

Andy Gray, who'd done nothing all match, and had been nowhere near the speculative punt, was left at the Wolves end with an unmissable tap-in which he celebrated ad nauseum in front of their delirious supporters, and without a hint of embarrassment. Our dog would have scored it. The embarrassment was all Forest's and despite some desperate huffing and puffing we never threatened to save the match, and retain **our** trophy.

So we bade goodbye to the League Cup – for a few seasons, anyway – and trooped dejectedly away, leaving the exultant Wolves fans to their celebrations.

That was it, then. Mediocrity in the League, relatively speaking (amazing how quickly expectations change – a few years back we would have thought 5th place in the top division was paradise), early exit from the FA Cup (nothing new there), League Cup Final disappointment, and about to exit Europe. Just the European Super Cup to show for our efforts, so maybe it's a more prestigious trophy than I'd first speculated.

Unlike me, Forest hardly had time to feel sorry for themselves before Wednesday night's appointment in an icy Berlin, where progress could only be made by our becoming the first club in the European Cup to get through after losing at home. On a bitterly cold night and rock hard pitch Trevor Francis skated through the East Germans, scoring twice, and Robertson got another (surprise, surprise, from a Penalty) as we sensationally overturned the odds with a 3-1 win.

Encouraged by my absentee success in the League Cup 2nd leg at Anfield I left the radio well alone again and caught up with the result at full time, with a roar of delight that could be heard in Berlin. Wolves, and Andy Gray, were forgotten, and the season was re-born.

Our name came out of the hat first, as it had done for every round in 2 years of competing, apart from round two last year against AEK Athens. I was disappointed that we wouldn't be clinching a place in the Final with a glorious City Ground night of drama, but I wasn't disappointed with our opponents, the "foaming cleanser", Ajax. The first leg tie on April 9th couldn't come quickly enough.

Our bizarre sequence of results continued, and we managed to beat Southampton, lose to Brighton (again), beat Man Utd and lose to Aston Villa in successive games, before the big night arrived.

31,244 (less the extrovert Ajax support, one of whom displayed a cutting edge in fashion by wearing his underpants outside his jeans) hoped the pendulum would swing back to "win", and were ecstatic when the Berlin combo of Francis and Robertson-Pen gave us a cracking 2-0 win and one foot in the final.

I was euphoric, celebrating with a quick drink in Downtown Sneinton before dashing home for the TV highlights, collecting fish, chips and mushy peas en route from the Chinese on Carlton Hill. (Apparently they moved North for a better lifestyle, from Harrow). Seldom has victory tasted better.

It was obvious to anyone that we hadn't played enough

games or done enough travelling, so the squad were flown straight out to the Middle East for a couple of vital friendlies, returning in the nick of time for a testimonial match at Sincil Bank before facing Derby in the League at the City Ground.

We were out to avenge our 4-1 Baseball Ground thrashing and Frank Gray duly obliged, with the game's only goal, sending the Rams back up the A52 with their tails between their legs.

That was Saturday, and on Wednesday night 65,000 packed the Olympic Stadium, Amsterdam. I wasn't one of them. Mortgage under control, but still no spare cash for foreign football jaunts, I'd long since resigned myself to "domestics" only as far as away games were concerned. In any case, I never expected Forest to repeat last season's glorious European run.

Besides, we were no longer the trembling, blushing, European virgins, and having been bridesmaid to last year's adventure the disappointment of again being exiled from the travelling Red army was less painful, although it still hurt.

I risked ordeal by radio again, anticipating the away goal that would leave Ajax needing four, but it didn't come. Instead, we were forced into a rearguard action, hanging on for a 1-0 defeat.

I just about hung onto my sanity, jibbering into the radio, legs twitching involuntarily with every defensive clearance, until the final whistle brought merciful relief, roars of delight, and a celebratory lager or two.

Our opponents in the Final were to be Hamburg, at the famous Bernabeu stadium, home of Real Madrid, and unlike last year we were the underdogs – practically written off by some sections of the media. All rather strange, considering our phenomenal record over the past three seasons, and that we'd already seen off German opposition twice in the competition.

Then again, we didn't have our very own Roy of the Rovers, and Hamburg did, in the diminutive shape of the honorary Scouser, England star, and all round good guy, Kevin Keegan. Still smarting from Liverpool's exit at our hands last year, the mighty K was assuring all and sundry that revenge would be sweet and Hamburg would demolish us.

His comments were given added credence by a serious injury to Trevor Francis which was to rule him out of top level action for over eight months. If that wasn't enough, we had to pack in an exhausting itinerary of 6 League games, plus another crucial friendly (in France), the County Cup Final, and John Robertson's testimonial, all between our Ajax 2nd leg on April 23rd and the Final on May 28th.

Francis sustained his injury on May 3rd (my wife's birthday) against Crystal Palace in the League. We were well into the second half with the game already won. Attacking the Bridgford End down Forest's left he burst clear of the square Palace defence, just below us, in pursuit of what looked to be his certain hat trick goal.

He was accelerating away from the last defender when he suddenly went down in a heap as if he'd been shot. I knew straight away that his season was finished and the post match verdict of a ruptured achilles tendon confirmed our worst fears.

Despite this enormous setback, a tired and jaded Forest still lost only one of their six remaining assorted fixtures – Wolves stuffed us again, 3-1 at Molineux in our last League game – before Madrid, and Hamburg, beckoned.

I abandoned my black and white TV for the Technicolour spectacle of Lynn's parents 26 inch screen, jogging from Carlton to Bestwood Park ahead of a gathering thunderstorm. Watching in colour was a treat at that time, but at the cost of being on best behaviour – strictly no abuse and histrionics to be hurled at the set.

As a spectacle, the game was little better than Malmo, but our 1-0 victory, courtesy of Robbo's grubber just inside the post, was immensely more satisfying. Deprived of Francis and O'Neill, and with our squad fully stretched and exhausted after the rigours of a third consecutive non stop campaign – something like 80 games, including those essential friendlies – we defended grittily, with Ian Bowyer sticking like glue to Keegan.

Garry Birtles, working his socks off as usual, became increasingly isolated and physically shattered up front. I thought he'd seal it at 2-0 when he had a great chance, well into the second half, to run through on goal, but he was absolutely shot and his legs just wouldn't carry him clear.

Shilton and Co at the back were magnificent, as was Ian Bowyer, and every Reds player gave their all, but it was indicative of our limited resources, and Clough's penchant for the unexpected, that the young and overawed Gary Mills was in our starting line up.

After the match Kevin Keegan explained why his confident predictions had come unstuck – Ian Bowyer kept tackling him!!

Every time the honorary Scouser was about to perform a spectacular party piece there was the spoilsport Bowyer, taking the ball off him, blocking his attempted shot, or just generally getting in the way and making a nuisance of himself – all desperately unfair, and aided and abetted by a referee who condoned that sort of thing.

If only Bowyer – and Forest – had read Keegan's script and played the game in the right spirit – perhaps taking a leaf out of Keegan's erstwhile Liverpool colleague, the sportsmanlike Graham Souness – then all would have been sweetness and light. Keegan, all post match smiles and winners medal, could have "sportingly" patronised unlucky runners up Forest whilst waving a cheery "I did it for you, lads", back to Merseyside.

We upstaged him, and even though it wasn't a cup final for the neutral – one of many, and two in a row for Forest – it completed a sensational, unimaginable, three years of glory for the Reds, still the only club to win the European Cup more times than their own Domestic championship.

Thus ended the final season of the 1970s.

~

Ian Bowyer

"Ian, Ian Bowyer, Ian Bowyer on the wing" was the Trent End greeting to our new signing, a young player who'd never quite fulfilled his potential at Manchester City, or as a future England prospect.

I was amongst the meagre 8,101 who saw him make his first Reds appearance, at a rain drenched and windswept Bloomfield Road, Blackpool, on October 20th 1973, where he rewarded us with a debut goal. Duncan McKenzie got the other in a hard earned 2-2 draw after John Galley replaced the injured Jim Barron in goal early on.

Bowyer came to Forest as an out and out left winger – hence the Trent End chant, which endured throughout his career, even when he played at left back – but even at that early stage his lack of genuine pace was a handicap, and he didn't have the wingers repertoire of tricks to compensate.

What he did have in abundance was unrelenting bravery, determination and enthusiasm, strength in the tackle and when running with the ball, and an eye for goal, with a flair for digging out his trademark left footed drives from almost nowhere.

He made 28 League appearances in his first season, scoring 6 times, but it took a move inside from the flanks, under the Clough-Taylor stewardship, to realise his full potential, the tubby Scotsman taking Bowyer's number 11 shirt. As he matured, his leadership qualities came to the fore – a wiry, ginger haired dynamo, leading by example – cajoling, clapping, shouting and urging his teammates on.

With Bowyer in the team, digging in fiercely – sometimes too fiercely – and sparking his colleagues we always had at least one proper captain on the field, whether or not he'd actually had the official honour of leading out the team and tossing the coin.

Like John Robertson and Martin O'Neill he had an affinity with Reds fans borne out of a lengthy apprenticeship in our struggling Second Division days and subsequent fruition as a top class player at the very highest Club level throughout our glory years.

He scored 97 Forest goals in total – 68 in the League – which is phenomenal considering that he was also our recognised "utility" player – not in the disparaging "not quite good enough to claim a permanent position" sense, but because he could be relied upon to step seamlessly into any position – provided of course that he could favour his left foot.

He started out as our regular number 11, is best remembered in his familiar number 6 shirt, but also featured prominently at number 3. He's also worn 10, 9, 8, 7, 5 (in a friendly) and 4, plus at least one mid-match emergency transfer to goalkeeper. It all adds up to a total of 564 appearances, second only in the club's history to Bobby McKinlay.

Everyone remembers his winning header in the European Cup semi final in Cologne. It's surely the most important in his career, and arguably in the history of Nottingham Forest, but it was only possible thanks to the efforts of our 1976/77 promotion side, squeezing up in 3rd place, with Bowyer's invaluable contribution of 12 goals from 41 games.

What value his 2 goals in our 4-3 home win on September 11th 1976 against Hereford United, in front of just 12,081? One of them was crashed into the Bridgford net following a storming run through the Hereford defence in a typical Bowyer combination of skill, determination, and explosive finish.

His final Reds season was 1986/87 when he fittingly scored his personal 100th League goal, on December 28th in our 2-2 home draw against Luton Town. He played his last proper game in our City Ground League fixture on April 20th 1987, a 1-1 draw v. Norwich City. We finished 8th in Division 1, but a paltry 14,446 were evidence that an era was coming to an end, and not just for Ian Bowyer.

13 seasons had flown by since I stood shivering on that bleak, open, Kop at Blackpool as our Maine Road reject made his first appearance for a struggling 2nd Division side, and now he was suddenly playing his last game for the Reds, with a League Championship and 2 European Cup Winners medals in his cabinet, a host of other assorted silverware, and that magnificent appearance record.

Manchester City's loss was one of the biggest transfer successes in Forest's history.

One special memory – January 27th 1974. The sheer delight with which he acclaimed his FA Cup 4th round tap in against his old club after Duncan McKenzie's mesmerising run.

~

The 1980s

The 70s had turned into the 80s on the crest of a tidal wave of success that was almost unbelievable in its magnitude. On December 28th 1974 I'd left the City Ground early – almost sacrilegious, as I was a martyr to the full 90 minutes, no matter how dire.

This time, on a chilling, dark, drizzly, Winter's day I couldn't stand any more as we were outplayed by Notts County, a team lower than pond life. We were heading for Division 3, financial disaster, and the kind of future all too familiar to supporters of fallen giants such as Wolves, Portsmouth or Huddersfield.

By close of play on May 28th 1980 I could reflect on a mind blowing roll of honour, achieved in just 3 breathtaking seasons :-

League Champions
League Runners Up
League Cup winners (twice)
League Cup Runners Up
Longest – probably for all time – top flight undefeated run
European Super Cup winners
European Cup winners (twice)
Plus a host of other accolades, conspicuous amongst them
Kenny Burns Footballer of the Year award.

All thanks to that humiliation by Notts, the catalyst for the departure of Allan Brown and the arrival of Brian Clough. It's the greatest achievement in Notts County's otherwise dismal record which, like Forest's undefeated League run, is unlikely to be beaten, given that the Magpies have been playing, and achieving nothing, for longer than any other League club.

Still, they've got Tommy Lawton and Don Masson to reminisce over, plus ....well, that's about it, really.

I revelled in our glory, self righteously proclaiming our

success as the preserve of true supporters like me, who'd loyally stuck with the Reds on sparsely populated terraces at distant outposts. Hypocritical bullshit, of course, and besides I'd have been the first to complain if our hardcore support of 8,000 were the only ones to turn up at Wembley.

As it was, supporters drifted away again. Our bubble didn't exactly burst – we were to maintain 1st Division football throughout the decade, with only one finish outside the top ten (12th, in 81/82) and three 3rd place finishes – but it deflated as Forest's high flyers sank back to the ranks of the ordinary mortals. The pervasive fear of hooliganism, and blunders in the transfer market were coupled with a sharp decline in entertainment value.

I groaned when Ian Wallace arrived, in what seemed a desperation purchase, and despaired when Justin Fashanu completed the other half of a "strike force" unequalled in its embarrassment factor.

We made our first round European Cup defence against CSKA Sofia and for once the away leg came first, which meant I'd be able to witness our progress to the next round live at the City Ground. We went down to a surprising 1-0 defeat in Bulgaria, but the lack of an away goal didn't seem important as we'd surely sweep them aside on Trentside, even without the still recuperating Trevor Francis.

It suddenly assumed monumental significance when CSKA stunned us by scoring in the second leg and we needed an improbable 3 to go through. It never looked on, and despite lots of huffing and puffing we looked very ordinary, and it was all over.

It was all over for a work colleague, and season ticket holder, distraught at the purchase, for huge sums, of allegedly star players who "couldn't trap a bag of cement", and intimidated by the permanent threat of violence which threatened to destroy the game. The arrogant, but impotent, lecturing and posturing of the clueless Thatcher didn't help.

There were 3 City Ground League gates below 20,000 in 1980/81 and an alarming 11 in 1981/82, including a scarcely credible 17,323 and 18,449 against Everton and Man Utd respectively.

The euphoria of the late 70s had rapidly evaporated and the early 80s were a disillusionment, not because we expected Forest to keep winning European Cups, but because the standard of play had fallen dramatically, against a background of warring groups and obscene chanting. Our first match as defending League Champions in 1978/79 had set the scene and many had vowed never to return on the strength of that one experience alone.

On the field, our European dumping was followed by League Cup disaster at Vicarage Road, where Watford avenged their previous exit at our hands with a 4-1 thrashing. In view of our indifferent League form – oh for such "indifference" and a finish of "only" 7th in the Premier today – that left us with just the FA Cup. Perhaps this would be our year.

For some inexplicable reason I'd overlooked the fact that we were already guaranteed one final, a one-off against Nacional Montevideo of Uruguay for the pretentious title of World Club Champions, a meaningless sideshow for most supporters but lucrative for the clubs, and prestigious for the football mad host nation, Japan.

The first I heard about it was when it was announced in a match programme that sponsors Toyota were running a competition to send 6 winners to the game, which was scheduled for only a few weeks hence – on 11th February 1981, at the Olympic Stadium, Tokyo.

As I gave it a cursory glance I couldn't begin to imagine that the bitter disappointment and self recriminations of the missed European excursions would be blasted away by the highlight of this, or any other, season.

The Orient

It slowly dawned on me that none of my colleagues and acquaintances, many of them fellow season ticket holders, were entering, unable or disinterested in taking a short notice week in the Far East, even if handed to them on a plate. Besides, the questions, a combination of Football and Toyota related facts and statistics, couldn't be answered without urgent research, including telephone calls to Toyota UK.

I overheard a group of supporters at the Jubilee Club unanimously deciding on the wrong answer to one of the Football questions and decided there and then that statistically I'd never have a better chance of winning such a superb prize.

Allowing for 6 winners out of, say, 25,000 regular fans, and discounting perhaps 90% as non starters, with 50% of the rest getting one of the answers wrong, the odds might be better than one in a hundred. A tie-break slogan was required and I reckoned on a further percentage getting that wrong (too many words, spelling mistakes, inappropriate slogan, name and address missing).

The Olympic Stadium, Tokyo, via exotic Hong Kong, suddenly beckoned tantalisingly.

Confident that all the questions were correctly answered, it all hinged on the slogan, and I took best advice from Bob, who wasn't entering, but was a past winner of competitions, including a visit to Lord's to see a cricket final. (It rained all day and his host, a well known International cricketer, disappeared to the pub).

It sounded simple :-

"Make it punchy. Stick rigidly to the theme. Don't exceed the maximum number of words. If possible, make it rhyme."

So, the seeds of my "designer slogan" were sewn and at

3am one midweek morning, after days of frantic chopping and changing, my masterpiece was finished. Modesty – and the possibility of using it again if suitable circumstances arise – prevents publication, but I knew it had a fighting chance, despite never having previously, or subsequently, won the proverbial tripe supper.

A voice on the 'phone, a couple of days after the deadline, interrupted another compelling afternoon in Insurance with the news that I had been selected as one of the six winners.

I was confident that I stood some sort of chance, but still couldn't believe after so many near misses in multi-million pound Readers Digest Prize Draws that Toyota were about to fly me half way round the world to see the definitive Forest away match. I called them back to check that it wasn't a set up and secured permission to tear myself away from files and 'phones for a week.

Forest away trips combined my passion for the Reds with my love of travelling. Forest v. Nacionale Montevideo, travelling out via Bahrain and Hong Kong, was the ultimate.

A brief presentation to the 6 winners took place at the City Ground, outside the players tunnel, prior to the League game against Everton, with Brian in attendance, albeit reluctantly.

As we awaited the formalities, the living legend appeared from the tunnel, face like thunder :-

"Come on, I've got a fucking match to win", he barked impatiently before, presentation quickly over and photographs duly taken, he disappeared again at speed.

We'd shared a couple of minutes in the professional Life of Brian and I could appreciate how he could terrify even seasoned professionals. It was also an insight into the pressures that were perhaps beginning to terrify him.

The strain of maintaining success, and living up to expectations, is immeasurably greater than its initial accomplishment, and the responsibility for re-investment of huge sums of money and resources into an ever evolving squad of disparate human beings would turn most of us into blubbering wrecks.

Our all male party of 6 were introduced to each other and hotel arrangements agreed. My room mate Richard was genial and knowledgeable, but was to display a somewhat unfortunate lack of planning with regard to his packing arrangements.

The night prior to our morning flight from Gatwick was spent in a nearby hotel and after breakfast we were set for the short coach journey to the airport. Or at least, I was. Richard was searching through his jacket pockets before emptying his flight bag and frantically ferreting through the contents. He had an air of quiet desperation.

"What's up?"

"Can't find my passport".

We systematically ransacked the entire room. Nothing.

We sat and talked it through. Maybe it had been dropped in the bar last night. A 'phone call to reception drew a blank. Unless he'd dropped it on the coach on the way down there was nowhere left to look.

Tony, our tour guide (soon to be nicknamed "fabulous" for his liberal use of the word) instigated a thorough search, including the coach. Zilch.

Richard despairingly accepted his fate. He must have left it at home, a fact confirmed subsequently by a 'phone call. He accompanied us to Gatwick but despite Tony's efforts and the evidence of his travel tickets and itinerary he wasn't allowed to travel and we had to leave without him.

It cast a shadow over our forthcoming epic, but fortunately his trip was only to be delayed, not cancelled.

In the meantime our Cathay Pacific 747 climbed into the February sky, next stop Bahrain.

We were seated in Economy, Smoking (with the emphasis

on the thick, choking variety, reinforced by pipe and cigar behind us) and the prospect of 17 hours of this was unthinkable.

The plane was packed, but the resourceful and equally non Smoking Vinny disappeared for a minute or two before returning triumphantly :-

"All sorted. Follow me".

Leaving the smog behind, the improved visibility only revealed row after row of occupied seats, but Vinny had worked his North Notts charms on two Australian girls occupying three seats and we squeezed together into a cosy foursome.

The friendly Aussies were great company and apart from a return to Smoking, in and out of Bahrain, for compulsory seat belt routine, we spent the flight together, arriving in Hong Kong the following morning, local time.

The approach to Bahrain over mainland Arabia was a magical experience. Night fell almost instantly, as a black, star studded, curtain, to the left, whilst to the right – our side – a spectacular orange sunset painted the rippled blanket of desert sands. It was a dramatic and awe inspiring sight.

Bedouin tribes would be settling down by their camp fires 36,000 feet below, as they had for centuries, in a world whose time was fast slipping away. Could their way of life survive another 30 years?

Night swept across the horizon and stole the show and soon the pin prick lights of Bahrain sparkled brightly below us through the clear desert air.

Sometimes I think I could spend my entire life watching the world through an aircraft window.

The daylight approach to Hong Kong some 8 hours later could hardly have been more of a contrast, but was equally spectacular. Sweeping and banking over desert islands, busy shipping lanes and urban sprawl, we dissected the tower blocks of Kowloon on the descent onto the narrow spit of concrete that jutted into the South China Sea as Kai Tak Airport.

I caught a glimpse of the infamous Kowloon City, a walled slum of festering tenements, and an abandoned island of neglect within urban Kowloon since neither British nor Chinese, due to the vagaries of past politics, accepted responsibility.

A no go area for tourists and most Hong Kong citizens alike, it housed the poorest of Hong Kong's poor, including many illegal, and often criminal, entrants from mainland China. Scarcely one hundred feet below us, and equidistant from Kowloon's vibrant streets, its inhabitants were as remote as the desert Bedouins.

It held a morbid fascination, but the glimpse from the plane was to be my only view, and it's now been razed, explosives bringing down the unstable and tightly packed warren of vermin infested squalor.

We bade farewell to our Aussie friends, who were heading out to the New Territories but said they'd look us up at our hotel if they could get back. We transferred to the Hong Kong Hotel where three of us, notwithstanding in my case 24 hours without sleep, dumped our luggage, showered, changed, and hit the streets. It was something like 4am English time.

The yellow-grey murk cleared obligingly and glorious warm sunshine bathed Hong Kong Harbour. Forest's World Club Championship decider, the vehicle by which we were here, seemed irrelevant, and by the time of our departure to Tokyo a couple of days later I'd have almost preferred staying on and merely collecting the flight back at the end of the week.

The famous Star Ferry, a couple of minutes walk from our hotel, carried us over to Hong Kong Island in just a few minutes, but lived up to its billing as a compulsory experience for any would be world traveller.

At a fare of two pence it was also one of the cheapest, and in a "money no object" gesture of Western decadence we threw in an extra penny to travel first class.

Hong Kong Island's Central District of high rise glass towers, housing its white collar prisoners of Insurance, Banking and Finance, resembled that of any large, modern, Western city but the paradoxically named Western District, a few short blocks away across an invisible boundary, was a different world.

It was a slice of the "real" China, if such a thing existed after the changes brought about by Mao's Cultural Revolution and other turmoils. Insulated by the protection of a Western Colonial power, this little enclave had a "purer" Chinese culture and tradition than most of the mainland.

The smell of incense and spices pervaded the air. Live chickens, snakes, locusts and other delicacies awaited their fate. The empty eye sockets of a fly infested bovine head were evidence of a back alley slaughterhouse, and official notices warned that rat poison had been laid, so best to ignore any tantalising morsels that may have found their way into the gutter.

Cardboard boxes were everywhere – in transit on the backs of hunched and scurrying shopkeepers, in transit in Transit vans, heaped in doorways, piled up on the pavements - in fact they were a bloody nuisance.

Minders impassively watched over their consignments of foodstuffs, clothing, electrical goods, cameras, cosmetics, or whatever – if it had been invented, it was there – and it was all "top quality". We knew it was true, because not only did it say so on every box, but the shopkeepers enthusiastically endorsed their written guarantee.

Hong Kong was cardboard box city.

It was also, especially in Western District, a city of barter, and after the novelty wore off I got a bit fed up with this ritual.

I stormed out of one shop after offering a fair price, which I knew to be more than generous, for a couple of films, defeated by minutes of futile haggling. A hundred yards down the street I was gripped on the shoulder from behind :

"Here, you take" insisted the shopkeeper, thrusting the films into my hand. I gave him the money, which I'd originally offered some fifteen minutes previously, and, transaction duly completed and honour satisfied, we went our respective ways.

On this basis it would take about a month to do a week's shopping.

Imagine the scene outside the City Ground. It's a cold, wet, January night and mid table Forest are playing mid table Wimbledon.

"That'll be £100" says the turnstile operator.

"I'll give you 2p" I reply.

Turnstile attendant convulses in mock hysterics.

"Alright, £95".

"10p".

"£90, and I'm robbing myself".

"What, to watch this crap, and in this weather?"

"£80, not a penny less – and don't let on, they'll think I've gone soft".

After another 30 minutes, with the game already under way, we compromise at £19 – co-incidentally the average price of a seat at the time of writing.

"Done" – and I probably was.

Evening beckoned and the Star Ferry threaded its way across the harbour through the maze of assorted shipping – the water borne equivalent of Hong Kong's frantic, bustling, streets – back to mainland Kowloon.

Return to hotel. Watch local news on TV then back out onto Nathan Road, now alight with neon as early evening turns, within minutes, to night.

No need for sleep. No time for jet lag.

A kaleidoscope of colours, smells and sounds assails the senses. A withered Chinaman pedals cheap knicknacks outside Benetton, incense burns in shops traditional and modern, and disco beat vies with the traffic noise.

We end up in Ned Kelly's bar, which sees another Australian encounter, this time of the male variety. Aussies packed the bench seats, but I was sportingly offered a place.

"Sit down here, Pom".

"Sure?"

"Yeah, it's some gorilla who's gone to the dunnie".

I hesitated.

"Sit down, willya".

I squeezed in amongst them.

"Bloody brave geyser, that Pommie".

"Six foot four he is, and wider than a barn door. He'll murder him when he gets back"

The wind-up continued, but an unsolicited pint arrived, with the words "get that down yer neck", and I felt comfortable again.

Seconds later a 16 stone giant loomed from the direction of the toilet and made towards where I was sitting.

"Here, mate, this Pommie bastard's got yer seat".

"Wouldn't be told. Just pushed in and grabbed yer place".

"Tried to tell 'im, but he wouldn't listen".

I made to get up, but he insisted on standing, sharing the joke with his mates, and on getting the next round :-

"No point any of you lads going, some Pommie bastard'll nick yer seat".

Next morning, "refreshed" by some three hours sleep, and not yet sober enough to appreciate my hangover, I answered a knock at the door to be greeted by my delayed room mate, Richard. He'd returned home to collect his passport and succeeded in arranging a transfer to a British Airways flight the next day.

Our winners complement of six was restored, and the party

also included a group who'd paid for the privilege of following Forest to Japan, including a Villa fan from Birmingham and two London based Chelsea supporters.

Hong Kong flew by with scarcely time to draw breath, and even less for sleep, and Forest's big game didn't cross my mind again until we were gathered in the foyer of the Hong Kong Hotel awaiting our coach transfer for the Tokyo flight.

We were also anxiously awaiting one of the paying travellers, who'd disappeared without trace a day or so earlier and, as the minutes ticked down, seemed certain to miss the flight. Shades of Richard's debacle at Gatwick, but with more serious implications as no one knew where the hell he was, and in a city of six million we could hardly send out a search party. The Police had been notified once his absence had become a matter of concern, but had not surprisingly drawn a blank.

We could only hope that he was OK, and that he'd re-join us on the way back through Hong Kong when, literally at the death, and looking like the living dead, an apparition shuffled into the crowded foyer. The wanderer had returned, but clearly hadn't been bathing in the warm sunshine – Jimmy White would have looked suntanned by comparison.

It appeared that he'd "been to a party" with some new found Chinese friends, taken something, deliberately or otherwise, and made it back, by taxi, to the hotel in the nick of time – nothing less than miraculous, given the state he was in. His fellow party goers had presumably found his travel itinerary and put him in the cab.

He spent the next couple of days like a zombie, and I'm not sure whether he even saw the match – he was on another planet.

All ready for the off then, except that I simultaneously received a message that I was to report to reception desk immediately.

I'm about to catch a plane to Tokyo, it's God knows what time in Nottingham, and any contact from home can only be bad news.

Before I reached the desk I got the message – a friendly Antipodean face greeted me.

"Hello again. Thought we might have a day together, and a few drinks tonight."

That wasn't in any doubt, but I'd got a Forest match to watch, and if she was disappointed, it was nothing to the way I felt. Cursing my luck, I made my reluctant and abject apologies and within minutes our coach was en route to Kai Tak airport.

My very own "brief encounter" was scarcely in the Trevor Howard/Celia Johnson league but I felt miserable leaving her there and was relieved when our Tristar climbed away from Hong Kong towards the Land of the Rising Sun.

We arrived in the Land Quite Some Time After the Setting Sun after a tedious flight enlivened by brief aerial views of Taiwan and a round the world drinking extravaganza courtesy of Cathay Pacific's free bar facility. I conceded defeat after a modest three or four but the serious drinkers visited alcohol from every available Continent and a variety of countries.

Tokyo's Narita airport contrasted sharply with Kai Tak. Brand new – but built only after concerted and violent opposition – spacious and quiet, it stood well outside the city sprawl on a "greenfield" site. It could have been any state of the art facility, anywhere, but for the inscrutable faces of the Japanese, who politely and efficiently shepherded their Western guests, formalities at a minimum, to the waiting coach.

We felt important, and as Forest supporters for Tokyo's prestigious, Toyota sponsored, World Club Championship Final, we were special guests. In Hong Kong, no-one noticed us.

The match was on the agenda again.

So was Winter clothing, Tokyo's chill night air inducing a collective shiver as we queued to board the coach.

Different airport.

Different climate.

Different culture.

The coach journey seemed endless, at first bowling briskly through the empty blackness, then collecting the scattered lights and traffic of the outskirts, before joining the clogged highways and urban sprawl of the city for our final excruciating crawl to the Tokyu Hotel.

Dehydrated and knackered after the journey, and shivering from the cold, I forced down a couple of glasses of revolting, yellow tinged, over chlorinated tap water, joined the others for a late evening skirmish with the local bars, and ended up with my customary three hours kip.

Our stay included the obligatory coach trip of the traffic jams, calling in at a temple and the Emperor's palace, before rediscovering the real Tokyo – traffic polluted canyons sprawling anonymously in all directions, with the cramped and ugly flats of the world's most revered economy (as it then was) comparing pitifully with the average semi and garden of poor old Britain.

It was back to the hotel for evening, where I should have stayed in and had a good night's rest. No chance.

Different country, same routine.

Shower, change of clothing, watch local news on TV – it's surprising what can be gleaned from the pictures only.

Night falls.

Multicoloured neon transformed the city and we hailed a taxi outside the hotel, armed, courtesy of Reception, with the name of Tokyo's equivalent of the West End.

There were five of us and we dived in, squashing four across the back seat. The driver made it clear that he was only licensed to carry four. We made it equally clear that we weren't splitting up – we'd no chance of meeting again if we became separated.

With a shrug of the shoulders the driver turned his back and stared fixedly ahead through the windscreen. He kept this up for a few minutes.

We refused to move.

He got out and tried to cajole us onto the street.

We stayed put, repeating the name of our destination.

He lost his temper, and ranted and raved.

We feigned indifference, which made him madder than ever.

The universal language of his sheer, pissed off, not answerable for my actions apoplexy as he stormed back into the driver's seat, slamming the door behind him, told us that we should have respected his wishes and evacuated the vehicle.

Too late.

He'd started the engine, floored the throttle, crashed the gear lever into first, and released the clutch.

The overloaded car catapulted forwards, tyres squealing.

I'm sure we took the first bend on two wheels, and things deteriorated from there. This man was seriously possessed and we were seriously worried. A rear door burst open as we slewed across the carriageway and we nearly lost a passenger.

Weaving manically through the traffic, all reason gone, our chauffeur seemed hell bent on killing us all. Perhaps he was from a long line of Kamikaze warriors – then again, perhaps that's a bit of a contradiction.

Perhaps he might stop at a traffic light and we could all bail out.

Perhaps not.

No escape.

As an ancient Japanese proverb might have it :-

"Smell of dung, sign of interesting journey."

It was like being in a film – a cross between an American car chase (except that we never saw the two blokes carrying the huge pain of glass) – and that four minute black and white train journey from London to Brighton.

Fate had mysteriously chosen not to extract the ultimate price and we were delivered, miraculously unscathed, into the neon of "Downtown" Tokyo. Our driver stepped solemnly out of the car and his face dissolved into a huge beam.

Honour satisfied, and as surprised as we were to be still alive, he accepted his fare with exagerrated grace and courtesy, bowed his farewell, and we escaped into the crowds.

Stomachs settled, McDonalds beckoned – to me, at least – but was waved aside, despite my misgivings, in search of traditional Japanese Sushi, which proved surprisingly difficult to find. Such establishments seemed to be invariably closed, their trade intended for the earlier waves of office workers and shoppers, but to my disappointment, enquiries of two passing businessmen bore fruit – or rather, raw, fishy things.

In answer to the simple question "Sushi?", which exhausted our working knowledge of Japanese, they marched us through the busy streets to a small restaurant that had just closed.

Hammering away at the door, they were unfortunately successful in negotiating our admission, and the excited owners couldn't do enough to welcome their Western guests, for which they were rewarded with a Forest scarf, which they proudly hung on the wall. I like to think that it's still there.

Our reward was a "Chef's Special" Sushi with meticulously prepared chunks of multicoloured raw and rubbery underwater flesh, augmented by cubes of compressed, cold, rice. Revolting.

Unable to cope with these traditional morsels, but careful not to cause offence, I managed to transfer my meal, one piece at a time, into my jacket pockets, from where it was subsequently deposited into a Tokyo litter bin. Nice hosts, shame about the meal.

We went to McDonalds afterwards.

Drinking was a different kettle of fish – or glass of Saki.

We stumbled upon a locals bar, discreetly hidden away in a narrow alleyway, which seemed to be a typical setting for "genuine" drinking places with authentic Japanese atmosphere. We had to knock to gain admission, but our welcome more than matched the Sushi bar, although initiation involved the eating of an evil tasting gherkin-type object followed by the relief – comparatively speaking – of a glass of hot Saki, which I downed in one. (Big mistake.)

The open plan room was fashioned, including a central bar, a la "Cheers", and was constructed entirely of wood in a style that I took, rightly or wrongly, as archetypal Japanese. Basic, but intimate, and hugely hospitable, it was a perfect venue for a social night of drinking and fraternising with the natives.

Our Forest tops, plus an amount of "poetic licence", led to a belief that we were Forest reserves/non playing party out for an illicit night on the town. We swore the locals to secrecy, signed dozens of autographs – with belated apologies, I was Garry Birtles for the night – and got back to the hotel well into the early hours.

Tokyo is by far the ugliest city that I have visited, but the warmth of our welcome, and the apparent lack of street crime, was a heartening contrast. I was surprised by the number of young women out on the town who were quite nonchalantly, often alone, strolling through even the dimmest lit thoroughfares without a thought of danger – as it should be, of course – as yet without the paralysing fear of verbal or physical attack.

The match itself took place in the Olympic Stadium and Winter turned to Spring, on a balmy day of warm sunshine. We were treated as VIPs and even the mighty Brian favoured us with a cheery wave from his position below in the dug-out. (I've got the photo to prove it.)

A capacity 70,000 filled the somewhat featureless and largely uncovered bowl and the pitch, although flat and perfectly playable, was the colour of sand, with not a blade of grass to be seen.

There was a tiny group of Nacional Montevideo supporters – I swapped a complimentary Forest flag for a huge Nacional banner – but otherwise the support was almost 100% for Forest, and large pockets of red and white were scattered throughout the stadium.

Forest were the better side, took the game to the opposition, but were unable to score, going down 1-0 to a goal against the run of play.

Defeat was all the harder to take because we hadn't managed a goal, and the crowd's muted reaction to Nacional's effort emphasised their backing for the Reds. It would have been nice to celebrate an equaliser, and if Forest had broken through I reckon we'd have gone on to win, and the crowd would have gone mad. I felt that we'd let them down.

After the final whistle I homed in on the biggest steward I could find and negotiated an exchange of my scarf for his special issue top, distinctive in white with red piping, Toyota logo, and commemorative motif. Unfortunately, some thieving bastard stole it from the locked boot of my car, together with my spare wheel, in broad daylight in Nottingham City centre.

Our post match reception featured some distinguished company, including the touring pop megastars Queen, who were affable and unpretentious - chatting, diving in at the buffet, and exchanging views on Forest's performance.

The diplomatic guests were more aloof, and the stunningly attractive daughter of a South American ambassador – El Salvador, if I remember correctly, – immaculately and very expensively dressed, clearly wished she was at a gathering more befitting her status of privilege and power.

In clipped, but otherwise perfect, Queen's English she explained that she was attending out of diplomatic duty and I decided that throwing the offside decision against Peter Ward into the conversation might just be a waste of time. So would my asking her out to McDonalds, or a little Sushi restaurant that I knew, and I reluctantly decided that our date was off.

In contrast, the victorious Nacional team welcomed us onto their bus after the post match nosh, and were delighted to autograph their individual photos in the match programme. The subdued Forest players left quietly, glum faced at the windows of their coach. If they played for our Sunday team they'd have looked upon a one nil defeat as a moral victory and be heading to the pub to celebrate.

Three or four of us decided, in time honoured "it seemed like a good idea at the time" fashion, to walk back to the hotel. It hadn't been far on the coach, and a warm, quiet evening was following the afternoon sunshine.

By the time we'd trudged for what seemed miles through grey, traffic-fumed streets, darkness was falling, a chill wind had sprung up, and Spring had turned back to Winter. Despite my extra layer of clothing, courtesy of my new Toyota top, I was shivering and cheesed off, and promised myself an early night if we ever made it back.

I crawled back to my room, showered, changed, and, my brain clearly malfunctioning due to the effects of exhaustion, went out again an hour later to answer the call of the neon. It was hardly an inspired decision after several days of travel, sightseeing, late nights – or early mornings – changing time zones and climates, but I was determined to extract every last minute from my Far East excursion.

The morning of our departure saw our little group arrive back at the hotel as early breakfasts were being served, and in less than two hours the coach was due to depart for Narita airport.

It occurred to me that perhaps I'd slightly overdone it.

If the journey out was an adventure, the return trip was an endurance test. A total of 37 hours continual travel – in real time – lay ahead, from the hotel lobby to my house in Carlton.

First, the long coach trip to the airport, arriving ridiculously early for our flight – no doubt to allow for the traffic grinding to a complete halt – followed by flight to Hong Kong, stopping off this time in Taipei, Taiwan. Finally arriving Hong Kong God knows when, after delays due to strong headwinds. Hours of waiting around before flight to Gatwick, via Bahrain again. Coach back to Nottingham, and taxi home from Slab Square.

If I'd been mentally capable of contemplating the enormity of the forthcoming ordeal I would have booked a room in the nearest airport hotel and crashed out, worrying about getting home when I was coherent again.

I still managed, for some absurd reason, to get my passport stamped "Peoples Republic of China" (or something similar) after temporarily disembarking into Taipei airport. It was a sad and rather pointless exercise, just to prove that I'd been there.

No such need at Hong Kong, where, trapped for hours inside Kai Tak airport awaiting the Gatwick connection, I was totally shattered and somewhat disorientated. Dozing at the bar – like a High Court judge – I was engaged in conversation by a craggy Australian, slightly the worse for drink (him, not me). The airport clocks showed something like 2am local time, but between us we couldn't work out what day it was, and decided that it didn't really matter.

Over tired, unable to sleep, and with a pounding head, I endured the slog to Bahrain and stretched my legs in another hot and oppressive Transit lounge. The floor was littered with prostrate Arabs in traditional robes. I envied their ability to snatch sleep, seemingly oblivious to everything, cocooned and mysterious in their desert garments.

The tiny Gulf island of Bahrain displayed in its airport a microcosm of the Middle East which, even in my zombie state, left an appetite to return and explore, as yet unfulfilled.

Back on the plane, passport unstamped – "not possible" – I couldn't face another eight hours cramped in Economy. Cathay Pacific, hospitable as ever, came to my rescue in the guise of a sympathetic stewardess who showed me into Marco Polo class where I was allocated a row of three seats, blanket, pillow and refreshments. I must have looked like death warmed up - I certainly felt like it.

(I wrote to Cathay Pacific afterwards, expressing my appreciation, and have continued to recommend them ever since.)

Drifting in and out of sleep I eventually became aware that chinks of light were sneaking past the edges of the plastic window blind. A quick look revealed a stunning panorama of the Alps, smothered in heavy Winter snow and beautifully illuminated by the early morning sunlight.

The pilot, equally captivated, awoke any remaining sleepers with news of the magnificent Alpine views and pointed out Mont Blanc, somewhere to the left of the aircraft. I couldn't swear as to which of the dozens of equally magnificent peaks he was referring, but took a photo anyway.

A week ago the Alps were a foreign holiday destination. Now it seemed like home, or at least just up the street, and soon we'd be commencing our approach to Gatwick.

Descending gently across the Channel, the English coastline for once clearly visible in the crisp Winter air, we were soon down on the tarmac.

The chill of wintry Britain, with a heavy frost still evident, came as a nasty shock, and the four hour coach leg back to Nottingham just about finished me off. We arrived back early Saturday afternoon, with a couple of hardy souls dropped off on Trent Bridge for our 5th Round FA Cup tie against Bristol City.

For the first time that I can remember, I had absolutely no interest in Forest's proceedings, and barely managed to organise myself a taxi home, where I collapsed straight into bed. I reckon I'd had no more than 15 hours sleep in the whole week.

I woke up in darkness, just in time to catch "Match of the Day", and highlights of Forest's 2-1 victory but, head still spinning, could make little sense of what was happening – reminiscent of when I learned that we'd paid £1m for Justin Fashanu, apparently on the strength of one freak televised goal at Carrow Road.

I went straight back to bed again, slept for another 12 hours, and apart from a dry, niggling, cough, which persisted for a couple of weeks, normal service was, sadly, all too quickly resumed.

~

It was definitely a case of after the Lord Mayor's show once I recaptured my interest in our remaining Cup competition. The 6th round favoured us with a home tie against Ipswich Town, although Martin O'Neill wouldn't be available for selection, having been transferred a couple of weeks earlier to Norwich City.

Ipswich, backed by a huge following in a gate of almost 35,000, didn't give a stuff about Cloughie's Wembley dream, which turned to nightmare when we lost the Portman Road replay 1-0, after an exciting 3-3 on Trentside.

So the season fizzled out without another trophy in the cabinet, but 1980/81 still goes down in my book as one of the most memorable ever.

By contrast, 1981/82 was unmitigatingly dire, over by January 18th when Spurs knocked us out of the League Cup, 1-0 at White Hart Lane. Trevor Francis had been sold after just two games, but that was good business as Manchester City repaid our initial outlay for a player who never recovered form or fitness after that injury against Palace.

Replacing him was another matter, and the contrast with Fashanu couldn't have been starker. The unfortunate youngster, confidence drained and at odds with himself, supporters and management alike, could only muster a pitiful 3 goals in 31 League appearances.

It was embarrassing to watch, and painful to hear the terrace taunts and jibes that compounded his misery. It wasn't the benefit of hindsight that prompted despairing "told you so" mutterings, and there was no point barracking the player – Clough and Taylor had dropped a nuclear proportion clanger and Fashanu suffered more than anyone.

Four home League gates of less than 16,000 bore testimony to the decline, and only 15,649, including a sizeable Welsh contingent, turned up for our 3rd round FA Cup tie at home to Wrexham on Jan 2nd 1982. Maybe <u>this</u> would be Clough's FA Cup year.

Maybe not.

Forest have a tradition of FA Cup humiliation against minnows and we weren't about to dishonour that legacy. We were simply awful, losing 3-1, and the hecklers couldn't even take it out on Fashanu, who wasn't playing.

I've intentionally avoided regular punctuations with team listings, which can be found in any statistical record, but it's worth noting the Forest selection on the day, as a reminder of our rapid fall from grace :-

Peter Shilton, Viv Anderson, Bryn Gunn, David Needham, Willie Young, Colin Walsh, Jurgen Roeber, Ian Wallace, Peter Ward, Mark Proctor and John Robertson.

Just Shilton, Anderson and Robertson remained from the glory days (and McGovern, who came on as sub) and I don't think it's being unkind to say that none of the other eight would have threatened for selection.

Ward, alongside Davenport, was sensational in the reserves, but for some infuriating reason couldn't turn it on in the first team, despite having pace and tremendous natural skill. Walsh had a "cultured" left foot, hit a mean dead ball, and often – but not often enough - looked the part. I was sorry when we released him.

Needham was perhaps the most effective of the rest, remembering that he played in an era when the 20 yard sliding tackle from behind, 2 seconds before the forward received the ball, was deemed legitimate.

I drifted away with hundreds of fellow sufferers well before the final whistle, the celebratory singing of the Wrexham fans fading into the distance as I became ever wetter in the pouring rain.

I squelched despondently back to the car, where I sat and steamed until the cold blast of air from the euphemistically termed "heater" reached its lukewarm best and cleared a navigational window of opportunity sufficient for the long journey back from Sneinton to Carlton.

In a dismal season, Forest v Wrexham on Jan 2nd quickly established that, at least as far as Forest were concerned, it wasn't going to be a happy New Year. In a season of low points, Wrexham was the lowest by a country mile. As quickly as we'd rocketed to the heights of success we'd plummeted back to mediocrity, albeit the kind of mediocrity we dream of in 1999 – firmly established in the top flight and not a relegation battle in sight.

Even the Pies, temporarily out of their depth in the 1st Division, beat us 2-0 at the City Ground, just 3 weeks after the Wrexham disaster, although we gained revenge of a sort – nothing less than victory home and away is really satisfactory – by beating them 2-1 in April at Meadow Lane, and thrashing them 7-1 in our grand finale, the prestigious County Cup final. So prestigious that 3,970 turned up, not including me.

I renewed my allegiance for season 1982/83 more in hope than expectation, but with hooligans and Thatcher still rampaging unchecked, and memories of last season all too fresh, even more supporters deserted. Seven League games drew less than 15,000 to Trentside, including 13,709 and 13,461 against Brighton and Southampton respectively.

Away from home West Brom (13,657), Sunderland (14,716), Birmingham City (12,987), Stoke City (10,880), Coventry City (9,760) and even Arsenal (only 21,698) were indicative of the general malaise. There was an all pervading atmosphere of violence.

No-one in their right minds would want to take wives, girlfriends or children, and the ceaseless, ignorant, denigration of football and its supporters by "she who must be obeyed" was nauseatingly offensive. The average supporter wanted firm action against the thugs – instead, all they got was semi coherent lectures about identity cards.

It was a dreadful time for football, and it's a sobering thought that it all seemed to disintegrate so quickly.

Could the current Premiership pack of cards collapse so rapidly?

If Hooliganism was the blight of the 70s and 80s – and it remains a permanent threat even today – sheer naked, arrogant, uncontrolled greed is the current evil. Whether the parasites can be purged is unlikely, given that recent newspaper articles of the "you ain't seen nothin' yet" variety contrasted the obscene earnings of our "superstars" unfavourably with the ransoms paid to the top US professionals.

I can't find the words to express the depth of my contempt for these mercenaries, and to those who say "good luck to them", and their £20,000, £40,000 or whatever per week, plus bonuses, sponsorships, "loyalty" payments, etc, etc, I can only wish an infestation of tapeworms. It's also a slight on the majority of professionals, often unfairly tarred with the same brush. Many of those in the lower divisions hardly make an average wage.

Back in 82/83 I anticipated the arrival of Manchester United for our first home League match, heartened by the overdue departure of Fashanu, but not by a daft refereeing directive that "deliberate handball" would be a sending off offence. Never mind the double footed launch, studs first, into an opponents shins, as practiced by at least 2 celebrated "hardmen", you touch the ball with your hand, son, and you're off.

Echoes of a similar stupidity today, when instinctive handball in the box is punished not just with a Penalty, but with a dismissal. Even a booking would sometimes be too harsh.

The directive of 1982 was short lived, as common sense prevailed, but not in the case of Colin Todd, who had already forgotten the new ruling when he leapt to intercept, goalkeeper style, a flighted ball over his head as Man Utd attacked the Bridgford End.

We went on to lose 3-0, before a modest – considering the opposition – 23,956, instant deflation after our encouraging start to the new campaign, a 2-1 win at West Ham.

Todd was our 2nd player to be sent off, following Willie Young's dismissal in a pre season friendly, and by October 9th Ian Bowyer and Steve Hodge, both in League games, had joined our early shower brigade.

Perhaps the dismissals were indicative of a collective determination, as Forest's squad, no doubt encouraged by a few words from Brian, went on to earn European qualification, albeit by virtue of a storming late run which saw us clinch 5th place.

Strong finishes became something of a Clough hallmark, but 82/83 was exceptional. When we lost 2-1 to Southampton, before our lowest home attendance, it was our 9th successive League game without a win, and the season was effectively over. Seven wins, including Everton and Liverpool at home, and two draws in the last nine catapulted Forest to a EUFA Cup spot and put a long overdue smile on our faces

The FA Cup was the low point for the second season running. Our 2-0 defeat at Derby ended the annual "will this be Cloughie's year?" headline, but at least Bob and myself escaped unscathed.

The atmosphere was one of the most hostile that I can recall, with trouble brewing for days ahead of the match. Clough's previous team had fallen from grace and their supporters were desperate to give Forest a bloody nose – in any way possible.

By the time our train had reached Long Eaton – just inside the Derbyshire border, it carries a Nottingham post code – scores of Police were evident. They were lining the trackside, station platforms, footbridges and level crossings, all the way into Derby station, to avoid bombardment of the Forest specials.

Exiting Derby station, scuffles and punch ups were breaking out all around us, with marauding gangs everywhere looking for Reds fans. A Police helicopter throbbed incessantly overhead, increasing the tension and air of menace. Two isolated Forest fans hurtled past us, hotly pursued by a gang of Rams. It could just as easily have been us.

We'd caught the earliest train, with the naïve intention of enjoying a couple of pints before the match, but instead we took sanctuary in an unlikely venue, the Theatre coffee shop, with not another football supporter in sight.

There we stayed, before joining the crowds on the Osmaston Road, where a massive police presence kept most of the warring factions apart. Even when we arrived behind the Forest end a frightening crush developed, and we were glad to escape unharmed (see "Police Intelligence").

Like local rivals everywhere, Forest-Derby fixtures are intense affairs, but the hostility inside the Baseball Ground was quite exceptional. Forest deservedly lost, 2-0, and never looked likely, but were baited incessantly. We were fortunately well up in the seats behind the goal, and I didn't envy the players in Derby's notoriously cramped and intimidating surroundings.

The scene was set early on, when Robertson went to take a throw in and had a pint of beer – or worse - thrown over him. He showed character by impassively walking away.

We left early to avoid the post match mayhem, with Forest's own yobs equally fired up, especially since the match was lost, and plodded silently back to the station amongst hundreds of fellow Reds. At least we felt safer than we had all day.

A triumphant roar in the distance confirmed that we hadn't staged a sensational fightback with two in the last three minutes. Yet again, we'd gone out of the Cup against a team from a lower division.

At least Rams fans speak the same language, so none of the "excuse me, can you tell me the time" traps as encountered on trips to Merseyside or the North East. Nor was it necessary to sit tight mouthed, whilst simultaneously feigning relaxed indifference, as happened when a gang of chanting, tanked up, Chelsea skinheads boarded our tube from Earls Court to Fulham Broadway.

Our twosome exchanged "keep your trap shut" glances, whilst inwardly rehearsing typically Cockney expressions such as "gor blimey, strike a light, me old sparrer" for possible emergency use.

By contrast, one of the Chelsea fans on the Tokyo trip assured me that I'd get a warm welcome, Forest colours and all, in a particular pub on the Kings Road, which was a favourite meeting place for Blues fans. I never took him up on the offer, but it's fair to say that whilst I've always been particularly cautious at Stamford Bridge I've personally had no real problems with Chelsea.

If we weren't going to win the 1982/83 FA Cup there was always our familiar standby, the League Cup, and my theory about West Brom games was reinforced when we overcame them in a two legged defensive struggle, 7-4 on aggregate. We walloped them 6-1 at home and lost 3-1 at the Hawthorns.

Watford popped up again in the next round and it got even sillier, as we beat them 7-3 over a mere 90 minutes. I stuck with my policy of returning to my terrace roots for low key Cup games – it made a change from the Exec – and stood in the Trent End.

Unfortunately, night matches gave full scope to the electronic scoreboard, glaring compulsively at me from above the Bridgford terrace, its irritating birthday messages and adverts flickering relentlessly right to left, minus the usual quota of faulty bulbs. At least this time it came in useful for keeping tabs on the ever changing score.

We beat mighty Brentford 2-0 at home in the next round before getting thrashed 4-0 at Old Trafford by the even mightier Manchester United. If nothing else, our League Cup run produced a glut of goals, although worryingly a good proportion were at our end. Sutton, Young and the veteran Todd hardly had the authority of Shilton, Lloyd and Burns, and our defence didn't exactly frighten the opposition to death.

Our late flourish in the League coincided with the return from injury of Hans van Breukelen, who missed the middle chunk after tearing a cartilage at home, where, so the statisticians tell us, most accidents happen. Van Breukelen, keen to prove them right, knackered himself kicking the cat, or tripping over his clogs – I forget exactly, but I know it sounded ridiculous – and the commanding Dutchman's welcome return soon shook our defence out of any complacency. Oh for such a dominant personality in the squads of the late 90s.

1983/84 was another season without a trophy, but the disappointment has to be measured against the long years since the 1959 Cup Final during which, as the man in the green tracksuit might have abrasively remarked, "we'd won nowt".

As it was, we were only robbed of European glory by two inexplicable refereeing decisions which, many years later, were dramatically revealed to be the likely result of a bribery scandal. Ironically, we'd already met the team concerned, Anderlecht, in our final pre-season friendly, losing 4-2 before a modest crowd of 90,000 (Barcelona were next on) in the Nou Camp.

Our squad was much stronger for this new season, and there were four goalscorers in double figures, Birtles, Davenport, Hodge and Walsh, plus a useful six apiece from Anderson and Bowyer. Kenny Swain partnered Anderson at full back in front of van Breukelen and the uncompromising

Paul Hart bolstered the centre. Chris Fairclough was later to replace Colin Todd, and the side had recaptured much of that missing element of pace.

Unfortunately, Peter Davenport's brain couldn't keep pace with his feet and he spent much of every game looking perplexed as the referee's whistle yet again stopped him in his tracks. In the unlikely event that you're reading this Peter, it's what's known in football as "offside", and I had bald patches from tearing my hair out in exasperation.

Speaking of pace, a young, nervous, East Ender was blooded towards the end of the season at right back as replacement for the injured Viv Anderson. 18 year old Des Walker first appeared in our 1-0 win against Everton at the City Ground on March 14th 1984, and given that we were on course for a 3rd place finish in the League and a EUFA Cup semi final the attendance of 13,647 almost beggars belief.

Walker made a quiet debut, and then more or less disappeared for a full season, re-emerging as a central defender in 1985/86 after playing the last three games of 84/85. The rest, as all Reds fans know, is history.

We were dumped out of the 83/84 League Cup in the first round by Wimbledon, whose combative, no frills, style overpowered our ineffective attempts over the two legs to "out-football" them, much to the frustration of Cloughie, who passionately believed that his purist, play it to feet, style should always embarrass unsophisticated devotees of the aerial bombardment.

Not so, of course, and Wimbledon's rise to the top flight proved that it was no fluke. Derided for their heavyweight spoiling tactics, they had the last laugh as they continued to infuriate the big boys, first surviving, then consolidating, on attendances barely up on their non-League days.

The Dons are without doubt the team of the 80s and 90s. The fact that they've consistently dented the egos of those who'd like their own cosy, artificial, prima donnas League makes it all the better, although their pretensions on a move just up the road from their rented premises at Selhurst Park, to Dublin, didn't do much for their "homespun" image, especially as their hardcore support has slowly built up to respectable levels. Maybe there was never much substance in it.

Another "homespun" club, Southampton, knocked us out of the FA Cup, 2-1 at the City Ground, making it a hat trick of 3rd round defeats. That left us concentrating on Europe, notwithstanding our excellent third place in the League, which only came about thanks to a sneaky finish on the rails, winning our last three, against Watford, West Ham and Man Utd respectively.

The EUFA Cup trail began quietly. We overcame East German side Vorwaerts, 2-0 and 1-0, home and away, and PSV Einhoven, 2-1 in Holland ("interesting" fact – I cycled past their ground on my first ever trip to Europe) and 1-0 at the City Ground. Only 14,994 and 16,934 bothered to turn up for the home legs, particularly disappointing in the case of PSV, one of the more prestigious names in the competition.

The Forest faithful – or should that be fickle? – weren't to be easily enticed back, even in Europe where the threat of hooliganism was minimal, but the draw for the next round catapulted us into the spotlight, locally and nationally. A titanic England v Scotland clash was thrown up when Glasgow Celtic popped out of the hat.

At last we'd got a match to anticipate, and a guaranteed full house for the City Ground first leg, albeit bolstered by some 12,000 Scots – they had half of the Bridgford terrace plus the whole of the Executive lower tier.

14,979 saw us beat Ipswich 2-1 on Saturday 19th November, but 34,084 packed into the City Ground on Wednesday night for a match that shouldn't have been played.

After the weekend the weather had turned progressively colder, with a series of penetrating overnight frosts. By Wednesday the freeze was so intense that the temperature couldn't even struggle above zero during the day, plummeting rapidly from mid afternoon onwards. There was no undersoil heating at that time and although the fog thankfully spared us it was obvious that the match couldn't be played.

So obvious, that when it was announced that it would definitely go ahead I could scarcely believe it. The decision was clearly taken for the sole reason that thousands of Celtic fans were already pouring into the city and the authorities, not unreasonably, were desperate for them to get their eagerly awaited crack at the English out of the way, and back home to Glasgow, Corby, Ireland, etc.

We parked in Lady Bay for a change, hopefully to avoid the worst of the incoming Scottish tide, but the razor sharp night air announced their huge presence, the alcoholic fumes redolent of the Home Ales brewery in Daybrook. We were swept along amidst waves of midsummer decked Bhoys, flimsily clad in their green and white hooped tee shirts, and insulated by drink, pre match adrenalin and bravado against a bitter East Midlands night.

They created an atmosphere which could literally be tasted, unmatched by any visiting support, and it was one of those nights where the football was almost incidental.

A good job too, as the pitch was unfit, resembling a skating rink on the Main Stand side, which is shaded from any weak Winter sunshine. Despite rudimentary pre match protection, in the form of bales of straw, or such similar high tech. treatment, the entire surface rapidly froze.

The largely uneventful nil-nil that followed was almost inevitable, as both sets of players struggled to stay on their feet, but as the match slithered to its frostbitten conclusion the Celtic fans prematurely roared out their "victory" acclaim, the strains of "It's a grand old team to play for" reverberating around the City Ground.

Like me before our shock exit to CSKA Sofia in the European Cup, they'd underestimated the value of an away goal. Nil –nil is always a vulnerable first leg scoreline for the away side, and the icy conditions arguably did us a favour.

We were cast in our favourite role as underdogs for the second leg a fortnight later, and 66,938 – less a modest Reds contingent – revved up to sweep us away in a barrage of noise and emotion. Playing conditions were ideal and we were set for an epic encounter.

The radio commentary only lasted a couple of minutes before my nerves went, and familiar mutterings of "I can't stand any more of this" were the cue for the dog to rejoice as we went for a tension busting jog across Carlton Forum.

When I switched on again, with about ten minutes to go, the eerie lack of crowd noise and low key commentary set my pulse racing – we must be winning! – and we were, thanks to Steve Hodge and Colin Walsh, which meant that Celtic needed three in the closing minutes.

Van Breukelen livened things up a bit by dropping a Neville Southall type clanger, stupidly conceding a free kick for time wasting. We scrambled the ball away, but Celtic scored from the resultant corner. Fortunately, time ran out before any further damage could be done.

Europe then went into hibernation until March, when we saw off Sturm Graz, 1-0 on Trentside and 1-1 in Austria.

In the League, Notts stole a lucky 0-0 against us at Meadow Lane, but we'd already taught them a footballing lesson at the City Ground, 3-1 back in October, when Fashanu (looking equally out of place in his Magpies strip) and Hunt were sent off as the Pies tried desperately to combat our overwhelming class.

It wouldn't be so easy against our EUFA Cup semi final

opponents, Belgium's highly respected Anderlecht, but we beat them 2-0 at the City Ground, Steve Hodge's double surely securing our place in the final.

Events then took a bizarre twist, to be put under the spotlight again 14 years later. Forest played badly, and lost 3-0, going out 3-2 on aggregate, but even in the context of our feeble performance we were robbed by two refereeing "mistakes". The first turned out to be irrelevant, given the enormity of the second, but both assumed tremendous significance in the light of those subsequent revelations.

The first happened when an Anderlecht player threw himself down just inside the Penalty area, without a hint of a Forest challenge, and the referee unhesitatingly awarded a spot kick, to the disbelief of the Forest team.

Incident number two was the real crippler. With barely a minute to go Paul Hart rose to head home a cross and put us into the final on away goals. As Forest turned away in celebration, and Anderlecht stood dejected, the referee urgently blew for a fictitious "offence" and awarded Anderlecht a free kick.

There was no question of offside – defenders were clearly between Hart and the goal as the ball came over – and no question of a foul – he was unchallenged, as the Belgian marking disappeared.

I watched the TV recording on Midlands sport the next evening and was furious at the injustice of it. It was bad enough finding out the result at 5am that morning, somewhere on the North Sea, without appreciating the travesty that had been inflicted.

We were returning from Rotterdam to Hull after a motoring tour of Holland and I couldn't believe it at first when the information desk told me that Forest had lost 3-0. I mumbled a cursory "Thanks" and returned in a daze to our cabin.

"Lost, three nil."

Lynn didn't take the news quite so badly. She was more interested in whether the steward had left the breakfast tray, so I was left to sulk in semi-disbelief on my own, trying to appear adult and unconcerned by the result of a trifling football match as we clattered off the ferry and dashed back to Notingham, returning at a sensible breakfast time of 8am.

Back to the future, and in 1998 a dramatic development at Anderlecht brought those decisions sharply into focus again. A former Anderlecht president, Constant van den Stock, admitted paying referee Mura £18,000 the day before the game. Forest immediately sought compensation from Anderlecht, and asked that they be given their place in Europe when they next qualified.

Unfortunately, the referee had died, and proof absolute that the payment had influenced those decisions could never be obtained. Circumstantially, Anderlecht hardly had a leg to stand on, as paying a referee £18,000 (at 1984 values) is hardly your typical goodwill souvenir, usually a pennant or a ballpoint pen.

Nevertheless it was somewhat hypocritical of the Forest board to endeavour to evade the FA "bung" allegations by claiming "It's nothing to do with us, guv, we weren't in charge at the time", whilst simultaneously crying "foul" over the equally remote Anderlecht affair.

At the time of writing, (23.13, 15.9.99, and wondering if I'll ever finish this typing slog) the outcome of both matters is still in the air. All I do know is that we'd have stuffed Spurs in the all English final and Forest's cabinet would have another European trophy.

As it was, we'd won nowt again, but with Europe guaranteed next season, thanks to our high League placing, things were looking up – or so it seemed. Johnny Metgod arrived, and earned his place in our hall of fame, but so did Trevor Christie, listed with Gary Bannister and others as fully paid up members of the Nottingham Forest Retirement Home for Discarded Veteran Strikers.

The Belgians arrived again, this time in the shape of F.C. Brugge, who dumped us out of Europe in the first round of the 1984/85 competition, 1-0 in Bruges after a 0-0 at the City Ground. So much for away goals, but at least we weren't robbed by the ref.

In the League Cup we crashed out to Sunderland, 1-0 at Roker Park after a 1-1 at home. The writing had been on the wall since our two legged first round tie against Portsmouth, where we'd struggled through thanks to a flattering 3-0 City Ground win, but only after extra time, following a 1-0 reverse at Fratton Park.

The relatively high home attendance of 18,182 was thanks to a vociferous contingent from Hampshire, including a sizeable number in the lower Exec, down into the Trent End corner. An unpleasant atmosphere prevailed throughout the match, and I was able to watch at close quarters from just left of the Trent End goal as the Police allowed Pompey fans to direct continual obscenities and threats in our direction.

Many of the Trent End needed little encouragement to respond and one Neanderthal spent most of the match in tirades of insults and fist waving, unchecked by threat of arrest. No wonder supporters had turned their backs on the game.

For all that, it wasn't total despair. I went to the Sunderland tie with a work colleague, Alan, an exiled Newcastle United fan from Lynemouth, near Ashington. To say he had a noticeable Geordie accent would be an understatement.

We stood in the Trent End, and he attracted some interesting looks, but no hostility, although he betrayed his Magpie roots by supporting Sunderland, and cheering when they scored. Fortunately, they didn't go on to get a winner, and I didn't have to pretend I'd never seen him before.

The EUFA and League Cup exits left us two down, and with League form indifferent, only one to go.

Would this be Clough's FA Cup year?

Do pigs fly?

Does John Motson know the past tense of "spin"? (clue – it's **not** span!!!!!)

The answer, of course, a categoric "No", but we avoided our fourth successive 3rd round exit by beating Alan's Magpies 3-1 in a St James Park replay after a 1-1 on our patch. Again, we needed extra time, not to mention Hans Segers saving a Peter Beardsley penalty.

What we didn't need was Wimbledon in round 4. We fought out a frustrating nil-nil at the City Ground, in one of those games where everyone knew after 20 minutes that we weren't going to score, and lost the replay, one nil. Curiously, our 4 game Cup run was concentrated in consecutive matches from January 6th to 30th.

There wasn't much else to do for the rest of the season except turn up out of habit, and only 12,649 of us bothered for our penultimate home game, on May 4th, against Watford. They missed a significant goal (although I can't remember anything about it), Nigel Clough's first in the League, since his Boxing Day debut at home to Ipswich.

We lost our final game, 1-0 at White Hart Lane, and that was that. Not a hint of promise in the three Cup competitions, 9th in the League, and not even the prospect of another bash at Europe next season.

1985/86 was almost an exact replica for mediocrity, but there were at least significant improvements in the quality of our squad, which were to bear fruit in later seasons, notably the signings of Stuart Pearce and Neil Webb, and the meteoric rise of Des Walker. Nigel Clough became established, and Johnny Metgod was strutting his stuff.

Garry Birtles didn't need any introduction.

Garry Birtles

I first heard the name Garry Birtles when a work colleague announced that Long Eaton had a cracking player on their books who'd just been snapped up by Forest, and that he was definitely one to watch for the future.

I've scarcely known him more enthusiastic, and his confident prediction was fully vindicated as Birtles went on to become one of the best ever to pull on a Reds number 9 shirt.

He was a very late starter in League football, particularly given that he moved straight into the top flight, Forest plucking him from obscurity when his expectations of a full time career in the game must have all but disappeared.

It ought to have been a lesson to other top clubs – and one that Forest would do well to remember – who seem content to risk multi million pound fees on established stars with lucrative contracts, but unwilling to gamble relative peanuts on unearthing a gem from the non-League ranks.

He'd been picking up his part time football wages as a supplement to his trade as a carpet fitter, before serving a couple of years anonymous apprenticeship behind the scenes at the Reds, during which time I was disappointed that my colleague's massive build up seemed wildly optimistic.

It was anything but, as Birtles suddenly burst into the first team spotlight in 1978/79, with a series of superb performances. He scored the opening goal against Liverpool in our first ever European Cup game, taking his chance like a seasoned veteran.

For one awful moment I thought he might be offside, as he found himself in the clear, but the officials were spot on, and we all went mad as he coolly dispatched a precise shot firmly into the Trent End net.

Clinical finishing, with his favoured left foot, was to be a Birtles trademark, the ball almost invariably driven low and deliberately – rarely did he succumb to a wild, hit and hope, rush of blood.

His effortless and instantaneous control was an absolute joy to watch. His style was lazily fluid, reminiscent of the archetypal gifted Continentals, as he'd almost casually kill the pace off a pass before spraying the ball to the feet of a teammate. Robertson was the master on the ball, but Birtles was one of the finest receivers with his back to goal, and like Robbo had the perfect temperament and footballing brain.

"One Garry Birtles, there's only one Garry Birtles" broke out in tribute from the Trent End as he ran Liverpool ragged, but it would have been equally appropriate off the field.

The sartorially challenged Birtles chose to announce his imminent presence visually, rather than audibly. At the cutting edge of fashion, his boldest outfits were more dangerous to the naked eye than the 1999 eclipse. "Large checks" was a description of his dress sense, rather than his salary.

It wasn't his avant garde tailoring that offended Brian Clough, as Birtles once overstepped the mark on the team coach heading for the airport for another critical long haul friendly. Birtles was complaining - with some justification – about the unnecessary trip, when Clough made the driver stop the bus and summarily delivered G. Birtles Esq. out into the road, from where he could make his own arrangements.

His Reds career seemed at an end when he was transferred to Manchester United, on the crest of a wave, but he had a miserable time at Old Trafford, as his goalscoring touch, and confidence, deserted him. Cloughie gave him a chance to return to the East Midlands and he jumped at it.

His second spell with the Reds included action as a makeshift centre half, but after a promising start he was less than convincing in this unfamiliar role. He was hampered by a niggling back injury, which plagued him relentlessly and was no doubt responsible for his noticeably upright stance.

Whether his back problems were in part a legacy of his carpet fitting days, I don't know, but even in his final season, 1986/87, and at less than 100% fitness, his contribution was a goal every other League game, with 14 in 28.

He always gave 100%, and no Reds fan will forget his performance against Hamburg in our second European Cup Final as he ran himself into the ground as our lone forward. He was practically on his knees late in the second half, desperately trying to run clear onto a through ball, and finish the game at 2-0, but going backwards all the time as the Hamburg defence chased him down.

With Birtles, we always knew that we'd got a genuine Forest supporter in the team. His roots have remained red and white and his local media reporting of the Reds current fortunes – and refereeing standards – is refreshingly outspoken.

Personal highlight - the Southampton League Cup Final, when Birtles turned the match, and made it my best ever Wembley occasion.

~

1985/86 saw a familiar pattern of disappointment, despite our strengthened squad. QPR evicted us from the League Cup, 3-1 at Loftus Road, and Davenport was sent off, presumably for arguing about an offside decision.

In the FA Cup we couldn't emulate last season's stirring run to the 4th Round, Blackburn Rovers drawing the lucky number that represented Nottingham Forest. Still, we got our money's worth, squeezing two games out of one tie, succumbing 3-2 at Ewood Park after a 1-1 at our place.

13th January 1986 was the specific date on which the season finished, bumbling along unconvincingly in the League for the next four months to finish a mediocre 8th, one place better than last year.

Metgod provided the highlight with his piledriver free kick against West Ham, and Franz Carr appeared, bamboozling defenders, the crowd and himself with a combination of lightning pace, erratic control, and uncanny knack of choosing the wrong option. That aside, I can't remember much happening, although Pearce and Walker were steadily endearing themselves as the season progressed.

The Public weren't exactly flocking back, and home gates of 13,000 or less were a dismal feature. The visit of Aston Villa, for example, attracted only 12,993, and it was a similar story away, including Arsenal (17,756), Villa (15,315), Leicester (14,247), Coventry (9,500) and West Brom (7,901).

Football, thanks largely to the yobs, and Government inaction, was on its knees. I can't help wondering though if today's headlong rush into saturation Europe and saturation TV won't see similar – and deserved – derisory gates, especially for unattractive first leg ties. I also wonder how we can have a "Champions League" when a good half of the entrants are anything but.

Back in the mid 80s Bill Murray should have been a Reds fan. These were Forest's Groundhog Days :-

In 1986/77 we won nothing – again.
We finished 8th in the League – again.
We failed in the League Cup – again.
We lost in the FA Cup 3rd round – again.
The season was over by January – again.
Attendances were pathetic – again.

And I drove from Carlton to Trent Lane, Sneinton, walked down via Lady Bay Bridge, climbed to the concrete heights of the Exec Stand, and parked my bum in my white plastic seat – part of the "O" in "FOREST" – again, and again.

For the record, there were subtle variations – it was Arsenal who knocked us out of the League Cup, 2-0 at Highbury, after we'd had a promising run, overcoming the respective might of Brighton, Palace (after a replay) and Bradford. Palace got their revenge in the FA Cup, 1-0 at Selhurst Park before a paltry 11,618.

At the time, Forest sold discounted season tickets at Christmas. I should have asked them to consider a similar option, valid from August to January.

Then again, I should have known better. We didn't win anything in 1987/88 but we broke the spell. Metgod had gone, but his towering presence had been replaced, late in the previous campaign, by the equally towering Colin Foster, and Paul Wilkinson was introduced in attack.

Six others made debuts – Terry Wilson, Steve Chettle, Tommy Gaynor, Gary Crosby, Darren Wassall and Garry Parker, but only Chettle and Parker stood the test of time, although Clough persevered ad nauseam with Crosby.

The injury plagued Terry Wilson was continually mooted as a future star, although my opinion was that he'd never make the grade. I remember him fiercely smashing one in at the Bridgford End – unfortunately we were attacking the Trent End at the time.

Nevertheless, we were firing again, and would have qualified for Europe, thanks to our 3rd place finish, but for

Heysel, and England's ban. Maybe the others weren't trying, because we were to do it again next season, with the same result.

Against logical expectations, the FA Cup came to the rescue, and for the first time since 1966/67 Wembley seriously beckoned. The League Cup deserted us again, 3-0 at Maine Road after an aggregate 6-1 over Hereford, but by February we were amazingly through to the 5th Round of the big one.

We cruised past Halifax Town, 4-0 at the Shay, which hardly caused any waves, but after a scrappy 2-1 against Leyton Orient at Brisbane Road, and with the bogey month of January out of the way, there were a few ripples on Trentside.

Birmingham City away, at least from a playing point of view, wasn't the most intimidating, and we'd suddenly got every chance of making the 6th Round, a mouthwatering prospect after so long in the wilderness. Could Cloughie be about to break his FA Cup duck?

Our clash was eagerly anticipated, and just under 35,000 packed St Andrews, definitely not including me. I'd been on a previous midweek League visit to this grim relic, with its hostile tribes of hooligans looking for easy prey in their familiar territory – a dark and depressing semi derelict wasteland, heavily littered with bricks, lumps of concrete and other missiles.

St Andrews is now rebuilt, thankfully, but I can't vouch for its surroundings, and I've never been tempted to return.

On the day, Forest shaded a hard fought encounter 1-0, with Gary Crosby getting the only goal, and there were distinct signs of Cup fever amongst Reds fans. We were drawn away at Arsenal, to groans of disappointment, but with Halifax, Leyton Orient and Birmingham gone we'd run out of small fish to fry.

Saturday March 12th saw thousands of Reds heading

optimistically down the M1, the belief having grown during the pre match build up that we could do it. I desperately wanted to go, but Highbury still remains as one of my missing London grounds, along with Brentford, Leyton Orient and Charlton.

In a masterstroke of clever timing and irony I'd booked as our Easter holiday a return visit, with Lynn, to Hong Kong. A day in London with Forest was pushing it a bit, especially as I'd fully extended my VISA limit, a decision that didn't go down too well when I'd casually introduced our holiday arrangements into a discussion about decorating the house.

I stayed in and watched Grandstand, punching the air in jubilation when the "Cup latest - Arsenal 0 – Forest 1" flashed onto the screen, and went barmy when it showed us 2-0 up, well into the 2nd half.

We were on our way, but I could scarcely believe it when it showed a "Cup latest" of 2-1 when according to my reckoning the game should have been over. Instant deflation, followed by endless minutes of nervous twitching, then merciful release as it's announced as a final score.

Liverpool were our semi final opponents, scarcely 40 minutes up the MI at Hillsborough, scene of our defeat against Spurs in 1967, and my personal despair when I queued all night for a ticket, only to be gatecrashed by thousands of late-comers.

I wouldn't be there this time either, but given the choice I'd have taken the Hong Kong trip. Typical of Forest though, to save their first semi final in 21 years to coincide with my Far East holiday.

We arrived the day before the game and I was chuffed to find that it was being shown live on local TV. It was almost surreal, watching late at night in our hotel room whilst the Reds were battling the Scousers in bright Spring sunshine on an English afternoon. We'd only been here 24 hours and already I was beginning to feel like an ex-Pat.

When we went 2-0 down I thought it was curtains, and my nerves disappeared. I was back on the edge of my seat – or rather, the bed – when Nigel Clough pulled one back, but no amount of shouting at the screen could conjure up an equaliser, and that was that. It wasn't Brian's year after all.

It was a blight on the holiday, but from Lynn's point of view massively overshadowed by the trauma of finding that Kowloon's brand new Marks and Spencer wouldn't be opening until after we'd arrived home. It's strange the significance that women can attach to such trivia.

Forest's FA Cup run had been far and away the highlight of the season – of several seasons – and was the catalyst for future glories. Despite being a season ticket holder, my only "live" game in our cup run had been via a TV set in a Hong Kong hotel room.

I didn't let it happen again, missing none of our 6 FA Cup ties in 1988/89, and only 2 of our 9 in the League Cup, but it was a season of both glory and darkest tragedy.

It started poorly in the League, 2-1 defeat in our opening fixture at Carrow Road conspicuous only by Steve Chettle's first goal. We drew the next four, all 1-1, and then couldn't even break our duck in the next one, an "easy" home game against Luton, the match finishing scoreless. Nowadays, that kind of start generates hysterical press coverage and puts mangers under absurd pressure.

Thankfully, we beat QPR 2-1 at Loftus Road and Brian was safe, but following Paul Wilkinson's departure before the season we were lightweight up front until Lee Chapman's complicated arrival in October, after contractual difficulties with French club Niort.

Other debutants were Brian Laws, Mark Crossley – what a loyal servant he's been – and Gary Charles, the latter defying all expectations by continuing to play in the top flight after leaving us.

Once we'd discovered the winning habit the season began in earnest and by Christmas we'd consolidated in the League and battled through to the last 8 of the League Cup.

Our League Cup run began easily enough, walloping Chester City home and away, 6-0 and 4-0, followed by a 3-2 City Ground win over Coventry. The attendance of 21,301 was an encouraging pointer to better gates overall, with "only" two League crowds below 16,000, against Luton (15,340) and Millwall (15,982) respectively.

We were at Filbert Street in the next round, biting our nails under the gloomy canopy of Leicester's bike shed, a feeble apology for a football stand that hides its entrance, embarrassed to be seen in public, within a row of terraced houses. Psycho was sent off for a late tackle, but we hung on for a nil-nil, and shaded the replay 2-1, the Foxes succumbing to the perils of the "Cs", namely Messrs. Clough and Chapman.

The Leicester victory came amidst an undefeated run of seven, ended abruptly – surprise, surprise – by Wimbledon, 1-0 at the City Ground. We lost our next one too, 2-0 on Boxing Day at Old Trafford, before embarking on an astonishing run of 10 consecutive victories, incorporating no less than 4 competitions – League, League Cup, FA Cup, and last, and by some considerable distance least, the Simod Cup, a contrived affair introduced in the absence of European competition.

For the record, we beat Chelsea away and Ipswich at home in the Simod, Ipswich and Leeds at home in the FA Cup 3rd and 4th rounds, and QPR at home in the League Cup 5th round (that was the night that Lee Chapman scored four).

In the League it was Sheffield Wednesday away, Everton at home, Spurs away, Villa at home and Luton away. To put it mildly, things were looking up, and we stretched our run to 19 undefeated before losing 2-1 in the League at Spurs on March 22nd 1989.

We were at home to Bristol City in the first leg of the League Cup semi final, but despite a poor display in a 1-1 draw I was not too downhearted as I still felt that we'd be too good for them in the second leg.

The games came thick and fast and on the following Sunday I went to Watford for the FA Cup 5th round, accompanied by English speaking Alan from Why-Aye land. He insisted on staying in the pub until we'd got less than ten minutes for the dash to the ground, barely taking our seats as the teams lined up.

I was surprised at the amount of support for the Reds, given also that it was on TV, and also when Alan produced a miniature set from his jacket pocket so that we could simultaneously watch the BBC coverage, a unique experience that provided the worst of both worlds.

The mesmeric compulsion of four square inches of black and white TV screen contaminated the real life technicolour excitement unfolding out on the pitch, but fortunately the batteries went after about 20minutes, so it was no contest. It was no contest on the pitch either, as we ran out easy 3-0 winners, courtesy of Webb, Chapman and Laws, Forest for once living up to an FA Cup billing as favourites.

I didn't go to Ashton Gate for our League Cup semi final 2ng leg – Chester away was the other one I missed – but sat glued to another live Reds TV appearance.

Garry Parker scored the only goal, in extra time, arriving unnoticed in his characteristic midfield poacher role to hit home a low centre. It had been a gruelling battle on a sticky pitch that turned into porridge in the driving rain, and I both envied and pitied the ecstatic but drenched Reds on the open Kop.

Luton were our opponents at Wembley, 30 years since we beat them 2-1 in our last FA Cup final, but first we faced the daunting prospect of our 6th round FA Cup tie, away at Manchester United.

Our party of three travelled across the Pennines in rain and drizzle, electing for the cross country route via Matlock and Buxton, the intention being to stop for a pub meal en route.

Fortunately we elected at the last minute to press on into Manchester, and a gut wrenchingly frustrating two hour crawl into, and through, Stockport emphatically vindicated our decision. We were caught up in a nightmare tangle of stop-start traffic, and at this rate we'd miss the kick off, as would thousands of others, including hordes from the East Midlands.

The motorway brought blessed relief, but the short dash was followed by another crawl, and we were sucked into the chaos surrounding Old Trafford, seeking escape down narrow, double parked, sidestreets, choked with supporters. My Company Metro, usually something of an embarrassment, came into its own for once as it fitted snugly on the end of a row at a T junction, barely ten minutes walk from the ground.

We were seated, knees wedged under our chins, by 2-30, behind the Scoreboard End goal, above the standing enclosure. Old Trafford was barely a quarter full, but a tremendous atmosphere built up by 3pm, thousands pouring in at the last minute.

It was some time after kick off before the Forest end was full, but thanks to a generous ticket allocation we had some 11,000 in a crowd of 55,052, and roared Forest on with a tremendous barrage. It's the best Forest support I've ever known at an opposition ground.

The game was predictably tight, and on a knife edge, with scarcely a clear cut chance, when Franz Carr went down the right late in the first half as we attacked the Stretford End. He slipped near the corner flag, to howls of derision from the home support, but their cries were silenced as he regained his feet, cut inside, and laid a perfect ball for Garry Parker, Bristol fashion, to sidefoot home.

Our end erupted, and I spotted Basharat Hassan, ex opener and loyal servant to Notts County Cricket Club, just in front of us, up on his feet in celebration as we all went mad.

We expected, and got, frantic second half pressure, but the nearest they got to scoring was an effort hacked away on the Forest line. United claimed it was over, but TV evidence proved that the officials were right. Late on, Franz Carr burst clear on goal at our end, and we were off our seats in anticipation, only for his shot to ricochet clear off the keeper.

It would have been party time, but as it was waves of celebratory noise poured down in the closing minutes as Forest looked increasingly comfortable, and United ever more desperate. Franz Carr,. goal maker and goal misser, surely had his best ever game for the Reds, continually harrying United defenders in possession with a non stop display as our first line of defence, deep in their half.

"We're on the march with Cloughie's army" roared out, until the final whistle took the roof off the Scoreboard End. After the bitter disappointment of the past it scarcely sunk in that I'd finally be backing the Reds at an FA Cup semi final.

After the match we reclaimed the car, trying to look dejected as we negotiated pockets of United troublemakers, before returning home by the motorway route. We achieved the sanctuary of the M62 before trailing our scarves triumphantly from the windows.

We were part of another Reds motorway exodus a couple of weeks later, this time south to Wembley for our League Cup final against the Hatters.

On a warm sunny day we made the most of our early arrival, basking on the grassy slopes outside the stadium, before an unexpected fracas broke out involving a few hundred Luton yobs, who were dispersed by a mounted Police charge.

It was as unexpected as it was disturbing, and a stark reminder that we couldn't take anything for granted, even on a balmy Cup Final day against lowly, outnumbered, Luton.

As for the match, it went according to script, after a shaky start. Clough got two, one from the penalty spot, and Webb our third as we finally cemented our increasing second half dominance with a 3-1 victory. Luton protested Webb offside, but our vantage point level with the play showed that he'd timed his run perfectly, finishing with aplomb at our end, which erupted in a riot of red and white.

Pscho lifted the cup, Forest did a rapturous lap of honour, and we crawled back up the M1, colours trailing, in a stop-start victory procession.

Six days later, on April 15th 1989, we were scheduled to play Liverpool in our FA Cup semi final, my first, long awaited, chance to see Forest clinch an FA Cup final place.

It was to be the blackest day in the history of English football.

Hillsborough

It was a repeat of the Old Trafford threesome that travelled in a red and white convoy the forty odd short miles to Sheffield's flagship Hillsborough stadium.

We picknicked in glorious sunshine amongst hundreds of fellow Reds, and a few Liverpudlians, detached from their maincore support which was approaching, as was the case last year, from the opposite end of the ground. It was a carnival atmosphere, and the crowd segregation was exactly as my brother had predicted following his experience in 1988.

He couldn't get a seat, and left us early to claim his spot on the Kop. Bob and myself claimed our seats in row "D", at the Kop end, before being removed to row "O". We weren't the only ones to be fooled by the 2 letters being printed in confusingly similar style, but it was an irrelevance compared with the debacle that was to follow.

From our new position, doubled up and with a partly obstructed view, I was puzzled – and said so at the time – as to why the middle section of the Liverpool end was full, and yet no-one seemed to be filling the end sections.

At 2.30 it seemed obvious to me that the clearly delayed bulk of Liverpool's standing support would feed into the end sections, reminiscent of the days in the 60s when two humble coppers, exercising what used to known as "common sense", would stand at the Trent End middle entrance and announce "sorry lads, section full – either end please".

By kick off I was so excited by the proceedings on the pitch that I'd ceased to bother about the Liverpool support, although I was conscious that it was absolutely solid behind their goal. When supporters began spilling onto the pitch, a few minutes after kick off – I think Lee Chapman had the ball at his feet, in their penalty area – I knew immediately that there was a severe crushing problem. Why else would it happen? There were no Forest fans at that end, and it made no sense otherwise.

What we didn't realise was the sheer horror of what was unfolding. We expected a few hundred fans to be removed to the less crowded sections, order to be restored, and the game to be re-started after a few minutes delay. Only when unconscious fans were brought onto the pitch, in ever increasing numbers, and the desperation of the rescue effort became clear, did the enormity of the tragedy become clear.

We watched the proceedings in shocked silence before filing silently away. My brother, trained in first aid, told us back at the car that he knew almost immediately that people were dying, but that his plea to help with resuscitation was refused by the Police. They were more interested in lining up across the pitch to prevent a supposed invasion by Reds fans than giving practical assistance.

The attempted cover up afterwards was bordering on the obscene, paradoxically only undone by camera evidence that disproved key allegations, when reliance on supposedly high-tech police cameras - at the expense of common sense - had arguably brought about the disaster in the first place.

Liverpool fans were bitter that their greater support had not been allocated, for logistical reasons, the Kop end, and it's a sobering thought that it might just as easily have been a Nottingham disaster.

There were problems at previous semis, and regardless of allegations of overcrowding - as far as I'm aware, peripheral, at worst – due to ticket forgeries, those already inside the ground are entitled to a guarantee of safety.

The book of personal accounts by friends and relatives of victims makes harrowing reading, but should be considered essential for anyone in pursuit of the full story.

~

It was decided, correctly in my opinion, to re-stage the game at Old Trafford, and after some discussion we decided that not only was it right that we went, but that Forest were fully deserving of all the support they could get.

By the day of the game, Sunday May 7th, our sympathies for the victims and families were quite properly and totally divorced from our footballing loyalties to Forest, and we desperately wanted to see the Reds at Wembley.

With Everton having won the other semi, it seemed that the entire nation, as represented by the emotional outpourings of the media, was somehow entitled to an all Merseyside "Tribute to Hillsborough", with Forest an incidental and acquiescing bit part.

Given that the decision was made to play the game, Forest were entitled to go all out for victory, but arriving early outside Old Trafford it felt as if the result was never to be in doubt. We experienced sporadic shows of hostility from Liverpool fans before the game, and the feeling that we were unwelcome guests at a private remembrance service. It was intended to be Merseyside's day of grief and Nottingham had better leave quietly by the back door.

Whether subconsciously or otherwise, the mood was reflected on the pitch, with Liverpool tearing into Forest, who gave scarcely an ounce of commitment and were easily pushed aside, 3-1, despite the lifeline just before half time of Webb's grubber squirming under Grobelaar into the Stretford End net.

It seemed as if no-one thought that we had the right to win, and the referee gave full licence to Steve McMahon – one of my all time disliked players, along with his role model Graham Souness – to give full, unchecked, vent to his "battling qualities".

We were sat not far behind the Liverpool dugout and after one of the Liverpool goals Kenny Dalglish reinforced my prejudices as far as he was concerned by turning to the

Forest support in a brief, but undignified and unnecessary, gesture.

Still, the media had their day, "justice" was done, and Forest did indeed leave quietly by the back door.

Our subdued journey home was brightened by an unscheduled stop somewhere off the Snake Pass where we spontaneously adjourned for disposal of the remaining rations.

My brother and myself scrambled up the Derbyshire hillside, leaving Bob behind at base camp, and enjoyed glorious views over the Peak District, evening sunlight flashing off the roofs of the returning Forest traffic winding silently home in the distance below our lofty perch.

I promised myself I'd return to this idyllic spot for a day's walking, but like most of my good ideas it's still in embryonic form.

Sandwiched between Hillsborough and the Old Trafford replay Forest had been at Wembley again. I boycotted the Simod Cup in its entirety, but 46,608 were recorded for our exciting 4-3 victory over Everton, and we'd got another trophy for the bulging cabinet.

I can remember exactly where I was at the time – I spent a damp afternoon listening on the radio whilst replacing a rotten window ledge in the garage. Surprisingly, I made quite a good job of it, and it was still as good as new several years later when we escaped the Alps of Carlton for the galeswept outer reaches of Arnold.

The tragedy of Hillsborough casts a permanent shadow over season 1988/89, but the records show that we finished 3rd in the League and picked up two cup trophies, so from a playing point of view things were looking up.

We didn't know it at the time, but the results of the Taylor report were to be a long overdue modernisation and rebuilding programme that by the turn of the century would see England's top flight stadiums amongst the best club grounds in the world. Ironically, Hillsborough has been left behind, although it still clings to its status as one of our showpiece grounds, for reasons which entirely escape me.

The 80s ended as I always knew they would, with season 1989/90.

It was a mixed affair, with a disappointing 9th place finish in the League, but hardly surprising with midfielder Steve Hodge finishing top scorer with 10, ahead of Nigel Clough's 9, Lee Chapman's 7, and Garry Parker's 6.

Chapman was on his travels again before Christmas, and with no adequate replacement on the horizon it was obvious that we'd struggle up front. Nigel Jemson took his place, but lacked a suitable partner.

Cloughie idiosyncratically persisted with the lightweight Gary Crosby down the right, and with Brian Rice, Toddy Orlygsson and Tommy Gaynor flitting in and out of the team we lacked quality. Colin Foster's departure before September was out didn't help either.

On the credit side, Jemson showed promise, Clough, Parker and Hodge were a force in midfield and Walker his by now customary magnificent.

Enough to have a shout in a Cup competition, but never enough to threaten in the League, and so it proved. We had a familiar 3rd Round FA Cup exit, at home in a live televised game, losing 1-0 to Man Utd, before just 23,068.

With the Zenith Data Cup blown in the second round, 2-1 at Villa Park – how we suffered at the tremendous disappointment, whilst 6,000 Villa fans rejoiced – the season was all about our old friend the League Cup.

We made an uncomfortable start in our defence as holders, scraping past Huddersfied Town on away goals, 1-1 at home and 3-3 in the return. Palace were next, hammered 5-0 on Trentside after we'd stuttered to a nil-nil at Selhurst Park, and I felt familiar Wembley League Cup stirrings.

We drew Everton at home in the next round, and it seemed all set for a Goodison Park replay when the Toffees came unstuck, late in the second half, in circumstances entirely of their own making.

They were undone by an act of stupidity from their experienced keeper, Neville Southall. Never one to take a few seconds over a goalkick when a couple of minutes would do – unless Everton were losing, when he'd move like greased lightning – he was up to his familiar tricks - pretending to remonstrate with his defence, walking back in freeze-frame motion, "accidentally" stepping over the ball – he had a full repertoire that used to drive me mad.

This time the referee had had enough of it and having already conspicuously warned him, to no effect, he had no choice but to penalise him when he went on slow motion walkabout again to delay taking a goal kick. Southall just couldn't help himself, and with the referee emphatically pointing to his watch and Reds fans screaming "Get on with it, you cheating, time wasting, bastard!" he was still incapable of getting the message.

A shrill whistle was music to our ears. Indirect Forest free kick, six yards out in front of the Trent End, Main Stand side. Everton packed the goalmouth. Forest mingled. Bodies everywhere, jostling and jockeying. I forget who took the kick - it might have been Clough – but it was craftily pushed across the face of goal for Chapman to smartly sidefoot home.

"YEEEESS!!"

I was off my seat in jubiliation. Justice. Instant retribution that tasted all the sweeter because it was so rare. It was too late for a preposterously disgruntled Everton, with Southall now getting on with it as if his shorts were on fire, to save it, and we went through, deservedly.

Next day at work a fervent Evertonian, who'd been at the City Ground, but watching a different match, was incandescent with rage – not, bizarrely, at his goalkeeper, but at the referee, and there was to be no discussing the subject.

Everton were back again, three days later in the League. They were thirsting for revenge, but as in the League Cup they weren't up to the task, losing one-nil again. This time Nigel Clough benefited from a piece of good refereeing, scoring from the Penalty spot.

Spurs at home was our reward in the League Cup quarter finals and over 30,000 generated a real cup tie atmosphere in a thrilling 2-2 draw. Crosby and Parker were our scorers, but a bruising encounter was indicative of a particularly mean Tottenham approach.

Their aggressive, no prisoners, tactics did them little credit, and it was a shame to see them abandon their traditional free flowing style. It was the ideal environment to allow the worst, most thuggish, excesses of a certain Mr. Gascoigne, as both Forest and Notts were to experience in the FA Cup.

Unlike Southall he escaped punishment, despite elbowing a Notts player in the face, jumping studs first into the chest of Garry Parker, and scything down Gary Charles in an appalling late dive. Still, he's England's misunderstood, persecuted, favourite jack the lad, isn't he?

As I pondered our replay prospects I scarcely gave a thought to a disturbance in the crowd, not far from us in the Exec Stand.

Next day at work we received the bombshell that it had been Harold Crossland who had collapsed and died. Harold was well known and respected in local Insurance circles, and a Forest fanatic.

Our telephone conversations always began with "Weren't they crap", "Great win on Saturday", "Why does he keep playing Crosby?", etc, - anything to do with Forest, and a bit about Insurance tagged on at the end.

It was a pleasure to know him, and a tragic irony that his passion for Forest was so intense that it eventually overwhelmed him. Sadly missed.

Spurs were over physical again at White Hart Lane, but a determined performance by Forest saw us clinch another thriller, 3-2, thanks to a brace from Hodge and one from Jemson.

An abiding tribute to Brian Clough is that he not only maintained Forest's traditionally high standard of sportsmanship, but in many ways enhanced them, the Reds almost invariably top of any unofficial referees poll for on field discipline. He proved that success at the highest level can be achieved without trying to kick the opposition off the park, or by cheating, and his philosophy does him immense credit.

We got Coventry City at home in the first leg of the semi final, and it was another knife-edge battle. Clough Jnr., with a penalty, and ex Coventry man Pearce secured a narrow 2-1 win. I was disappointed with the attendance of 26,153, given also that it was a local derby, but not with the scoreline, which we'd surely protect at Highfield Road.

Our threesome apprehensively set off on Sunday February 25th, concerned less about Forest's prospects than the immediate question of whether the game would be played. Heavy rain had put the match in doubt and it was still teeming down as we ploughed through the spray down the A46, wipers doing a Moses as the deluge persisted.

Subdued, with scarves apologetically hidden in a corner on the back seat, instead of their usual fresh air buffeting from the windows – I shredded three over the years – we anticipated a swift and unfulfilled return to Nottingham. We splashed on regardless, and into the terraced backstreets approaching the ground. The rain eased, then petered out as the skies miraculously cleared, and the thickening tide of local fans was surely evidence that it was still on.

Pulses quickened. Too late to air the scarves, unless we wanted to risk a brick through the window – the maze of narrow roads provided convenient parking, but past experience had taught the need for anonymity.

As the weather cleared, a strong drying wind lent a hand to the sterling efforts of the Coventry groundstaff. The heavy, sticky, pitch was just about playable, thanks to a liberal spreading of sand, but a less important match might well have been called off.

The game was a tense affair, Forest defending the one goal advantage and securing a nil-nil draw, but the last few minutes took an eternity as the Sky blues tried desperately to break the deadlock. It was Forest who came nearest, with a typically ferocious free kick by Stuart Pearce which crashed against the cross bar at the open Kop end.

At the final whistle Forest's travelling army celebrated another passport to Wembley, the taste of success still as sweet as ever. Once we'd cleared the suburbs out came the scarves, waving furiously in my mirrors and thumping against the roof. Not exactly an aid to road safety, but an integral part of the away trip experience.

For the second year running we were firm favourites in the Final, against unlikely opponents Oldham Athletic. We hit the motorway early for an easy run down, expecting to park in the residential area within walking distance of Wembley. My confident prediction that it would be a doddle, especially on a Sunday, proved to be slightly misguided.

To say that we weren't welcome was an understatement, yet we'd parked there without difficulty last year. Now there were signs everywhere warning that non residents would be clamped or towed away, and some streets even had barricades.

We toured the semi-detatcheds of Wembley in vain, taunted by hundreds of yards of empty spaces. Shit. We stopped to consider our options, which were basically limited to driving out to Harrow and getting the tube back, when a bloke, somewhere in his mid twenties, emerged from his house and came over.

"You know you can't park round here"

"Yes, we've been driving round in circles for half an hour. Is there anywhere around and about?"

"No way, mate, sorry, unless you want to get towed away"

We were about to move off when he suddenly came to the rescue with a suggestion that, as the Heineken advert would have it, made a refreshing change :-

"Hang on though, I'm going out this afternoon. Tell you what, you can have my resident's permit. Leave it inside your windscreen and post it back through the door after the match"

Absolutely brilliant - and trusting. We thanked him profusely, offered him a fiver for a drink – which he wouldn't accept – and posted the permit back afterwards, together with a match programme.

Wembley was now all seater, which meant essentially that the lower tiers cost more for an even crappier view, as we were to discover from our thin squares of plastic that we took to be what passed as "seats". The attendance of 74,343, despite the reduced capacity, was less than 2,000 down on the Luton final, as the Hatters hadn't shifted their total allocation.

The game went to script again, but as with all our 1989/90 League Cup games, bar Palace at home, there was no more than a goal in it. Forest were the better side, becoming more assertive as the match wore on, but incapable of turning possession into goals.

We were well into the second half when Nigel Jemson burst through, only to have his shot blocked by the keeper. Stifled celebrations were instantly resurrected when he pounced on the rebound to ram it joyfully home.

Our end exploded in relief, but the expected goal rush didn't materialise. I thought we'd finished them off a few minutes later when Pearce blasted a free kick around the Oldham wall. It was fizzing into the corner of the net, directly at us, and I'd already got us mentally home and dry at 2-0 when the keeper miraculously got a hand to it and pushed it round the post.

It was a wonder save that kept our victory celebrations on hold until the final whistle, and led to the usual nervous last few minutes that accompany a one goal lead, regardless of territorial domination.

We rejoiced as Forest paraded the Cup on their victory lap, and cheered them to the echo as they disappeared into the tunnel, before retracing our steps to the car. It was suddenly a quiet Sunday evening in our enclave of residential Wembley as we left the throngs behind and headed for the barricades.

All quiet, bar half a dozen Oldham supporters, ominously tagging us and closing in on our heels. Acting decisively – something of a novelty – we used the element of surprise, and turned to face them :-

"Bad luck lads, you had us worried near the end"

"Yeh, right" one of them grunted reluctantly back.

We continued to chat, well aware of their hostility, which thankfully began to evaporate as genuine conversation developed. As we thought, they'd homed in on us, as one of them put it, to give us "a good kicking". They were rough lads, but became friendly, and almost apologetic once we'd developed a rapport, and we parted company on good terms.

So we made it safely home, yet another Wembley visit under our belts, but with one more dramatic twist in this final season of the decade. We beat Sheffield Wednesday 3-0 away in our last game, and they were relegated.

~

Police Intelligence

As a generally honest and law abiding citizen, and coward to boot, I've always avoided trouble, or run away from it when it found me. I've preferred to travel away independently and incognito, sometimes arriving hours ahead of kick off, depending on the attraction of the venue.

Unfortunately, I've still fallen foul of arrogant, macho, policing on a number of occasions. Football's yob element, prevalent and often out of control in the 70s and 80s – and still simmering in the 90s – demanded tough policing, but all too often it was applied indiscriminately and unintelligently, alienating the moderate – majority – supporter and ultimately costing lives.

Some forces seemed to enact a local vigilante role, treating away supporters arriving on their patch with contempt, unable or unwilling to differentiate genuine fans from the riff-raff, or more significantly identify or react to issues of crowd safety.

So it was at Derby for our 3rd Round FA Cup tie on January 8th 1983, 6 years before the Hillsborough disaster. Forest fans were directed behind our stand towards the turnstiles, and we funneled into a narrowing gap which was partially obstructed further ahead by a large mobile hot dog vehicle.

There was no pushing, just a slow and orderly shuffle, but it suddenly became apparent that a crush was developing due to the dangerously positioned van. At first it was mildly amusing, and I remarked to Bob that we could be carried forwards simply by lifting our feet off the ground.

Then the crush intensified, the pressure visibly rocking the vehicle. Breathing became more difficult, and there was no escaping the frightening compression until mercifully, like corks from a bottle, we suddenly surged clear, gasping for breath. Several people were visibly distressed, some in tears.

A group, led by a middle aged lady, sought out a couple of Police officers, pleading tearfully with them to get the stall moved "before someone gets killed". They were basically told, under implied threat of arrest, to mind their own business. Tragedy was averted when the obstruction was subsequently pulled clear, but no thanks to the officers concerned.

Two simple questions arise – which brain dead authority sanctioned it being there in the first place, slap bang in the path of the away support, and why were supposedly trained Police officers arrogantly dismissive of pleas for help from the distressed public when any 10 year old could have seen the danger?

Answer – we were football fans, and away ones at that – part of Thatcher's despised legion of sub humans, and the seeds were well and truly sown for Hillsborough and its shameful attempted whitewash.

I was also with Bob one midweek evening at Leicester. We made our way quietly to the ground, feeling conspicuous in our suits following an early exit from work. After the match the Forest contingent was held back for what seemed like hours, awaiting their escort back to the railway station and, as it subsequently transpired, to allow time for marauding gangs of Leicester fans to set ambushes along the way.

Our problem was that we weren't going anywhere near the station, so we politely asked a senior officer – he had one of those "I'm in charge" cane cum swordstick things – if we could slip away and back to our car. No chance, sunshine, you're heading for the railway station with everybody else and if you don't shut up you'll spend a night inside.

So, two be-suited British citizens were herded like prisoners of war towards the Forest specials, shadowed by sinister groups of Leicester yobbos, and desperate for a chance to slip our escort and track back to the car without suffering GBH – by City yobs, or the Police, take your choice.

We darted away at a road junction as we approached the station, retracing our steps down streets long since empty of the comfort of the dispersing crowd, with only prowling groups of City thugs looking for easy pickings.

Bob was even more worried than me, legacy of the nasty eye injury received in an attack outside Anfield, but I reminded him that at least our accents wouldn't give us away, and as long as we'd not been spotted leaving the Forest support we were just two blokes out for a drink. Besides, we were heading back towards the ground, which hardly made sense if we were Reds fans.

We tried to look nonchalant, talked loudly – about work – and successfully negotiated several gangs of nutters (of the Filbert variety) before recapturing the car. Thanks to the boys in blue – both sets – we arrived home very late, but at least didn't end up eating hospital food.

Even at Hillsborough some years back two of us were aggressively prevented from entering a departing half empty service bus back into Sheffield. "Football Specials only" was the order, and despite explaining that we were Forest fans with a train to catch, and had been there 15 minutes, he insisted on overruling the driver's cheery "no problem, hop on lads".

He conspicuously escorted us to the back of another enormous queue which hadn't even been there when we'd first arrived, having raced from the ground bang on time.

We missed our train and spent an hour or so at Sheffield railway station thinking up appropriate adjectives for a certain Sheffield policeman.

Just a sample cross section, and in fairness I don't suppose it's much fun having to clean spit off your uniform after football duties, but most people respond positively to a positive approach.

A friendly search outside Old Trafford – "Sorry mate, just a precaution", followed by "Hope you stuff 'em, I'm a City fan" did far more for Police relations and public attitude – at least as far as this citizen is concerned – than any amount of intimidatory macho posturing.

I've never experienced the City Ground as an away fan, but rumour has it that Forest have now got it about right, which might be why – along with having the atmospheric Bridgford End – there's usually a strong away following.

I once made friends with a four legged member of our local constabulary which patrolled behind the Trent End, by the simple and time honoured expedient of bringing it an apple every week. A similar gesture at Derby in the 80s might well have seen me arrested for attempted bribery.

Let's hope that lessons have been learnt.

~

The nervous 90s

It never crossed my mind that I wouldn't be renewing my season ticket for season 1990/91 and I dutifully nipped down to the City Ground a couple of days before the deadline.

Forest could have my money, but I didn't see the point in letting them have it any sooner than necessary, and in any case I had to go through the ritual of telling my wife that I hadn't made my mind up yet.

I also went through the ritual of checking that all my numbered vouchers were there, since that opening match a couple of seasons earlier when I discovered at the turnstile that half of them were missing. Strange to think that in our three dismal relegation seasons of the nineties such tickets would be better value.

As it was, the writing was beginning to appear on the wall, although I can't claim to be amongst those few perceptive souls who began to mutter pessimistically about Clough's ability to keep us at the top. We hadn't threatened another Championship tilt, but neither had we been out of the top half. Our finish of "only" 8th at the end of 90/91 was disappointing, but it was one better than the previous season.

At this rate we'd be champions again in 1998/99, and we were – if you turned the League tables upside down.

The squad lacked strength in depth and we were reliant on a tiny nucleus of regulars, who more or less played every match, League and Cup alike. Looking back, it's a credit to all of them, whatever individual criticisms I may have made, to sustain such an effort.

It's hardly surprising that we looked jaded in our final, and biggest, match of the season. The bare statistics of first class matches played are as follows, predominantly shared out amongst just 16 players, with a few bit part contributions :-

Crossley (54), Chettle (53), Walker (52), Clough (52), Pearce (49), Parker (48), Keane (48), Crosby (39), Laws (35), Jemson (30), Hodge (24), Wilson (23), Carr (18), Charles (16), Woan (13), and Gaynor (13). Only Glover, with 9 appearances, otherwise threatened double figures, and 7 players just about managed every game, with 2 or 3 not far behind.

Our total playing staff was about half the bodies on the bench at a current big match – just what do all those masticating clones, with their sponsors tracksuits, actually do, apart from meticulously turn the logos on their drinks bottles in the direction of the TV cameras?

Roy Keane's contribution was nothing short of phenomenal, and begs the question as to what might have happened if we hadn't struck gold that season. Clough threw the young Irishman in at the deep end at Anfield in only our second League game, and the radio reported our new find as having a highly promising debut.

Within a couple of weeks of seeing him I was proclaiming that we'd discovered one of the greatest stars in Forest's history, and by the end of his first English season he was nationally acclaimed. Keane was the find of this, or almost any, season, but I can't quite find a place for him in my player profiles as he was on his bike before we experienced his full potential. Suffice it to say that he'd make most Manchester United top tens.

The season was notable for some bizarre happenings, if not for any consistent – FA Cup excepted – run of form. In the League we had a 2-2 at Coventry, with both Sky Blue goals coming from the penalty spot, and another missed.

We beat Norwich City away 6-2, and home 5-0, the latter coming straight after consecutive 4-0 and 7-0 wins against West Ham and Chelsea respectively. We were caught up in the Chelsea support on Lady Bay Bridge afterwards, and they were great, taking the proverbial out of their own side, and chuffed that we'd thumped West Ham in the Cup.

Our League Cup defence ended in equally strange fashion, and again Coventry were involved. We overcame Burnley and Plymouth before a visit to Highfield Road gave the Sky Blues a chance of revenge for last season's semi final.

Coventry went berserk, going an incredible 4-0 up with just over half an hour gone. Amazingly, we pulled it back to 4-4, with Clough getting a hat trick, before the abject despair of a Coventry winner, and goodbye League Cup. I'd been convinced that history was about to repeat itself, and that for the second time we were fated to appear in three successive League Cup finals.

Barnsley knocked us out of the Zenith Data Systems Cup, 2-1 at Oakwell on January 30th – what a blow that was – and only one path to Wembley lay open. It was also our only chance to salvage something from what was apparently to be another mediocre season.

We were tired of the same old headline, but surely it might happen one day :-

Would this be Cloughie's FA Cup year?

FA Cup 1991 – Wembley at last

Our 1991 FA Cup campaign got off to an inauspicious start when we were drawn away at Selhurst Park against Crystal Palace in the 3rd Round.

Palace were always a tough nut to crack and their South Norwood location was a pig of a place to get to from Nottingham. A dull nil-nil draw vindicated my decision to stay at home, although it was never really in doubt, with kick off put back 24 hours to accommodate live TV coverage.

There then followed an extraordinary, probably unprecedented in the British game, sequence of postponements, due to three different extremes of weather.

I was half way out of the front door – literally – for the first scheduled replay, fully kitted out against the unrelenting heavy rain, when a 'phone call from my father in law, George, announced that it had just been called off due to a waterlogged pitch.

Second time round, heavy frost penetrated deep into the playing surface, but at least the postponement was early enough this time to save the Palace support from another wasted trek.

Third attempt, and the match was actually played, but Mark Crossley spoiled our premature celebrations by conceding a last minute equaliser. His mishit clearance found a Palace player who superbly returned it straight back over Crossley's head and into the Trent End net. No-one could break the deadlock in extra time, but Forest's double headed coin - with Stuart Pearce remembering to call "heads" – won us another home replay.

We drove down in perfect conditions, parked, and met a thick blanket of fog as we approached Lady Bay Bridge. The ground was enveloped in a filthy, impenetrable, murk, and after a reasonable delay the referee had no choice but to call it off. I barely made out a small group of Palace fans in the gloom, but their chants of "Eagles, Eagles" were almost immediately followed by a large splash, and we never saw or heard from them again.

It's impossible to legislate for fog, especially of the swirling and malevolent "now you see it, now you don't" variety, and conditions were infuriatingly perfect, and remained so, no more than a mile from the ground. By the time I'd returned home, the view from the lofty heights of Carlton showed thousands of urban lights studding the Trent Valley, the fog having enjoyed its little joke, and scarpered.

After rain, ice, and fog, I half expected a plague of locusts to disrupt the fourth re-arrangement, but apart from a derisory moth we were spared, winning 3-0. Crosby's crisp drive into the Bridgford net, after a superb move, was the pick of the goals.

Even then, there was more drama to come. I arrived home to find my wife somewhat distraught, having summoned the Police following a disturbance, and apparent attempted break in, by intruders in the back garden.

Our Golden Retriever, Sally, although approaching veteran years – she finally reached a ripe old 16 – and soft as soap, had come to the rescue in an uncharacteristic display of ferocious canine protectiveness, and sent them packing over the fence. If only she'd dished out the same treatment to the neighbourhood cat population, instead of befriending every last one – not to mention the fox that used to kip under one of the shrubs.

Palace in the 3rd round had packed in more incident than we'd had in 5 consecutive years back in the early 80s, and we hadn't even been knocked out yet. Needless to say, our 4th Round tie, away at Newcastle, was postponed – I think, just for a day, due to ice – and Forest were also slow starters, only just pulling it back, from 2-0 down.

The equaliser came with barely a minute left. I was listening on the radio, and had given it up as a lost cause, when the commentator's voice took on a sudden shrill excitement :-

"And Clough's in the clear. He's through on goal. He's scored!!!"

I went demented, frightening the dog half to death, and began to anticipate victory in the replay, and through to the 5th Round. With two recent semi finals under our belts it might just be the year to go one better, and lay the ghosts of FA Cup failures past.

Mind you, watching the TV highlights I was glad that the linesman gave Clough the benefit of the doubt as he made his run onto Terry Wilson's through ball.

The replay was plain sailing, a surprisingly easy and low key 3-0, thanks to Hodge, Clough and Pearce, the latter two repeating their contribution at St James Park. I was relegated to the Bridgford End, accompanying two "out of town" visitors, a French lad on an exchange visit, and a certain Evertonian still smarting after the Southall debacle, and firmly rooting for Newcastle.

Next stop The Dell, and my brother travelled alone as "our" representative for the Monday night fixture. It was echoes of St James Park, with somewhat lucky Forest – we borrowed some off Arsenal that year – saving themselves thanks to a late Steve Hodge equaliser, and we were all set for yet another City Ground replay.

This time I stood in the Trent End, and saw Nigel Jemson, returning after injury, hit a storming hat trick in a 3-1 victory. I always thought that Jemson - strong, well built, skilful and two footed - had everything needed to become a memorable centre forward for the Reds, and the Southampton performance looked like the launching pad.

Clough thought otherwise – he always seemed to be at loggerheads with "big head" Jemson – and for whatever reason he left him on the sidelines again when we were crying out for someone up front capable of running at the opposition, or manufacturing a goal out of nothing. It might even have cost us the Cup.

The quarter final draw threw up a highly attractive fixture, away at Norwich. Carrow Road was a ground I hadn't visited, and anticipating a huge demand for Forest's allocation of some 6,000 I descended early on the City Ground, en route to work, on the first day of sale. Fortune smiled for once and I got 2 of the last half dozen seat tickets, before "Terrace only" was called, with huge queues still snaking back across the main stand car park.

The Norwich trip was one of those rare Reds excursions which was just about perfect. Accompanied by my brother, and in ideal, quiet, weather we set off early by car, scarves flapping as we headed for Gunthorpe Bridge, gateway to Norfolk.

Not a motorway in sight, and with Saturday relief from the weekday plague of lorries, the A17 and A47 were a comparative pleasure. We bowled along with a good number of fellow early rising Reds, like us looking to make the most of a trip to Norwich.

One look at the map reveals that, with the possible exception of Leicester, Forest were the most accessible top flight team in a huge triangle from Nottingham to Immingham and Kings Lynn, and the match day coach park used to bear witness to Reds from the likes of Newark, Grantham, Sleaford, Boston, Spalding, Skegness, etc.

Nowadays they stay at home, or the new generations support Manchester United, instead of their local non League club, which is particularly distasteful. At least the Reds were geographically logical, and most of the triangle (north of Spalding and Kings Lynn) spoke the same language.

Scunthorpe raised Kevin Keegan, for example, has an accent that could easily pass as typical Nottingham. It's fascinating how the East Midlands accent, presumably descending from a particular strain of Vikings – the main shopping street in Stockholm is called Drottinghamshavn, or something similar – extends in its narrowing triangle from the North Sea, south of the Humber estuary, picking up Nottingham, Derby and (just) Leicester, before turning West Midlands/Potteries.

Anyway, at the time that part of Eastern England was significantly pro Forest, and it felt like home territory, even as we skirted the Wash, picking up locally based buses full of travelling Reds.

Somewhere approaching Kings Lynn we passed a handicapped lad having the time of his life, sitting by the verge in his full Forest regalia, waving at the Reds support, and thrilled to bits when we hooted and waved vigorously back. Football was obviously a great therapy, and he couldn't have been more excited if he'd scored Forest's winner at Wembley.

Early arrival in Norwich – as planned, for once – saw us park centrally and easily, with loads of time to explore the attractive City centre, break for refreshments, and wander up to the Cathedral.

Having done, and thoroughly enjoyed, the touristy bit, we asked directions to Carrow Road of two formally dressed gentlemen walking purposefully across the Cathedral forecourt. They were Norwich supporters en route to the game, and immediately offered to walk down with us.

Further conversation revealed that it was no less than the Bishop of Norwich and his son, and that furthermore, and ominously for us, his Bishopness had yet to see Norwich lose that season. Was God, or fate, or both, on the side of the Canaries?

As a born again Atheist, but typical football supporter, I

felt an uncomfortable pang of superstition – maybe, there was a divine intervention at work, and it was to be the year of the Canary, and Robin Hood would have to flee back into Sherwood Forest, from where to emerge again when fate was smiling.

Funnily enough, Spurs fans were rabbiting on – it might have been Chas and Dave - about fate, convinced that their name had been on the Cup since the third round because it was 1991, one of their lucky and mathematically guaranteed years. What an absolute load of unadulterated crap.

Our hosts were excellent company, bidding us farewell and good luck outside the ground. Within minutes we'd exchanged our convivial pleasantries with the clergy for the gutteral chanting of the Forest masses squashed into narrow seats under a low and echoing roof – tremendous for atmosphere – and swaying in the tightly packed corner of away terracing down to our right.

Norwich's "end" occupied the rest of the terrace behind that goal, and for the first time that day I was aware that they had a hard core of yobs out for confrontation, but retained in check by a large Police presence and an even larger mesh fence partitioning the respective enclosures.

Forest's vocal support was at its best, and when Roy Keane put us ahead with a low scuffling shot our corner of Carrow Road exploded. The celebrations began, inspired by a Primary School standard forward roll by Keane after he scored – Peter Beagrie can sleep in comfort – and despite lots of huffing and puffing by Norwich I never felt that we'd let it slip.

We didn't, and about one minute into injury time I thought I heard a lone and plaintiff voice from the Norwich Directors Box :-

"Oh Father, why hast thou foresaken me?"

Rapturous celebrations at the final whistle.

A walk on air back to the car, where we demolish the last

of the food and drink. On with the radio, and the match report.

Two hours stuck in traffic before getting out of Norwich – who cares, it helps prolong the taste of victory.

The open road.

Drinks in Leadenham, joined by other returning Reds.

Back home for a couple of lagers and a re-run on Match of the Day.

Perfect.

Thank you, God.

West Ham in the semi final at Villa Park was a different prospect altogether. For a start, Birmingham isn't Norwich, and the short trip, through urban and industrial sprawl, is more of an irritation than a proper awayday.

I travelled with Bob, and we arrived in good time, parking within the shadows of the Gravelly Hill Interchange, a planning nightmare come true. An easy walk took us within a few hundred yards of the ground before we saw anything of the West Ham support. They weren't Norwich either, and didn't look likely to be intimidated or outshouted by the Forest contingent.

Our seats were in the upper tier behind the goal, opposite the Holte End with its huge expanse of terracing, possibly the biggest in England at the time, give or take Sheffield Wednesday. As usual for cup semis, it was split roughly 50/50, with the left side, as we faced it, a vibrant Red and White, contrasting with the dingy Claret of the Hammers.

The Hammers had the Main stand, and Forest the diddy one opposite, but on balance we seemed to have the best of the ticket allocation, including the lower tier at our end. The Claret half of the Holte terrace looked more packed than Forest's, and there was no doubting that the East Enders were up for it.

On the pitch, Forest, attacking our goal, were beginning to assert their authority, when West Ham's Gale was sent off for an innocuous foul on Crosby. It seemed to knock the stuffing out of the Hammers, whilst simultaneously arousing their fans to new heights of passion as they got behind their outplayed team.

Our support, despite the valiant efforts of a few determined would-be cheerleaders, was strangely muted, and failed to reach the crescendo I had expected, possibly due to its spread over three totally separated stands. Our end never got going, although Forest were running riot on the pitch.

Crosby – not the most popular player with the West Ham supporters – Keane, Pearce and Charles – not the most popular player with the Forest supporters – all scored once as we overwhelmed them in the second half on a surprisingly heavy and "patchwork" surface.

One of my all time Forest ambitions, a glorious FA Cup semi final triumph, was actually happening, after more than 30 long years of disappointment, and I was ready to join 20,000 Reds in a rousing victory party.

It wasn't to be.

As Forest coasted it, the Hammers fans, in a defiant, rousing, and sustained chant of "Billy Bonds Claret army" raised the roof for an unbroken last 10 minutes and I for one was bloody annoyed.

West Ham fans had "got their noise in first", completely unprecedented and unrelenting, and had gatecrashed and spoilt our party, just as it was about to gather momentum. It took the wind out of our sails.

Nevertheless, the final whistle was greeted with a huge roar from the Reds fans, and my hands were sore by the time our victorious heroes had finally disappeared into the dressing room.

Wembley, here we come!

Spurs were the other half of the 1991 Cup Final, and the papers were full of it being their year – hadn't I heard something similar before?

Obtaining tickets, courtesy of our season ticket vouchers, proved relatively easy, in terms of there being enough to go round, but a painstaking process of recording names, addresses, etc, in an attempt to stifle the black market, made the actual purchase agonisingly slow.

Forest had posted regular, idiot proof, notices in programmes and local papers, but it was still beyond the intellectual capacity of some.

"Do we need the actual vouchers?"

Girl at ticket window – "Yes, please"

"'Ere, Steve, I said we did"

"Well you've gorr'em – they're in yer jacket pocket"

"'Ang on"

Produces vouchers, after much fumbling about, and dropping of about £10 in loose change onto the floor.

"'Ere y'are, duck"

"You've not filled them in"

Fumbles about, and produces pen.

"'Ang on, this dunt write"

Girl at ticket office produces pen, and vouchers are slowly completed.

"What's yer post code, Steve?"

"Doesn't matter", insists the girl at the window, in a schoolteacher type "you're the 50th today" kind of voice.

"Which part of the ground?", she enquires.

"'Ere, Steve, where are we sitting?"

Much agonising and studying of plans of Wembley, and comparative prices, before Steve actually makes a sensible comment :-

"Don't want to sit behind a post"

Sensible, but given the antique nature of our National Football Slum, difficult to guarantee, unless you sat in the shallow lower tier of plastic squares, in which case you could see bugger all thanks to the low level view and a bloody great perimeter fence.

Ten minutes later, transaction somehow completed, Steve and colleague triumphantly leave the scene :-

"Wemberley, Wemberley……."

It was sometimes a similar story on City Ground match days. At the time, Bob and myself occupied seats 82 and 83, row 11, Block J. Suddenly, a couple of lost souls would stumble along our row, looking puzzled, before re-examining their tickets.

"Is this Block "C", row 22, seat 51?"

"No, this is J,11,82"

Blank look.

"You want Block "C" for Block "C". It's between "B" and "D". This is "J". It says so on the entrance."

"What row is this?"

"Eleven. It says so. Look."

"Where's 22?"

"Go and find Block "C" first. Then look for row 22. It should be between 21 and 23. Then look for the seat numbers. They're on the back of the seat. 51 should be after 50, but before 52, unless you're walking in the other direction. Tell you what, ask that steward."

All painfully reminiscent of my first efforts on a computer a year or so back, so I shouldn't mock. Anyone watching me painstakingly type this text, or curse in blind outrage when "Word 97" decides to do its own bloody minded and inexplicable thing again, would no doubt pass similar comment.

The main thing was that I finally had the definitive dream ticket – Nottingham Forest F C, appearing in the Football Association Challenge Cup Final on May 18th 1991 against Tottenham Hotspur F C.

My brother, a non season ticket holder due to frequent Saturday working, managed to acquire a ticket late on, and arrangements were duly cemented for him to travel down with us.

The great day dawned grey and murky, and stayed that way, but our car was brightly festooned in red and white, including a debut UK appearance of a Forest souvenir flag from my Tokyo trip. (I should have known better – we lost that one, too).

Resolved to extract every last drop from Forest's Cup Final day, we were well down the M1 by 9am, surprised at the early volume of Reds traffic, which was diluted by occasional northern based Spurs followers. We passed a packed and arthritic coach, boldly proclaiming "Forest on tour", spluttering along asthmatically in clouds of belching black diesel at all of 20 mph. At that rate it must have been en route since about 2am, and might just about make Wembley by kick off.

We were there just after 10am, and in the absence of any pre-conceived plan – especially after the last visit – just kept going until we were scarcely 100 yards from the Twin Towers. I spotted a wide and empty forecourt on the left, and pulled onto it, suspicious that the incredible absence of any parking restrictions or other vehicles must be a trap.

We checked and double checked that it wasn't, and dropped anchor. Within minutes fellow Reds were following our example, and we soon had a forecourt full of late breakfasting Reds.

We tubed into the West End, skirting the semi-deserted stadium, and wary of the scattered groups of Spurs fans desperate for tickets, thanks to the traditional and scandalous "touts charter" allocations. Whenever we were approached we quickly replied "just about to ask you the same question", which even gained a sympathy vote as we'd journeyed all the way down from north of Watford.

As we surfaced from the tube station into the West End Bob commenced a sneezing bout that lasted, off and on, and despite medication from a sympathetic pharmacist, until we were halfway back up the M1.

There was a thick, grey-yellow murk hanging over the capital, visible in my rear mirror as we left "The Smoke" behind after the game, and I reckon it must have triggered Bob's hay fever.

He was to see the game through tear stained eyes – as were most of us by the final whistle – and sneeze his way through half a dozen packets of Kleenex. We even thought about having him auditioned in Theatreland for Snow White and the Seven Dwarfs. (No prizes for guessing which part).

Having done the West End, and enjoyed a pub lunch in Chinatown, we arrived back at Wembley to find it transformed. The whole area was heaving, and I couldn't wait for Forest to win the FA Cup.

Cloughie held hands with Terry Venables as the teams came out, but I don't think there was anything in it, and there was certainly no fraternising on the pitch.

"Psycho" put us ahead with a typical, fiercely curling free kick, aided and abetted by a crafty Steve Hodge nudge in the Tottenham wall, but that was as close as it came to my dream coming true.

The inadequate refereeing of Mr. Milford, unwilling to deal with the manically wound up Gascoigne, was shameful, and begs the question as to why referees are rarely subject to retribution by the authorities in the way that players are.

Spurs were allowed to substitute England's favourite cheeky chappie after he'd committed his second blatant and entirely unprovoked sending off offence. The infamous Mark Dennis got banned for weeks for less, although he was of course guilty of being less "gifted", and played for less fashionable clubs.

It's football's equivalent of Tennis's "John McEnroe syndrome" – he should have been sent packing after his first on court tantrum – and West Ham's Gale, if he was watching, must have wept in despair.

Miraculously, neither Parker nor Charles were injured by Gascoigne's assaults, but he shouldn't even have been on the field to commit the second offence, and ironically was the main victim – apart from it probably costing Forest the Cup – of Milford's nightmare.

The pattern of the game after we scored was one of Spurs becoming increasingly dominant, helped by the travesty of Gascoigne's substitution. Once Paul Stewart – another one near the top of my Graham Souness led scrapbook of all time favourites – broke clear down the right and scored with a precision shot I knew it wasn't our day.

Crossley's penalty save from Gary Lineker gave us brief hope, but with Forest, and supporters, drained, extra time saw the unfortunate Des Walker head the Spurs winner neatly into his own net.

But for a couple of "For Christ's sake hit it!" half chances falling late on to Clough, and Clough dribbling and losing it instead, that was that.

With Bob's nose lighting the way like a beacon, the final whistle saw us slip quickly and quietly away down Wembley's dingy steps, too dispirited to wait to applaud the Reds off. We found sanctuary back at the car and comfort in the remains of our respective food parcels.

Passing Spurs fans took the proverbial, and also some of our food - by invitation, and to their surprise, after they'd cheekily asked us, but it's doubtful if Messrs Milford and Gascoigne, the bastards in the black, and white, respectively, would have been invited to tea.

Arriving home knackered I was left to ponder how, after every away trip, the interior of the car looked as if a family of East European refugees had been stowed away for weeks. Like Mr Milford's 1991 FA Cup Final decisions, it was inexplicable.

~

Des Walker

Des Walker's decisive own goal in the 1991 FA Cup Final was the first time I'd seen him put the ball in the back of the net. His attempt to head the ball behind for a corner saw it cruelly sail past Mark Crossley and the unfortunate Walker finished on the scoresheet at last, but for the wrong reason.

It was his penultimate season for the Reds, following his debut at home against Everton on March 14th 1984, since when he'd become something of a local legend, not just for his defensive prowess, but for his inability to score a goal.

The young Londoner had played his first senior game at full back, before more or less disappearing until season 1985/86, when he stepped into Chris Fairclough's shoes, and almost immediately became a revelation in his new central defensive role.

Like Fairclough, to whom he'd played second fiddle, his strengths were his pace, and an ability to read potential danger and snuff it out with the minimum of drama. Fairclough was a decent player, but Walker proved to be truly exceptional, and by Christmas 1985 the number 4 shirt was his property.

"You'll never beat Des Walker" was not just a Trent End (and subsequently Hillsborough) chant, but almost a statement of fact. Walker saved Forest's bacon time and time again with vital interceptions and tackles, appearing from nowhere when a goal seemed inevitable.

He usually played alongside a conventional centre half, such as Colin Foster, Carl Tiler or Steve Chettle, although he also featured in a lightweight pairing with Chris Fairclough. Walker was the quickest defender I've seen in a Reds shirt and his lightning pace and reactions on the ground complemented the aerial strengths of his partners.

One typical scenario sums up his staggering ability to

rescue us from disaster :-

Opposition striker bursts clear on goal, mentally celebrating his imminent finish past the exposed keeper. Walker, who isn't even the nearest Reds defender, arrives from nowhere in a blistering burst of acceleration and, immaculately as ever, toe pokes the ball cleanly away just as it's about to be slotted into the net. The gobsmacked striker can only curse in frustrated amazement.

There's surely been no better exponent at Forest of how to play as the last line of defence. "Where the hell did Walker come from", became a cliché for Reds and opposition fans alike.

I would expect most fans to name him in any Forest top ten over the last 30 years, and deservedly so, but the bizarre anomaly is that he never seemed comfortable, at least to me, in possession, or kicking the ball.

I'd go as far as to say that when it came to taking a place kick I'd put him at number eleven in most teams. His method of hitting a dead ball looked clumsy, even amateurish, and his stirring runs upfield, roared on by an expectant crowd, always looked out of control, as evidenced by their usual anti climactic conclusion.

He jogged on tiptoe in the warm ups, a most unlikely and unconvincing, almost mincing, style that was an incongruous contradiction with his rocket powered surges once the game was underway.

Superb timing and an unflappable temperament kept him out of trouble with referees and opponents alike, and despite a phenomenal number of crucial challenges in the box, I can't remember him conceding a penalty. (That's not to say he didn't, before anyone writes).

A strange thing happened on New Year's Day 1992. Des Walker scored a goal for the Reds, a late equaliser in a one all City Ground draw against Luton.

It meant that his total of one goal, in his last season with

Forest, was his best ever, and was maybe the confidence booster that prompted him to leave for Italy at the end of the season.

Along with Roy Keane and Teddy Sheringham, who were also to depart for pastures new, he'd been valiantly papering over the cracks in a weakening Reds squad, but Serie A exposed his lack of pure footballing ability, as I predicted it would.

He was absolutely magnificent, game after game, in his role at Forest, for which he was perfect, and quickly recovered from his Italian nightmare to pick up where he left off, just 40 miles up the road at Sheffield Wednesday.

He spent 8 years with the Reds, and his place in Forest supporters affections hasn't diminished, as evidenced by his welcome on Trentside whenever he's returned with the Owls.

~

Season 1991/92 saw a generally mediocre squad flatter to deceive, with an 8th place finish in the League, a 6th round FA Cup appearance, and yet another League Cup Final. Those bare statistics hide the fact that only Pearce, Walker, Keane and Sheringham were top quality, and all bar Pearce would soon be gone.

With Crossley lacking consistency, and Gary Charles and Carl Tiler hardly inspirational, Pearce and Walker had their work cut out in defence. Roy Keane had midfield support from Scot Gemmill, with contributions from Kingsley Black and Ian Woan, whilst up front it was usually Crosby, Clough and Sheringham.

Sheringham top scored in the League with 13 from 39, followed by Keane and Gemmill, both with 8 from 39. Pearce, Woan and "our number 9", Clough Jnr, came next with 5 each.

Injury and tactical uncertainty saw additional appearances by Chettle (17), Glover (12), Laws (10), Wassall (10), Brett Williams (9), 6 apiece from Jemson and Marriott, and 5 each from Parker and Orlyggson. A certain S. Stone played once, in our final League game, a 3-0 defeat at West Ham.

Looking back, it's a wonder that we did so well, and little wonder that next season, without Des and Teddy, and with Brian sadly past his prudent retirement date, would be a disaster.

As it was, we were still too good for the feeble Pies, stuffing them 4-0 at Meadow Lane on August 24th, in what was to prove probably the highlight of the League season. Lucky Notts scraped a 1-1 at the City Ground in the return on January 11th before our best home crowd of the season, an amazing 30,168, well up on the likes of Liverpool, Man Utd and Arsenal.

Our charge (if that's the right word) to the 6th round of the FA Cup was as flattering as our League position, the Reds coming out of the hat first against a trio of lowly opponents, before a fourth, Portsmouth, had the audacity to draw home advantage.

We struggled past Wolves 1-0 in the 3rd round, thanks to Clough's late goal, Hereford 2-0 thanks to Pearce and Sheringham, and again after an undignified struggle, and Bristol City with a comfortable looking 4-1 (Clough, Pearce, Sheringham and an own goal).

Thoughts were turning to the possibilty of a second successive FA Cup Final – after all, that was the pattern with the League Cup – and just maybe Brian Clough's name was at last on the world's most famous Cup.

I didn't go to Fratton Park for the 6th round, and our expected march into the semis - even if, as some pessimists predicted, it might take a replay. I'd been to that corner of Hampshire before, in our 2nd Division days. "Rough" was an understatement.

"Rough" would be just one assessment of Forest's feeble performance, calling on our traditional reserves of incompetence in the Cup against supposedly inferior opposition. Mark Crossley was the unfortunate villain of the piece, dropping a tame centre from the right onto the feet of a Pompey player, who couldn't believe his luck, and tapped home the winning goal.

The semi derelict Fratton Park exploded, and so did Forest's FA Cup dream. Yet another disappointment for Brian – and the rest of us - and maybe, coupled with the frustration of the Spurs Cup Final defeat, it was partly instrumental in him deciding to have one more, ill advised, crack at another season, with the saddest of consequences.

Pompey went out in the semi final at Highbury against Liverpool, robbed by a piece of Scouse chicanery. Liverpool were awarded a direct free kick some yards outside the penalty area, and in typical and well practiced fashion – I've seen it time and again against the Reds – they smartly plonked the ball down right on the edge of the box.

Equally typically, the weak referee let them get away with it, John Barnes scored direct, the commentator went into raptures, and I sat screaming at the TV in pointless outrage :

"Look at that, the bastards have done it again, and no-one's noticed."

Lynn told me to calm down, and went on about something to do with men never growing up, whilst I quietly seethed. The newspapers were full of John Barnes magic the next day, but if I'd been writing the headline it would have been "Pompey are cheated".

If I remember correctly, they were a goal up at the time, with only a few minutes left, but it seemed too good to be true, and I knew that Liverpool would somehow fluke it – or worse. They shaded it, predictably, after extra time.

I remember them once taking a free kick – I think Dalglish had fallen over – at the City Ground, some 15 yards ahead of the incident, with a moving ball, and whilst the ref was still lecturing the would be Reds defender. Needless to say, they were allowed to play on, exploiting a non existent Reds defence, and almost scored.

I suppose it's all part and parcel of the winning mentality, but without wanting to sound too sanctimonious I can honestly say that I was proud of the high standards set by Brian Clough, without compromising a fiercely competitive approach. Messrs Lloyd, Burns and Pearce are three examples that immediately spring to mind.

As for the League Cup, we just couldn't help ourselves, and arrived at Wembley yet again, this time to meet Manchester United. En route we overcame Bolton, 9-2 on aggregate (4-0 at home, 5-2 in the second leg), Bristol Rovers 2-0 at home, Southampton 1-0 at the Dell after a goalless affair at the City Ground, and Crystal Palace, also in a replay, 4-2, after a 1-1 at Selhurst park.

That left Spurs in the semi final, and for the second time in the League Cup we came up trumps at White Hart Lane, 2-1 in a tense affair after a 1-1 on Trentside.

I went with Bob to Wembley, but I don't think he was relishing it any more than me. It had been obvious from when I first purchased the tickets that United fans would be intermingled in some numbers with Reds fans, not just because many had apparently engineered the use of Forest tickets or vouchers to claim an allocation from the club, but also from the number of "tickets wanted" adverts in the local press.

Given that the latter scenario would be reflected nationally, and that hordes of London based Man U fans would be using their local connections, it was obvious that Reds supporters would be heavily outnumbered.

I wouldn't have minded if we'd been playing, say, Spurs, Chelsea or Arsenal, but the thought of the bloke round the corner hitting the road in his latest Manchester United kit annoyed the hell out of me.

I might have overdone the anti Notts wind-up (it's not meant to be taken too seriously, please!), but Magpies fans are the essence of local pride in football, from where stems the game's history and tradition.

They can wear their shirts with pride, all the more despite being heavily outnumbered in the streets of Nottingham – as are Reds fans, these days – by the "look at me, I'm a Manchester United supporter" brigade. Instant "success" and gratification are the curse of the modern game and many of its bandwagon followers.

After all, if my father had messed up my own football upbringing, I'd be defiantly singing the Wheelbarrow song, (the thought makes my blood run cold) but at least I'd have saved a fortune on big match tickets and Wembley trips.

As it was, Bob and I found ourselves sitting on a wall within walking distance of Wembley Stadium, eating our lunch surrounded by clusters of "gor blimey" accented "Mancunians".

Coach after coach streamed by, unashamedly displaying their banners, testimony to local betrayal from the West Midlands, Norfolk, London, the West Country, and even the East Midlands and Yorkshire.

It was a case of "spot the Reds fan", although Forest's 25,000 or so were thankfully in evidence as we worked our way round to our end of Wembley. So were an alarming number of Man Utd followers, queuing at our turnstiles.

There was little expectancy or sense of occasion, but a tangible undercurrent of hostility, heightened by the usual excesses of alcohol in the wrong hands. Backstage Wembley seemed even more squalid and dingy than usual, with sporadic trouble already breaking out.

We were glad to take our seats, knees wedged under our chins, necks craning for a view of the pitch around an obstructing pillar, in the familiar surroundings of our National Hovel. Thankfully, we were a few rows away from the nearest trouble – although not the nearest Man U contingent – but were continually distracted by the nearby aggravation and baiting, which broke out in vicious fighting in the toilet and refreshment area at half time.

I was glad to hear the full time whistle, less upset at our one nil defeat in a disappointing game than concerned to scarper quickly back to the car.

I believe passionately that opposing fans should mix freely and peacefully, but there's something about the worldwide legions of Man U followers that gets up the noses of supporters from every other club in the land.

I've sat alongside Leicester fans at the City Ground and shared an afternoon of friendly banter and rivalry, but that League Cup final did nothing to allay my dislike of those Sharp billboards parading the streets of Nottingham.

That was it then – not a bad season by recent standards, but for those who could read the writing on the wall, the warning was clear – "Beware of relegation".

Skittles

As a diversion from the intensity of the first time matches I lent my support to the Forest Youth team for a 2 legged Youth Cup semi final and had an experience of near tragedy that turned into black farce.

If I remember correctly, the opposition was Arsenal. I know that we lost over the two legs and that Reds would be hero Lee Glover attempted to run the show, and failed miserably.

I was with my brother, and we were returning home across Trent Boulevard towards Sneinton Dale. Cars were double parked, and an oncoming motorist flashed to let me through. Into second gear, accelerating uphill, when a little lad raced out from the left from behind one of the parked vehicles. He'd run full pelt, as I discovered afterwards, down the gitty and straight across the road.

There was no time for anything but a shocked gasp and a ferocious stamp on the brake pedal, by which time he'd already smacked into the passenger wing. I couldn't have been doing more than 15 or 20 mph, which sounds negligible. It isn't. The impact sent him into a somersault over the bonnet before he crashed down into the road in front of us.

"Shit, shit, shit".

I didn't want to get out of the car. The stomach churning shock that he was dead, or at best critically injured, was a hammer blow from nowhere. A split second had changed the world.

My brother got to him first, just in time. The little so and so was getting to his feet and was about to scarper, shocked and shaken, having miraculously landed on his shoulder. He was destined to be a stuntman.

He lived just around the corner, and we took him home. His parents weren't exactly hysterical with concern. He was cut and bruised, but we were worried that he might be suffering from shock, or even concussion. We needn't have been. When we suggested a medical check we were immediately reassured :-

"It's alright, he's been knocked down before. He's always dashing out into the road without looking".

That was OK then. He couldn't possibly be seriously hurt. No problem.

Next, report to the Police. Also, no problem.

By a bizarre coincidence a Police car was parked at the bottom of the road. Two uniformed officers occupied the front seats. A young man in plain clothes sat in the back.

I approached, and attracted the driver's attention. He wound down the window and glared at me.

"We're busy." (Local Constabulary-speak for "Can I assist you, sir?" – he didn't even know we were football supporters).

"Sorry, but I've just knocked a little boy over, just up the road."

"Yes, and we're in the middle of an arrest."

They both glared at me.

"Well, aren't I supposed to report it to the Police?"

"Is he injured?"

"Just cuts and bruises, I think, but he might be in shock. We've taken him back home. Just up there, if you want to call in."

They didn't.

All I wanted to do was record the incident, just in case – not to mention the legal requirement – and go home. They had other things to do.

Their "other thing" sat sullen and disinterested whilst I suggested taking my licence down to the Nottingham Central Police station on Monday (I hardly ever carry it with me, unless I'm driving abroad), which visibly cheered the officers.

I left them to their arrest and duly called in to make my report a couple of days later.

At the next home match I dropped by to check that the lad was OK.

He's fine, thanks. He's out playing."

With the traffic, no doubt.

~

1992/93 – End of an era

1992/93 was a watershed.

It was Brian Clough's last season.

It was Forest's first drop from the top flight in 16 memorable, unprecedented, seasons.

It was my last one as a season ticket holder.

We all knew that Clough couldn't go on for ever, and those who said he should already have stepped down were to be proved right.

Those who predicted at the end of August – i.e. my fellow Exec Upper ticket holder, Bob – that we'd be relegated were initially considered some sort of village idiot, and a particularly disadvantaged one at that. He might as well have claimed that Lord Lucan and Shergar were living together in his garden shed.

I took his words as typically provocative mischief, but Bob is nothing if not astute, and by mid September I was a convert.

Yet it all started so brightly.

Liverpool at home first match. August 16th, the Summer holidays in full swing, and an expectant shirt sleeved full house, albeit a miserly 20,038. The deserted Bridgford End rose in steep tiers of grey concrete, splashed red with clusters of shiny plastic seats, its highest reaches overhung by the steel claws that would counterbalance the roof.

I was transfixed by this imposing, compelling, structure, which throughout the match inexorably drew my gaze. I'd followed its construction during the close season, trespassing on site to sneak tantalising glimpses of our new stand.

I received for my pains dirty looks from the suspicious contractors, mistaking me for one of the group of local residents who'd reported them for working outside their officially sanctioned hours.

Our new Bridgford stand sparked in me a latent interest in stadia construction, and I even found myself wandering around Meadow Lane as Notts set an example to everyone by transforming a dump into a first class stadium, on a limited budget.

I've spent the odd lunchtime watching Nottingham's new ice stadium grow from the rubble, and have photographed Notts CCC's superb new grandstand, so I suppose I've qualified for my anorak.

As Burt Reynolds so succinctly put it in "Deliverance" - "Insurance – shit", but not everyone can be a sports architect, especially those like me who don't have any talent, but I can still stand in awe at our century's cathedrals of worship.

I leapt to my feet in awe when Teddy Sheringham scored the game's only goal, fittingly in front of that wall of concrete, and we went home on top of the world.

We were philosophical after we lost our next two, 2-0 at Sheffield Wednesday and 5-3 at Oldham, but then Clough dropped a bombshell that led to Bob's doomsday prediction and, in later years, newspaper allegations concerning Brian, Terry, and a "bung". Teddy Sheringham, reported as being homesick for London, was suddenly transferred to Tottenham without a credible replacement in sight.

Even without the benefit of hindsight our squad looked threadbare, with the lack of quality up front almost insulting. Clough fulfilled an ambition by bringing the veteran Gary Bannister to the City Ground, failing to catch the elusive – at least, off the pitch – Dean Saunders. We'd save him for another rainy day.

Despite having a miserable time, Bannister still finished second top scorer, with 8 in 27. Clough came top with 10, including 3 penalties, in a full house of 42. The young Roy Keane, already a cut above the rest, was next, with 6 from his 40 midfield appearances.

Stuart Pearce wasn't at his best, retiring through injury, to Clough's alleged anger, with almost half the season still to go, and Steve Stone, performing heroics in the reserves, was mysteriously thrown in far too late, when we were as good as sunk.

That left Crossley, Laws, Chettle, Crosby, Gemmill, Woan, Black, Orlygsson, Tiler, Charles, Glover, Rosario, Webb and Williams who more or less completed the season's squad, give or take the odd bit part. Hardly inspirational.

Terry Wilson's career was cut short after just 5 games, through injury, but I could never manage even 1% of Forest's oft stated belief in his potential, and his demise, though a personal tragedy, made no difference to our relegation battle.

Similarly, I failed to share the general enthusiasm for Brian Laws who, like the blessed Nigel, could give the ball to the opposition time and time again, with scarcely a murmur. On one occasion Clough gave the ball away five times in succession and no-one else noticed. Gemmill did it once and there was outrage.

"Get off the field, you're bloody crap, Gemmill", was one of the kinder comments, bawled out from somewhere behind my left ear. The lightweight Gemmill was a luxury we could ill afford in a relegation battle, managing one derisory goal in 33 League appearances, but he didn't deserve the vicious abuse of the barrackers. Apart from anything else, it only helps the opposition.

Clough's philosophy seemed to be to stick with what we'd got – the "you've got us into this mess, now get us out" principle.

It might also have been the case that his clearly failing health, and eccentric mannerisms, as Forest fell further into the mire, were hardly an advert for incoming quality players. All very sad.

By October 17th, when we lost at home, "one nil, to the Arsenal", with Gunners tackles crashing in unpunished from behind, coupled with synchronised arm hoisting, even the clearly befuddled Clough could surely see that we simply had to improve the team. In the 10 matches since that balmy opening day we'd drawn three and lost seven.

A short reprieve, courtesy of a one nil home win against Middlesbrough, was followed by another five without a win, including three defeats.

The unthinkable was thinkable – we were going down, I say we were going down.

The Forest management were like frozen rabbits in the headlights of the Relegation Express. Brian had clearly lost the plot, a forlorn figure on the bench, drained by the pressures and excesses of too many turbulent years in one of the most stressful jobs going.

The Directors were in an invidious position. Tolerant of Clough's eccentric, abrasive, dictatorship whilst we were riding the rollercoaster of success – although even then there was bitter resentment in some quarters – they daren't step in to forcibly remove the most successful manager in the club's history.

We'd finished 8th in the League last season, and reached another League Cup final, so if BC wanted another season in charge no one was going to argue, at least not in public. If the Directors had pushed him out the media would have had a field day, and there'd have been much airing of dirty linen, not to mention outrage from the fans.

If his replacement had kept us one point from relegation it would have been considered abject failure – "Bring back Brian", "It wouldn't have happened under Cloughie", "Heads must roll." The decision had to be Brian's.

As the months ticked by, and our plight became ever more desperate, an alarming number of fans still couldn't accept the situation :-

"Brian'll turn it round", "Cloughie knows what he's doing", "'E not lerrum gudahn".

The capacity for humans to attach unquestioning belief and commitment to their leaders never ceases to amaze and depress me. Even as Germany lay in ruins towards the end of World War 2 there were believers who "knew" with blind certainty that Adolf's secret weapon was about to turn the tide.

Our secret weapon was Robert Rosario, thrown into the fray for 10 League appearances at the tail end of the season, and inflicting damage to the tune of one solitary goal. Still, at least it counted, along with another from Kingsley Black, as we untypically secured maximum points with a 2-1 home defeat of Spurs on April 12th.

Typically, I was away on holiday, having donated my ticket to a work colleague, who told me that it wasn't a bad game. That meant that I'd missed a third of our decent home performances, counting Liverpool and Chelsea (3-0, on January 16th) as the other two. Our scrappy wins over Middlesbrough, Oldham and QPR were memorable only for the luxury of three points.

I remarked early in the season that defensively we weren't good enough to keep many clean sheets, and that we'd struggle to score more than once, which meant that we'd draw or lose a lot of low scoring encounters, and so it turned out.

There were 3 0-0s, 6 1-1s, 5 1-0 defeats, and 10 by 2-0 or 2-1, so we weren't being thrashed out of sight, it was just that we'd usually concede a minimum of one, and weren't generally capable of a potentially winning two. When we did, in a miserly 9 matches – that means a staggering, depressing, 33 games where we scored once, or not at all – we won 6 of them. If only we'd had a Stan Collymore.

We weren't going to have a Brian Clough after the season, but his belated confirmation that he'd be retiring failed to galvanize the Reds into the impossible – scoring often enough to give the defence a chance to concede one without knowing that it probably meant goodbye to three points.

I got absolutely pissed off and frustrated every time we let one in, thinking "that's it then, one point at best today", and trooping home dejected as my expectations were fulfilled.

Appropriately, it was the Blades who finally twisted the relegation knife, in our penultimate match, at an emotional and packed (26,752) City Ground on May 1st. It was the last occasion that Trentside would see that famous green tracksuit top and the media descended in droves, Clough more than ever before the focus of their intense glare.

He was a poignant and lonely contrast with the sunlit sea of red and white that had rapturously greeted his entrance from the tunnel, Sheffield United's huge support equally vociferous in their acclaim. Events on the field were a relative side-show, but ran true to form as Forest displayed their full repertoire of inadequacies, losing 2-0.

At the final whistle we drifted quietly away, sharing with a few hundred others a despondent disdain for the combined retirement party/relegation wake that followed. The chanting and singing faded away behind us, and a glance back from Lady Bay Bridge showed a thickening tide pouring out of the City Ground and streaming along the banks of the Trent.

There was the usual melee behind the Trent End as eastbound met westbound – Lady Bay versus Trent Bridge – and the scene reminded me of an ants nest, its inhabitants swarming out after an unseen thump from a giant's foot.

I watched the post match scenes on television, with Clough feted by the Trent End, itself a pale imitation of former glories. It was a sad finale, and the biggest mistake in Clough's Forest career was the timing of his retirement.

His last first team match was the following Saturday at Portman Road, where Ipswich fans paid tribute, the Suffolk club having enjoyed their own unlikely share of the big boys spotlight under the stewardship of the admirable Bobby Robson.

As Clough prepared for well deserved retirement Forest prepared for life in what used to be called the Second Division, and I prepared for life without a season ticket.

It was the end of a glorious, exhilarating, adventure.

After a period of intense speculation our new manager was announced, the unassuming and personable ex-Red Frank Clark, although the fans choice (and not for the last time) was for another ex-Red, Martin O'Neill.

Forest's best ever free transfer acquisition was to be less successful as manager, but was absolutely spot on in securing the key signing for our forthcoming promotion campaign.

Stuart Pearce

Early in Stuart Pearce's Forest career someone in the crowd, flinching at the sight of a typically "robust" tackle, must have voiced the thoughts of thousands :–

"That bloke's a psycho."

No doubt his mates joined in, and before long chants of "Psycho, Psycho" were to ring around the City Ground, Pearce acknowledging the Trent End, or our away support, with his trademark salute – arms aloft, fists clenched, face like Grant Mitchell on a bad day.

Pearce arrived from Coventry in a double swoop that also brought his team-mate, central defender Ian Butterworth. They made their debuts on August 7th 1985, along with our other new boy, Neil Webb, in the first match of the season, a 1-1 draw at all plastic, no away fans please, Kenilworth Road.

Pearce made a respectable start (Webb went one better, scoring our goal), and apart from injury was to wear Forest's number 3 shirt for the next 12 seasons, until the northern Magpies extended his Premiership career following our relegation season of 1996/97.

Like Garry Birtles he was a late starter. Pearce was an Electrician by trade, and part time footballer for non League Wealdstone, until Bobby Gould recognised his potential and unwavering commitment and snapped him up for Coventry City. Why they released him, I don't know, but we got the bargain of the decade.

Pearce took nothing for granted, continuing to advertise his electrical services in the Forest programme, and playing every match as if his life depended upon it. The latter trait never changed – apart from an indifferent spell during Brian Clough's final season – but the adverts were dropped and Pearce became 100% professional footballer.

He also displayed 100% professional attitude and quickly endeared himself with his bone crunching tackles, surging runs, and ferocious shooting, often performed in sequence as he turned defence into attack with an exhilarating one man rampage that lifted the team and crowd, and could change the tempo of a match in seconds.

All left foot, of course, but it's fair to say that only using his right one for standing on hasn't seriously diminished his career.

Pearce was Forest's Gladiator.

His pallid complexion belied huge reserves of stamina. Powerful thighs drove him forwards, and a single minded, fearless, commitment to the Reds cause raised our spirits, even on a crap day, and even when Pearce was having a bad game. He was an absolute cert to become club captain.

Supporters identify with a battler, and Pearce was that and far more besides, a Reds hero to stand comparison with Liverpool's Tommy Smith, "Chopper" Harris of Chelsea, Spurs Dave McKay or Wimbledon's Vinnie Jones – none of them endowed with the greatest of technical skills, but of an almost spiritual significance, and cult status on the terraces.

His early Reds days featured a glut of X-rated tackles, and the birth of that nickname, and word soon spread that Psycho took no prisoners. Any opponent wanting a seat for a Forest game had only to take him on to find himself unceremoniously deposited in row 13. It was enlightening to note which players, some with a reputation of their own, "disappeared" after a first encounter.

Liverpool's Danish Scouser, Jan Molby, of "brick outhouse" build, and with legs like pit props, stood his ground once and contested a 50/50 outside the Trent End penalty area. Both players went in like battering rams. The collision was nuclear, but there was only going to be one winner, and Psycho came away with the ball, to an explosion of acclaim.

His sledgehammer shooting was no less effective, and after he'd crashed in a couple of free kicks his dead ball specials became part of the folklore. He scored our only FA Cup final goal since 1959 – at least, at the right end – with a swerving 25 yard effort, but his best effort was possibly a blockbuster at Old Trafford in a League game.

At least 35 yards out, at the Stretford End, it seemed beyond even Pearce's prudent range, and his optimistic run up was accompanied by a crescendo of cat-calls, whistles and derision. Pearce responded by curling a screamer over the wall and into the top corner of the net, silencing the home support and triggering wild celebrations from the Reds behind the Scoreboard goal.

If he gave the opposition a hard time, he was never much trouble for referees, accepting his punishment for a mistimed tackle without question – that was almost the only offence of which he was ever guilty. Almost, but he uncharacteristically lost control against Middlesbrough at the City Ground, justifiably outraged as Ravenelli devoted his so called "talents" to a petulant, whingeing crusade to con the ref into booking the entire Forest team.

Ravenelli then hacked down a Forest player and Pearce theatrically waved an imaginary yellow card. The result - a booking for Pearce, and the guilty party got away Scot free. It was a distasteful pointer of things to come, as refereeing standards, apparently under some kind of senior "directive", plummeted to an all time low in an absurd orgy of card flourishing and banning of common sense. I'd ban those bloody cards, and John Motson would have to find something else to get hysterical about.

Nevertheless, Pearce adapted his game to the "cheats charter", no contact, regime – "It's football, Jim, but not as we know it" – and although sometimes vulnerable against a determined and pacy winger he's proved that he's still no mug, even well into his "veteran" years.

He's picked up the odd England cap, and the captaincy, along the way, not to mention the World Cup 94 and Euro 96 penalty dramas – missed one, scored one – but his biggest challenge is the broken leg sustained recently whilst playing for West Ham. As I type these lines, only time will tell whether he can make a full recovery, but time is unfortunately no longer on his side.

Off the field, his self conscious, hesitant, mumblings into the camera matured into assured comment, with dashes of dry humour, but despite exchanging jellied eels for mushy peas his accent hasn't got any better.

It was his signature that Frank Clark was after, not a speech, and Clark must have been doing mental cartwheels of delight when he committed himself to another season following our relegation in 1993, inspiring players and supporters alike to renew their allegiance.

His equalising close range header at Peterborough the following April set the scene for Collymore's stunning late winner, and our promotion back to the Premier League.

We've been privileged to have 2 legends at the City Ground in the modern era – Brian Clough was one, and Stuart "Psycho" Pearce was the other.

~

1993/94

The fixture list said it all – Southend, Derby, Grimsby, Crystal Palace, Luton, Barnsley, Stoke, Bolton, Portsmouth, Tranmere, Oxford, Leicester and Notts in successive League matches. Apart from a full complement of East Midlands derbies, which included the embarrassment of facing Notts on level terms, there was nothing to quicken the pulse.

I didn't renew my season ticket, but was glued to the TV for our opening fixture, at tiny Roots Hall, Southend, where our expected victory romp turned into a hard fought 1-1 draw. Our team was Crossley, Lyttle, Pearce, Cooper, Chettle, Stone, Black, Webb, Rosario, Glover and Woan, and it predictably took a defender, Stuart Pearce, to save our goalscoring blushes.

We drew 1-1 again in our first home League game, the Rams pulling in a crowd of 26,684. I wasn't tempted, but tuned in to our next live TV offering, on September 19th. Stoke were the City Ground visitors, the strains of "Delilah" ringing out from the Bridgford End as the Potters ran out 3-2 winners.

By the time we'd drawn 1-1 at home to Portsmouth on October 2nd our League record was dismal – played 9, won 2, drawn 3, lost 4 – relegation form. Time to make a personal appearance.

I'd relinquished my season ticket for a number of reasons, including the ever increasing cost, for a diminishing return, the luxury of having my weekends free, and, significantly, because Forest were making me miserable.

I was fed up of arriving home on Saturday evening thoroughly cheesed off, having effectively invested half my weekend in a ritual that was becoming more of a habit than enjoyment. I'd spent the last season gloomily anticipating relegation, and wondering why I bothered turning up.

Old habits die hard, and in my usual contradictory way, which even irritates me, so God knows what it's like for others, (as my wife frequently says, "you'll never hang yourself") I was already questioning whether I'd made the right decision. Other questions, such as :-

"Shall we go to Marks this afternoon?"

"When are you starting the decorating?"

"Don't you think it's time we thought about some new curtains?"

were also influential, and on October 16th I joined a friend, Ken, who'd got seats at the front of the Main Stand, in the Trent End corner. On a pleasant Autumn day it was bloody cold in that dark, draughty, spot, reinforcing my dislike for that side of the ground.

The opposition, Tranmere Rovers, although riding high in the table, weren't exactly a thrilling prospect, but one man stole the show, and warmed our hearts. An allegedly less than fully fit Stan Collymore scored one in our 2-1 victory, and maybe Forest's season was about to come alive.

We demolished the Pies 1-0 at home a couple of weeks later, the scoreline no reflection on our overwhelming superiority, and after a stutter against Millwall, losing 3-1 at home in our next match, we put together a storming run of 9 wins and 4 draws. Unfortunately, I picked one of the draws for my next visit, our New Years Day fixture against fellow promotion hopefuls Charlton Athletic.

With the Trent End redevelopment on hold, official ground capacity was approximately 28,000, but allowing for segregation, etc, the attendance of 26,543 was more or less a full house. It was one of six over 26,000, (Derby, Notts, Middlesbrough, Leicester and Sunderland were the others) and with most of the rest only a couple of thousand lower the City Ground still had a Premiership atmosphere.

I couldn't believe how frustrated and animated I became, nearly three months since my last visit, as Charlton rode their luck and escaped with a point, despite being outplayed for most of the game. The Reds looked re-born, and I made my mind up to be there if and when we clinched promotion.

We could give it our undivided attention after Tranmere Rovers knocked us out of the League Cup. We'd beaten Wrexham, West Ham and Manchester City, but didn't beat anyone in the FA Cup, losing the replay 2-0 against Sheffield Wednesday after Colin Cooper's last gasp equaliser at Hillsborough.

Another television Sunday saw us hammer the Foxes 4-0 at the City Ground, in a game memorable for a magnificent goal by Scot Gemmill, who superbly swerved a 35 yard drive straight back into the Bridgford net following a mishit clearance by the keeper. The Reds were beginning to look the part, after that dreadful start (David Platt, take comfort).

Meadow Lane next, on February 12th, and I was there, warming to our gathering Premier charge. 13 unbeaten, but Forest were awful, and a spirited Notts deservedly beat us, 2-1. I left the ground even more depressed than after the Charlton game, a harsh and chastising reminder of the paradox of still caring so much about Forest's fortunes – it hurt so much more when it all went wrong.

For our enigmatic, but exceptional, number 9, Stan Collymore, it could all go right and wrong within minutes. Deceptively laid back, he seemed to play when it suited him, missing games through injury and blowing hot and cold on the pitch. He seemed indifferent to any emotional attachment to the Reds cause, yet could explode in temper at the first provocation.

As our promotion push intensified, so did my commitment, my nomadic wanderings finding the upper tier of the Bridgford End, and a cracking view from the curving sweep that links it in with the Exec. (or rather, Brian Clough stand, as it's now called). It was March 19th, Bolton the visitors, and Stan waiting in the wings.

He' d been out through injury and only came on as second half substitute, with Forest struggling, and our promotion dash threatening to come off the rails against a battling Wanderers side. He appeared to a rapturous reception, immediately lifting the crowd, and the tempo of the game.

He scored with practically his first touch, latching onto a "route one" punt downfield from Mark Crossley and getting behind the suddenly flustered Bolton defence, to knock it into the Bridgford net. Minutes later, he was off the field again, summarily dismissed for elbowing an opponent, but during that brief, dramatic, appearance Stan turned the game, and we claimed all the points, with a 3-2 win.

Collymore was no doubt provoked, and if, as a colleague believed, he'd been spat at, then "illegal use of the elbow" was understandable. The problem was that everyone knew that he could be easily wound up, and used it to maximum effect. Even in our Tuesday 5 a Sides, the two "hard men" always concentrated their fiercest assaults where they knew they'd get the mardiest reaction – it finished in fisticuffs on several occasions.

Collymore returned from his suspension for our crucial game at fellow promotion hopefuls Millwall, and scored in a 2-2 draw, Steve Stone getting a late equaliser after Des Lyttle was sent off for nothing in particular. It was a terrific Forest performance, with Millwall fans sadly reverting to their infamous worst, screaming torrents of racial abuse at the players, and attacking Reds fans and vehicles.

It was the psychological turning point of the season, and showed that we weren't going to be intimidated by opposition teams or supporters, and I knew then that we'd be back. By the time we played Derby at the Baseball Stadium on April 27th a win would set us up for our promotion party at Peterborough next week. The Rams surprisingly put up little resistance, losing 2-0, and the champagne was on ice.

I'd had a look at our fixture list after the Bolton game, and predicted that Peterborough would be the promotion clincher, surprising for someone who came second bottom in our inter office pre season promotion/relegation predictions – Forest was just about the only one I got right.

I scrounged a couple of season tickets and was down at the City Ground the minute our allocation went on sale, and by Saturday April 30th I was a born again travelling Red.

A glorious sunny morning saw a middle aged resident of Arnold carefully stretching a large Nottingham Forest flag across the back window of his car before hanging a frayed scarf out of the passenger side, tightly knotting one end around the grab handle. His "best" scarf was laid conspicuously along the top of the rear seat, ready for wearing on arrival at Peterborough.

He picked up his work colleague, Tony, who was soon to move onto greener pastures, including work as stats man on Radio Nottingham's live Forest commentary (as in "we've had 68 minutes of play and Tony tells me that Forest have yet to test the keeper", or "bloody hell, is that a wasp?, I'm out of here.")

We followed the red and white flow east along the A52, sprinted down the A1, and became part of a carnival procession into Peterborough, parking easily in a side street and joining the masses of exuberant Reds already celebrating, 2 hours ahead of kick off.

Picnicking at the roadside, we were guests at a Nottingham street party, a slow tide meandering boisterously towards Peterborough's tidy and compact London Road ground, car horns and klaxons punctuating the general commotion.

"We are going up, I say we are going up!"

We settled on a spot just right of the goal, on shallow steps under the low canopy of what was now Peterborough's Trent End. It was heaving by kick off time, and a decent view was well nigh impossible.

It looked a similar story away to our left, with Forest support packed in on the open terracing. With a nucleus in the seats to our right, plus pockets dotted around everywhere else, it was as good as a home game, and we were as good as home, giving the Reds a storming reception as they trotted out.

The pitch was a credit to the groundstaff, more bowling green than tired, end of season, patchwork, and we prepared to roar the Reds back to the Premier. No chance of Posh spiking our guns on a dodgy surface.

With half time approaching we were swaying silently in stunned silence, Peterborough deservedly 2-0 up, and coming close to a third that would have seen us dead and buried. I was digesting the awful thought that 3 points from our last two games, Grimsby away and Sunderland at home, might not exactly be a doddle, and any less might not be enough, when Stan the Man suddenly pulled one back against the run of play.

From despair to jubilation in an instant, and with Forest surely pulling themselves together during the break we anticipated the victory onslaught. Forest pressed forwards, attacking our end, but roars of excited anticipation turned to desperate pleas for salvation as the minutes rushed by and we still couldn't break through :-

"Come on, we're losing!!!",

"For Christ's sake pass the bloody thing – left, man, left!!"

"Hit it!! – shit, why didn't he just hit it?"

As Forest's pressure mounted, their keeper came into his own, making a number of superb saves that he'd no right to. The result didn't matter to Peterborough, but no one would know – they treated it like their cup final.

We could only watch in exasperation, twitching and cursing in frustrated impotence as the game moved into its last quarter, and surging forwards in premature celebration as another effort was about to be beaten away.

Nothing outside of "real life" can, in my opinion, match the drama, emotional turmoil, and highs and lows that can be compressed into 90 minutes of football. It might "only" be a game, but without diversions from the humdrum – or worse – struggles of everyday life, be it sport, music, ballet, origami, or whatever, human society would die of boredom.

8,000 Forest fans were tearing their hair out in near despair, with about 10 minutes of our most crucial match of the season to go, devastated that an anticipated knees up to the Premier was slipping away.

For the umpteenth time, the ball came across the crowded penalty area, just a few yards in front of us. I think it was from a Reds corner, after another excellent save had intensified the agony, but I can't be sure – it had all become a blur of one way traffic. What I can remember is seeing the inspirational figure of Stuart Pearce getting his head to the ball, just a few yards out, watching it find the back of the net, and instinctively checking the ref's signal before, a split second later, going totally barmy in relief and delight.

It all happened within a couple of seconds, and we were transformed from abject wrecks into a chanting, singing, jubilant army, as Forest poured forwards for the winner that would surely come. It didn't, at least not until a precious few more minutes had ticked by, passions had subsided, and it was set to finish all square. Enter Stan.

He picked up the ball on the left edge of the penalty area. With no obvious options, and Peterborough's defence comfortably funneled back, he took a couple of paces, and suddenly exploded a ferocious angled shot into the opposite top corner of the net.

It would have been sensational in a pre season friendly, but in the context of our promotion clincher, with just a couple of minutes left, and after we'd trailed 2-0, it ranks second only to Ian Moore against Everton.

The Reds support went absolutely berserk.

Unfortunately, the eruption flowed over the barriers as hundreds of idiots poured onto the pitch, causing a lengthy delay before they were finally cleared back onto the terraces. At the final whistle, and despite pleas for common sense, over they came again, in droves, an unstoppable mass of infantile selfishness. They put paid to any chance of Forest acclaiming their support in a lap of honour, and deprived us of a climactic celebration of a wonderful footballing day.

I was furious and disgusted, as were many of the club officials and players, and we drifted quietly away, leaving a thinning rearguard to cheer the Reds when they finally made an appearance high in the safety of the stand - remote, static, but safe from the tossers on the turf.

Why do they do it? Just what is the point? It's not exactly the greatest kick known to mankind, milling about like some kind of village idiots convention at best, and threatening crowd disorder and the return of those murderous fences at worst. It was a shameful blot on an otherwise fabulous day, and if it might appear churlish to some that I've commented so strongly, I make no apologies.

Back home after one of those triumphant return journeys that should have lasted for ever, I eagerly awaited our season's finale, at home to Sunderland. We drew 0-0 at Grimsby, and then on May 8th Cotgrave was left to the Geordies and the City Ground was wall to wall red and white, in the season's highest crowd, 27,010.

In a carnival atmosphere, with many in now familiar end of season fancy dress, it finished 2-2, Pearce and Collymore fittingly scoring. "I can't help falling in love with you" echoed from the Mackems on the Bridgford Lower, and seemed an equally fitting end to the season.

~

1994/95

Despite my re-born enthusiasm during our promotion campaign I decided not to re-invest in a season ticket for our forthcoming Premiership challenge, unhappy with the direction of the game, (although that's nothing compared with my opinion now) and increasingly comfortable with the idea of not committing myself to every home fixture.

As I type these comments it's 8pm on Friday October 1st 1999 and Forest are playing Barnsley at home (to suit Sky, of course, not to mention the bank manager). It's blowing a gale and lashing down against the window, and it's exactly the kind of night, and opposition, that screams out "stay at home, Richard, Gardeners World's on in a minute" ("Alan Titchmarsh prepares his garden for the winter months").

Back in 1994 I was still drawn regularly to the City Ground before a ball was kicked, stopping by to inspect the new Trent End development. It's a symptom of my undiminished condition known as "Floodlight Pylonitis", a compulsion to investigate any stadium in the vicinity of my travels – Monaco FC, Shea Stadium New York, Hong Kong's Sha Tin Horse Racing Circuit, the Tartu Concert Stadium in Estonia, with its magnificent single span "seashell" roof, to namedrop but a few.

For anyone similarly afflicted, "Football Grounds of Britain", by Simon Inglis, is essential reading. It was a "surprise" Christmas present from my wife after I'd dropped a few dozen subtle hints.

In the early summer of 1994 the City Ground stood exposing itself on the banks of the Trent, the naked Trent End revealing a brown desert that would be a lush green carpet by kick off time, thanks to fast germinating seeds and Forest's irrigation system.

Nothing much seemed to happen for weeks, as site clearance and pile driving dragged on, then a latticework of steel suddenly sprang up and we had the framework of a real stand. I watched the arrival, and painstaking positioning, between two giant cranes, of the huge "goalpost" frame, below which the roof was suspended.

As the new double deck Trent End took shape we were only a new Main Stand short of a full set, and even now, in my cynical disenchantment with many things football, I can't wait for it to happen – if it happens.

As for events on the pitch, I initially welcomed, then ultimately despaired, at the thought of Bryan Roy, who complemented Stan Collymore, the pair of them scoring a prolific 35 out of our League total of 72, the 3r^d highest behind champions Blackburn, with 80, and runners up Man Utd, with 77.

Third, appropriately, was also our final placing, a superb and totally unexpected achievement, albeit in a poor standard Premier. Blackburn were surely the weakest title winners in its short history, as illustrated by their laughable European Cup efforts the following year. Still, at least Le Saux and Batty put up a bit of a fight.

My first live Reds match was November 5th, when I took the offer of a place in an Executive box at Anfield. With transport laid on, a reserved parking space behind the Centenary Stand, and dedicated hotel style facilities, it couldn't have been further removed from my previous Anfield visits. Our suite was practically on halfway, with a perfect view, through toughened glass, of a heavy pitch, a contrast with Anfield's usual close cropped, flat, surface, tailored for Liverpool's traditional fluid passing game.

Like the City Ground, Anfield was replacing its best loved stand. The new Kop stood to our left, substantially complete and partially occupied. I wasn't impressed. The single tier structure, intended to echo the atmosphere and intimacy of the old Kop, looked unimposing, with little style or dramatic effect.

Designed – as is all of Anfield – to suit Ken Dodd's Diddymen, it maximises capacity, and doubtless there were severe building constraints preventing the construction of an impressive double decker to rival those at Forest, Blackburn, Villa, Spurs, etc, but it still seemed like an opportunity missed.

Speaking of which, Jason Lee, in one of only 5 League starts (replacing the injured Collymore) missed our best chance, failing to control and convert a mishit clearance by the keeper just outside the box, and Liverpool went on to win a game of few chances one nil.

I was less disappointed than I'd have expected. Our sanitised, carpeted, capsule, even with the stereo crowd noise control turned up to maximum, rendered the proceedings on the pitch almost surreal, more remote and less involving than watching on TV.

We arrived before the crowd arrived, and left after they'd gone. We wined, dined, and watched Grandstand. The match took place somewhere in between, but the only cut and thrust in our group of mixed allegiances was whether to have red or white wine. Liverpool FC can be proud of their executive hospitality and catering – better, in my experience of one each, than Old Trafford – and I'd always be grateful of a return invitation, but as a regular option it's not for me.

That was it until February 4th, when I completed a Liverpool double. 25,418 crammed into the City Ground. Our new Trent End lower tier had rows of shiny red seats, all empty, whilst the upper tier was vibrant and animated as Reds fans tried to recapture the spirit of the old Trent End. As with Liverpool's Kop, it could never be.

It all looked pretty impressive from my latest vantage point bottom left in the Exec, in the corner adjacent to the Liverpool fans. We were top dogs when Stan (who else?) put us 1-0 ahead, and home and dry until, not for the first time on Trentside, the Scousers nicked one at the death.

The lower Bridgford went barmy, I muttered a few well chosen expletives, the ref's whistle went, and the Exec fans trooped funereally home. A few minutes earlier shrill whistles were ringing out all around the ground in anticipation of victory celebrations, now all that could be heard was the muffled singing of the Scousers, thankfully receding as I shuffled up the steps onto Lady Bay Bridge. I had to remind myself that we'd actually drawn.

Just to prove that I wasn't a closet Liverpool fan, I was there again at our next home match, albeit a month later, March 4th to be precise. Spurs were the visitors, and the new Trent End was fully open for the first time. On a bright sunny day I climbed to the upper tier, lingering in the bar area to watch through smoked glass the crowds drifting over Trent Bridge. Another new panorama greeted me from my seat just right of the goal, the City Ground looking superb as 28,711 almost filled it to capacity.

The game was less of a spectacle, memorable only for a thrilling, frantic, last few minutes. With Forest 1-0 down, and almost out, Frank Clark brought on "super sub" Jason Lee, to tremendous acclaim. With the atmosphere suddenly electric, he tore into Spurs as if his life depended on it, creating mayhem in their defence.

Spurs fell apart, and incredibly we turned the match around, with two in two minutes. Bohinen and Lee were the scorers, right in front of our new stand, Lee with a close range finish after he'd won an aerial battle with their keeper. The ground erupted, the Trent End taunting the huge Spurs following with a predictable, but no less enjoyable for that, "You're not singing any more".

Barely a minute left, but it was déjà vu, Liverpool all over again, as Spurs swamped our penalty area for a last ditch corner - Forest's Achilles heel, for many a season. If we were going to throw it away this would be it.

It all seemed to happen in slow motion, over 100 yards

away, in the opposite goalmouth. The ball came over, heads went up, and the first I knew that it had gently found the net beyond the despairing Reds defence was when the lower Bridgford erupted. Seconds later the ref blew the final whistle, the Tottenham end danced in celebration, we drifted quietly away, and I had to remind myself that we'd actually drawn.

As for the lanky Jason Lee, it was probably his most memorable appearance, albeit a very brief one. He was a contradiction, crowd favourite cum infuriating spurner of open goals. Seldom first choice, and short on Premier quality, he endeared himself with his effort, if not his ball control.

He also attracted attention for his eccentric hair style, opposition fans, to the tune of "He's got the whole world in his hands", aptly and humorously summarising the Jason Lee look with "he's got a pineapple on his head".

We finished the season with an unlikely run of 13 undefeated, including a 7-1 annihilation of Sheffield Wednesday at Hillsborough on, appropriately, April 1st. I didn't go, but was at the City Ground the previous Wednesday, with three Insurance acquaintances from Leeds. They had to rely on a post match drink for comfort, after Stan tore them apart in the first half, by which time it was game over – Forest 3, Leeds 0.

I made my final appearance on a scorching May Saturday for the visit of already doomed Manchester City, and our anticipated 3 points, and European qualification. The season's best crowd, 28,882, saw us struggle, but 1-0 was good enough. We sealed our undefeated run with a 0-0 at Wimbledon in our last game, and it was carnival time for thousands of Reds fans in a gate of 15,341.

Not a bad return to the Premier.

~

Stan Collymore

Brian Clough's loss was Frank Clark's gain as Forest finally got their man after months of speculation, and a relegation that might never have been.

My first sight of the enigmatic Mr. Collymore was our Division One encounter with Tranmere. He was allegedly only half fit, an uncertain starter after missing games through miscellaneous niggling injuries, a pattern that has been a hallmark of his career.

He was also a sensation, match fit or not, as he tore Tranmere apart with a virtuoso display, head and shoulders above everyone else on the field. Tall, lean, and muscular, with an almost casual, loping, stride, he simply cruised through the match. I can't remember a more exciting first impression of any player, apart from the world's greatest, George Best, and even allowing for the mediocre opposition it was clear that Stan was the man.

He scored in our 2-1 win, and was close on numerous other occasions. He sprayed crossfield passes nonchalantly out to the flanks like a latter day Jim Baxter. He drifted to the touchlines, surging past flat footed defenders before releasing, Robbo style, wickedly curling centres, with either foot. Picking up the ball centre circle he burst away from his markers as if on springs, accelerating into overdrive and leaving the opposition floundering in his wake.

The charge of excitement when he was in possession was reminiscent of Ian Storey-Moore. It was like watching the schoolboy progidy running rings around his inferior mates. Stan didn't so much steal the show, he was the show, and I went home awestruck.

To no-one's surprise, he finished the season top scorer, his charismatic presence the difference between Division One also rans and promotion back to the Premier, his stunning left foot rocket at Peterborough sealing our return. His Premiership goals saw us clinch 3rd place, and a surprise return to European football.

He was idolised by many, but those same simplistic worshippers turned viciously when their man converted to a rival faith, the old enemy, Liverpool, and worse, with the parting message that Forest weren't in the big League that his talents and ambitions deserved.

I was pretty peeved myself at the time, but reflected that he'd cost us £2m, we'd sold him for £6m, he'd finished top scorer two seasons running, got us back into the Premier, and Europe, and alone provided more incident – sometimes unsavoury – and entertainment than I'd sometimes seen from the entire squad throughout whole seasons.

His reception on his return in new colours was typical of the boorish, hateful, attitude all too prevalent today, with taunts and invective screamed out almost hysterically in blind rage. They merely vindicated Collymore's decision to leave, unlike his subsequent playing performances.

He couldn't, or wouldn't, produce it on his chosen bigger stage, as his temperamental shortcomings submerged his footballing talents, and his "personality problems" followed him to Villa, exploding into headline news after his shameful attack on Ulrika Jonsson, and stories of psychiatric counselling. Fulham were the latest club to take him on, and, sadly, he's probably in the last chance saloon.

His impact at Forest was arguably more intense and influential than any other player, and for a couple of dramatic seasons we had a number 9 who would compare favourably with a certain number 10 from Brazil.

Frank Clark may have ultimately lost the plot, but he gave us Stan's best years, as the unproven gamble from lowly Southend joined the elite ranks of Joe Baker, Trevor Francis and Garry Birtles at number 9 for the Reds.

~

To Europe – and Walsall

We started 1995/96 without Collymore, off to Liverpool for a record fee, proclaiming that Forest weren't big enough for him. In many ways he was right, given our subsequent failure to consolidate in the Premier, but in one way he wasn't big enough for Forest, deriding – if quotes attributed were true – the club that had risked a fortune, immediately after relegation, on a player who'd yet to achieve anything apart from a reputation that he could be difficult to handle.

I was concerned to learn that his replacement was to be Kevin Campbell, Ian Wright's poor relation from Arsenal. He had a patchy goalscoring record and I feared the worst, especially as he didn't come cheap, and we could ill afford to waste a penny in the Mad Hatters world of the Premiership.

Throw in Jason Lee and Andrea Silenzi, plus the untried Paul McGregor and Stephen Howe, and Premier defences wouldn't exactly be quaking in their boots. My misgivings proved correct, Campbell, short on confidence and beset by niggling injuries, managing a woeful 3 from 21. Roy and Woan top scored with 8 apiece, followed by Stone on 7.

It might have been more democratic, but the season's League total of 50, compared with last season's 72, was evidence of Collymore's immense contribution. We also conceded four more than we scored, on which basis our final placing of 9th wasn't bad.

Perversely, on loan Campbell saved Everton's bacon at the end of season 1998/99 with a spectacular and uncharacteristic goalscoring burst, whilst Collymore was allegedly suffering from clinical depression, his football career in the balance.

I made one solitary League appearance, for the visit of Blackburn on April 13th, a frantic, breathless, last minute dash after a phone call from a work colleague at 2.15

offering his ticket. I just made the Exec Upper Tier for kick off, gasping for oxygen like a beached whale, after a Schumacher drive from Arnold and a crippling jog from Sneinton.

Forest were gasping for air at the final whistle, on the wrong end of a 5-1 scoreline. Blackburn weren't 4 goals better, but had the run of the ball, plus Alan Shearer's theatricals. I'd taken a dislike to him since the first time I saw him in the flesh, and although I seemed to be in a minority of one at the time, I reckon I'm a member of a less exclusive club now.

It was Blackburn's day, just as it was Blackburn's season. It seemed they could do no wrong, but the pendulum swung back in 1998/99 when already relegated Forest as good as put the final nail in their Premiership run by reversing recent history – including another walloping – and winning at Ewood Park

We went out of the League Cup against Bradford City in our first round, and out of the FA Cup in the 6th round, losing one nil at home to Villa after Mark Crossley's heroics in our 5th Round White Hart Lane penalty shoot-out had raised expectations.

It was the EUFA Cup that held the promise of revisiting past glories, all the more so because all the other British teams were falling by the wayside, round by round, leaving unfancied Forest hogging the national spotlight and the television revenue. It was almost like the old days, and I was turning, with the passing years, into Mr. Nostalgia.

I went to all four home ties, opting for the Bridgford Upper on every occasion. We drew our 1979 European Cup Final opponents, Malmo, in the first round, and both matches were dour, close fought, affairs. We lost 2-1 in the Swedish leg, but Ian Woan's away goal proved vital.

A relatively modest 23,817 created a great City Ground atmosphere as the Reds pushed forwards for a winning one nil lead in the return, mindful of the potential disaster of a succesful Malmo breakaway. It looked increasingly desperate, well into the second half, when Bryan Roy, who was having a not untypical stinker, and was my favourite to be imminently substituted, picked up the ball outside the Trent End penalty area and suddenly released a fierce drive into the top corner. The ground erupted, and it was non stop celebration until the final whistle.

Little known – to me, at least – French side Auxerre came out of the hat first for the next round, and after Steve Stone scored the only goal of the first leg, following a good move down the right, we were all set for another special European night on Trentside.

28,064, including a thousand or more from Auxerre, gathered in expectation, but goal shy Forest had to be grateful for a 0-0 against the quick passing but equally impotent Frenchmen. The atmosphere, despite the extra 4,000 in the ground, was strangely subdued, but we headed home more than content to be through.

Another French side, Lyon, were next, but this time, due to a combination of live TV coverage and playing the first leg at home, only 22,141 were there, including a vociferous French contingent. They were a contrast with the mixed bunch from Auxerre, containing a significant nucleus of aggressive, possibly neo-fascist, young men, reminiscent of some of the worst excesses of Millwall (but still pussycats compared with the 100 or so Croatian military types in the Trent End at the City Ground's opening Euro 96 match).

There wasn't much quality football to excite them, or us, our 5th tie following the pattern of the other 4, but Paul McGregor, part aspiring Premier striker, part aspiring pop star, got us off our backsides with a late close range finish. It was captured and oft repeated in a dramatic few seconds of TV footage as he ran on to celebrate with Reds fans in Forest's half of the lower Bridgford.

It was the only goal of both games, gritty defence again our saviour in an intimidating atmosphere in Lyon – but no more intimidating than my one and only visit, when we did battle with the locals in the frantic Gallic mayhem that passed for traffic management in those parts. Fortunately, I wasn't driving, so I kept my eyes shut.

Unfortunately, it was the organised Germans of Bayern Munich in the next round, after Europe's winter hibernation. We were firm second favourites, but Steve Chettle was the unlikely hero in the first leg at the now decidedly old fashioned Olympic Stadium, sneaking home a far post header, in our 2-1 defeat. All we needed was a Malmo-esque 1-0 at the City Ground. As simple as that.

On a cold, grey, drizzly March day I spent my lunch hour eagerly anticipating what might be one of Nottingham's great European nights, the City centre already peppered with little knots of Bayern supporters.

They were no doubt disappointed, as I am ashamed, of our filthy Council House and run down Slab Square, with its squalid fountains and public "conveniences", not to mention millions of pieces of compressed chewing gum plastered to the streets.

Still, we can be proud of the City Ground, now superior, albeit with only half the capacity, to Munich's open, ageing, stadium, and I reckon that the Bavarians, boisterously filling their half of the lower Bridgford, were impressed.

A capacity 28,844 saw an early Pearce effort somehow deflected off the Bridgford End line, and the Germans infuriatingly rode their luck, going on to win in similar vein and identical scoreline, 5-1, to Blackburn.

I went home desperately disappointed, but even more so with the media, who reckoned that Forest were drubbed, and never in with a chance. I disagree. If Pearce had opened the scoring – and 99 times out of 100 it would have gone in - during our intense early pressure Forest could have sat back and dictated the game. Instead, Bayern got the first one, we were chasing the game, and it was tailor made for their quick breaks as we pushed desperately forwards.

Ifs and buts don't win matches, and our last European campaign until who knows when – anybody taking bets? – was over. So, as we were about to see, would soon be our temporary membership of the Premiership.

In the meantime I tried – and enjoyed – summer football, in the shape of Forest's hosting of three Euro 96 games. It threw it down for the first one, Turkey v Croatia, but the atmosphere was great, even if attendances were well below capacity due to the usual ticket mismanagement for such events.

Geriatric and depressing Hillsborough, with its superior capacity, was the main host, depriving Nottingham of Denmark's colourful and noisy support, but I reckon the City Ground would have won a vote as superior venue - and location – hands down from the supporters of Croatia, Turkey and Portugal (and probably Denmark, if they'd had the privilege of playing here).

It's a shame that the City Ground is unlikely to be in the running for any future tournaments, but I'm glad I made the effort for Euro 96, which whetted my appetite for a future overseas one.

On to 1996/97, and one look at our signings, before and during the season, spoke volumes. To a squad desperately short of Premier firepower was added Dean Saunders, Alan Fettis, Nikola Jerkan, Tommy Wright, Ian Moore, Brian O'Neil, Steve Blatherwick (from the reserves) and, second time around, Nigel Clough.

Pierre van Hooijdonk, who in my opinion was considerably overrated, especially by himself, arrived in a classic case of too little – one miserly Premiership goal – too late – eight games out of our last nine. Throw in Steve Stone's injury, out for the rest of the season after an awkward fall near the Main stand touchline against Leicester in only our 5th League game, and we were always going to struggle.

Bryan Roy couldn't be bothered, Chris Bart-Williams was in and out through injury and loss of form, and David Phillips, a stalwart of our 1st Division promotion season, was no longer up to Premier speed.

On the plus side we had Pearce, Cooper and Haaland. Crossley, Lyttle and Chettle could be relied upon to never give less than 100%. Woan usually flattered to deceive. Gemmill could perform a disappearing act that was worthy of the Magic Circle, and Chris Allen failed to score in 16 starts plus 8 as sub. Not good.

Campbell finished joint top scorer with 6 in only 16 played, Alfie Haaland sharing the "distinction" of matching his total. Pearce got 5, and Reds long coveted super striker Dean Saunders managed a scintillating 3 in 33 – I reckon I could have done better, and for less money.

We weren't just certs. for relegation, we were the surest thing since Noah said "I think it's going to rain". Frank Clark, our best ever free transfer acquisition, couldn't find a successful signing to save his managerial life, and down we went, to no-one's surprise. All this after we beat Coventry away, Campbell getting all the goals, and half his season's League total in one go. Our 3-0 win put us top of the table, and it was only August 17th.

Sunderland brought us crashing down to earth with a resounding 4-1 victory at the City Ground four days later, and it was the start of a relentless plunge to the bottom, with a record breaking Premier run without a win. We lost 9 and drew 7, before upsetting the odds and beating high flying Arsenal 2-1 in an early City Ground Christmas present on December 21st.

We hit an unexpected purple patch in January, with five wins from five played, including FA Cup victories over

Ipswich and Newcastle, but it was a false dawn, and one pitiful win in our last 15 saw us sunk without trace. Mighty Chesterfield put the icing on the cake, dumping us out of the FA Cup in the 5th round.

The post Clough managerial roundabout began to gather pace. Clark was out. After a short session in tandem, or whatever the arrangement was meant to be, the Stuart Pearce-Dave Bassett combination ended with Harry in charge and Psycho off to Why-Aye land. I was pleased to see the experienced Bassett given the reins, although the misgivings of many others concerning his ability to produce a sustainable Premiership outfit were to be proved right, at least as far as Forest were concerned.

At the time we had one question – could Forest bounce back yet again?

I stuck with my now familiar pattern of picking a handful of games for live appearances and otherwise following the excellent Radio Nottingham commentary. Late Winter Saturday afternoons became a self indulgent sprawl across the settee - radio on, TV pictures of the 5 Nations (soon to be 6) Rugby, and intermittent Ceefax football updates. (Radio Nottingham lost the rights to the 1999/2000 season, but so far I'm just about tolerating Larry Lloyd and co).

Our last home game of 1997/98 saw us needing to beat Reading to more or less clinch a fighting return to the top flight, and I couldn't believe how excited and committed I felt as I took my seat in the Trent End Upper.

As the initial carnival atmosphere turned into a stomach knotting, frustrating stalemate, with relegated Reading – bar a mathematical miracle – outplaying us, it brought home one of the three reasons why my visits had reduced. The older I got, the more, rather than less, personally I took the Reds performances, and here I was again getting wound up over a silly football match. I could do without it.

I could also do without sacrificing the time – half a day,

compared with a couple of hours on the settee during which I could also demolish my dinner. Last, but not least, the obscene money grubbing mentality of many “top” Premier superstars, most of whom are unfit to lick the boots of George Best or Ian Storey-Moore.

Despite which, I almost bought a £199 Bridgford Upper season ticket in 1999 so, to misquote Arnie, “I might be back”. To re-quote my wife, “You’ll never hang yourself”. I used to be indecisive, now I’m not so sure.

Anyway, it all ended in smiles, turning on the game’s two dramatic moments. Well into the second half Reading, yet again moving fluently forwards, finished a neat move with a cracking shot that beat Dave Beasant, and from my view, directly in line, was goalbound.

In the split second as it sped towards the corner of the net I thought “shit, that’s it then”, only for outrageous good fortune to favour the Reds as the swerve on the ball exaggerated and it ricocheted to safety off the inside of Beasant’s left hand post.

With two minutes to go I’d given up, resigned to a bad tempered trudge back to the car and – the thing I hate most about Sunday matches – work next day. As I contemplated this most comprehensively burst of bubbles, we won a free kick somewhere near halfway.

I think it was Steve Chettle who chipped it into the left hand corner of the Bridgford Penalty area, where Chris Bart-Williams, with his back to goal, defender tight on him, suddenly produced the moment of magic that we’d lacked all afternoon.

He controlled it in an instant, executed a Cruyff like turn, (father, not son) and with the defender flat footed in his wake was face to face with the keeper. My heart jumped. A surge of adrenalin, as Bart-Williams, from an angle to the left of goal, hit a crisp cross shot into the opposite corner.

I reacted to his, and the Bridgford End’s, reaction as the

ball found the back of the net, and the City Ground erupted in a joyous cacophony. "We are going up, I say we are going up!" reverberated from every side. Shell shocked Reading and their supporters legitimately cursed their ill fortune. As Millwall might have put it, we were lucky, and we didn't care.

Ipswich clinched promotion for us in midweek, defeating our closest rivals Sunderland, and I followed it on a Radio Nottingham special, sharing Steve Stone's anticipation of the forthcoming Premiership campaign. Surely, we'd learnt from our last experience.

Well no, actually, and a dismal re-run saw Forest, and Dave Bassett, as good as doomed by Christmas 1998. Mediocre signings and familiar lack of quality saw us heading for another record – the first team to be relegated three times from the Premier.

My visit to the City Ground on March 10th 1999 provided evidence of another 90s manifestation that, along with rampant, uncontrolled, greed, makes a grown man want to weep. The new refereeing directives at times make football a laughing stock, and here was an example.

Newcastle were the visitors, and English speaking Alan, now based back in Lynemouth, travelled down, as did another Geordie, a Manchester based work colleague. We met in the Larwood and Voce – "Geordies here, Geordies there, Geordies every………", and the atmosphere was excellent, a far cry from those grim "Jimmy Nail and Co" days of the 70s. Cotgrave was left to the Mackems.

On the field, feeble Forest, and Cup conscious Newcastle, scarcely raised the temperature, except in the eyes of the ref. I thought I was prepared for a typically poor display of Premiership refereeing, but Mr. Winter took me by surprise.

In a match that 5 years ago would have scarcely merited a free kick, let alone a booking, he flourished cards and interrupted what little flow there was with abandon. With Red Nose Day imminent, I thought he was on a sponsored stoppage.

Forest's Louis-Jean was sent off for making two tackles, Newcastle were awarded a penalty that even they didn't understand, and Dietmar Hamann, who got clean away with the game's nastiest offence, almost scored from a free kick awarded after a Newcastle player fell on his backside following an air shot - when I did it in Parks football all I got was derision.

It was the final straw, midway through the second half, to see the usually combative Andy Johnson, already booked for wiping his nose on his sleeve, or something similar, pull out of a 60-40, allowing Newcastle to run clear. He knew that "foul play" (i.e. physical contact) would result in red, and Forest down to 9 men. It was farcical.

I'm not accusing Winter of bias – Forest were merely unlucky to catch the worst of his absurdities. Headlines in next day's Evening Post attributed comments describing the worst refereeing display in years. I wouldn't disagree, but it must be seen in the context of those directives, whereby quantity of cards, often sprinkled liberally throughout games with barely a hint of malice, seems to be the yardstick for retaining Premier refereeing status.

It doesn't help that intense, melodramatic, "fashion victim", John Motson (where were you when Souness and McMahon were wreaking havoc?) has lost the plot, and seems besotted with coloured cards. "There, look, he raised an arm" – to another outbreak of "handbags" – "Surely that's red. You can't do that. He's got to go". Yet I often think he wouldn't recognise a dive if Brian Phelps was performing in his local pool.

I went home disgusted, and Forest returned to the dressing room, having lost 2-1, knowing that the ref was a joke, but, sadly, so was our third Premiership campaign.

Be it ever so humble....

To move, or not to move, that is the question – or at least it's back on the agenda.

Once again, the unsavoury prospect of the Reds relocating is being mooted, just as we've celebrated 100 years at the City Ground, and I for one don't like the thought of it. Unfortunately, the Council own the freehold, and some of them would love to see that side of the Trent smothered in a lucrative property development.

Clearly, they're entitled to a fair rent, and this may be an initial scaremongering smokescreen by the current Forest owners to set the scene for implementation of a hidden agenda, ahead of the next leasehold agreement. As far as I'm aware, Forest have shrewdly acquired the odd nearby parcel of land over the years, and if the Council were to demand a prohibitive tariff in anticipation of the arrival of the bulldozers we could presumably make it legally difficult for them.

My case for staying put isn't based on sentiment alone, although naturally supporters develop a deep affection and sense of belonging after years of paying homage at their sacred arena. Sentiment can't override squalor, and with regard to close neighbours Derby County their move from the cramped, dilapidated, Baseball Ground, which had no scope for redevelopment, was essential for their future.

No such constraints apply to the City Ground. Its capacity is already a comfortable – and at 6 foot 2 I should know, having sat bent double at overrated venues such as Anfield or Old Trafford – 30,000, and rebuilding of the Main Stand as a state of the art flagship would lift capacity above 35,000 – even more if the Trent End corners were filled in.

Without exception, supporters from Turkey, Portugal and Croatia were singing the praises of Forest's facilities, and its superb Trentside setting, at Euro 96. A work colleague recently had a similar reaction from a visiting Spanish friend at a League game. Away support is usually high, for similar reasons – Forest is always a popular trip.

We don't need to be plonked in the middle of some anonymous industrial park, and mustn't let any arguments for a new site gloss over the potential for serious traffic congestion and crowd segregation problems outside the ground, already evidenced alarmingly outside Pride Park and the Riverside.

Imagine the nightmare if the ill conceived groundshare with Notts had gone ahead on the site of the Wilford power station – that side of town would have ground to a halt after every Forest game. It's bad enough with the retail parks. The current location, whilst inevitably less than perfect, is a much better bet, and only a short walk from the railway station.

We've got the most attractive setting in the Football League – the views from Lady Bay or Trent Bridge never fail to quicken the pulse – and that little corner of West Bridgford is part of Nottingham's sporting heritage.

The Forest ground, Meadow Lane, Trent Bridge cricket ground – with its superb new grandstand – the T.B.I., and, just down the river, the National Water Sports Centre, are known with affection internationally. We'll soon have the National Ice Stadium barely half a mile up the road.

As the cliché has it, there are only three things that matter, "location, location and location", and Forest have got them all, in abundance.

In the words of the song - "don't throw it all away".

~

Steve Chettle

Two footed, with flair, pace, and natural ball skills – these are all attributes that belong to more gifted players, despite which Chettle's career with the Reds, his boyhood team, has spanned an unbroken 13 seasons.

He currently stands fifth in the list of all time Forest appearances, in the illustrious company of Bob McKinlay (whose record 685 will never be broken), Ian Bowyer, Stuart Pearce, John Robertson and Jack Burkitt (the last captain to lift the FA Cup) and looks set to climb even higher, barring injury – a troublesome back problem currently giving some concern.

My wife was the football catalyst, encouraging the junior Chettle at summer school in Bulwell (remember Miss Carrington? – "never mind Stephen, it's only a silly game, you just kick it with the left one.") She never said that of course – for a start, she gets left and right confused – but she does remember him as a pleasant and polite young lad, and he appears by all accounts not to have changed.

Chettle kicked it with his left one throughout his one club career, bar the odd rebound from the right. It never had the mesmerising magic of a Maradonna, or club hammer terror of a Pearce, but his belated responsibilities as penalty taker are proof that he can certainly hit it.

At 6ft 1, and a trim 13 stones or so, solid in the tackle and capable in the air, "Chets" is the archetypal "no frills" defender. He's enhanced his playing limitations with an impeccable temperament and unstinting loyalty and commitment to the Reds.

Chettle is "local boy makes good", someone to identify with in today's cynical game – everybody's Parks Football mate who was just that bit better, grabbed his chance, and stayed the course. More significantly, and unusually these days, he's kept his roots firmly in Nottingham soil (cue for his imminent transfer to Aberdeen).

He's had his critics through the years, and is the one player synonymous with our fortunes over recent seasons – just a cut above the First Division, yet not able to cut it consistently with the big boys of the Premier. His unassuming demeanour – even now he makes an unconvincing captain – has cost him glory, stepping aside at dead balls to such as Robbo, Psycho, Coops and Honky Tonk.

An assortment of Forest managers haven't seen fit to dispense with his services, and given the turbulent last few seasons that alone speaks volumes for his value to the club – his Forest future has hardly ever been an issue.

I can't wax lyrical over scintillating, match winning, performances – centre halves don't win that type of revue, for a start, and Chettle isn't that kind of player – but his goal at Bayern showed echoes of Martin Peters as he ghosted in at the far post. Maybe Chettle is ten years ahead of his time, in which case he'll be around for a few years yet.

It's entirely fitting that he completes my personal choice of player profiles, a perfect "book end" to my first, Bobby McKinlay.

Steve Chettle is in many ways a mirror reflection of that famous servant of Nottingham Forest Football Club.

~

With Dave Bassett gone and Ron Atkinson unable to perform an end of season miracle we started 1999/2000 back in the First Division. After a familiar "will he, won't he", Martin O'Neill didn't, but most Reds fans took heart from the unexpected appointment of David Platt as the Forest Directors turned to youth.

Platt has an enormous task ahead of him, and whether he's up to it remains to be seen. Brian Clough took nearly 3 seasons to get us back, and then it was only by the skin of our teeth, thanks to Kenny Hibbitt's goal for Wolves at Bolton. The rest, as they say, is history, but that history, as with our 3rd round escape against Tooting and Mitcham in the 1959 FA Cup, swung on the finest of knife edges.

History will again be the judge, but it's encouraging that the Reds seem to be following a youth policy on the field as well as off it, ex Red Paul Hart continuing the good work he put in at Leeds Utd. Our Youth Academy looks to be in excellent hands, and one thing that will tempt former diehards such as myself to return regularly is a vibrant, motivated, exciting team.

Speaking of youth, my one appearance to date in the final season of the 90s coincided with the loan debut of our first triple barrelled player, Ian Wright-Wright-Wright. I'd already bought tickets, on the instruction of an ex schoolfriend in Sweden, returning for the weekend desperate to kit out his 9 year old son at the Forest shop, in defiance of the Manchester Utd sickness infecting most local Swedish youngsters.

My mate Richard, in his first match for donkeys, was more excited than his lad, and we were all disappointed that Forest, squandering numerous chances, ended up only just scraping a 1-1 draw with QPR, who were reduced to 10 men on half time following the heinous offence of handball. Wright missed the resultant penalty, but despite him making his name at Arsenal, and being "controversial" at times, I've always admired his 100% commitment. He actually plays as if it means something.

It's indicative of my dwindling visits that Ian Wright was the most familiar Reds player, Mark Crossley and Steve Chettle excepted, although I did recognise a few others. Dougie Freedman impressed again with fine ball skills, if not sustained involvement, and is a natural goalscorer. Scimeca looks a good signing, and with youngsters breaking through, and Platt's overseas brigade looking promising, I'm keeping my fingers crossed that year 2000 will tempt me down again as entertainment levels rise – provided that we can knock those awful refereeing directives into touch.

In the meantime, I can reflect on the memories, and friendships, that football, and Nottingham Forest, have brought to me and to thousands of others.

It's also broadened my musical horizons. I discovered Bruce Hornsby thanks to Grandstand's results service. I discovered Shaun Colvin as a backing singer on one of his CDs, and saw her in concert at Nottingham's Royal Centre. She was support to Scottish Folk/Rock band Runrig. I fell in love with them, and never miss a local appearance. They're shamefully ignored by the media, but a recurring theme from "The Big Wheel" album, the unrelenting passage of time, says everything that matters.

It's been 40years since my first Forest match.

Where did it all vanish to?

~